LENIHAN

HIS LIFE AND LOYALTIES

LENIHAN

HIS LIFE AND LOYALTIES

JAMES DOWNEY

New Island Books
Dublin

LENIHAN: His Life and Loyalties
Published October 1998 by
New Island Books
2 Brookside
Dundrum Road
Dublin 14
Ireland

British Library Cataloguing in Publication Data
A catalogue record for this book is available from the British Library

ISBN 1 874597 97 9

Photographs courtesy of Independent Newspapers, Mrs Ann Lenihan,
Liam Lawlor TD, Westmeath Independent.
Cover design: Slick Fish Design, Dublin
Cover photograph: Independent Newspapers
Typesetting: New Island Books
Printed in the UK by Biddles Limited

James Downey has been one of Ireland's leading and best-known political commentators for the last three decades. After a career in the Irish Times (foreign editor, Westminster, and political correspondent) he is now a political writer with the *Irish Independent* and writes a political column for *Business and Finance* magazine. He was Ireland's European Journalist of the Year in 1996.

By the same author:

Them and Us: Britain, Ireland and the Northern Question 1969-1982
All Things New: the 1989 General Election and its Consequences

Foreword

I knew Brian Lenihan for twenty-five years or more, but came to know him really well only in the last ten or twelve years of his life. I do not wish, and it would be wrong, to exaggerate the depth of our friendship. He was on affable terms with vast numbers of people, but outside his family his truly close friends were few. One was Vinny Mahon, who figures largely in the early part of this book; in politics, his great intimate was Ray Burke. With Burke he discussed endlessly two subjects, European history and politics and the internal affairs of the Fianna Fail Party. The first he also discussed pleasurably with me over many a pint and many a dish, but on the second he would not have dreamed, while still a member of the party's front bench, of opening up fully to me, nor would I have expected him to do so. Only in his later years did he cast aside discretion and make such comments as, of a political associate, "he got greedy."

Nevertheless, our association was certainly one of such fellow-feeling as to warrant the use of the word intimacy. Although I did not support the party to which he devoted so much of his life, we both took it more or less for granted that our attitudes on most important issues of public policy were virtually identical. On world affairs, I would hardly disagree with a word of his analysis. On national politics, I liked to tease him for claiming not merely that he himself was a social democrat, which he unquestionably was, but that Fianna Fail is a social democratic party, an arguable proposition. I was proud of our friendship and of my ability to distinguish the serious statesman from the man who operated behind such a cloud of confusion that, in the words of Bertie Ahern, he sometimes confused himself. For his part, he read my writings and commented on them incisively and usually favourably. Writers are easily flattered, and it is possible that for that and other reasons I took too much for granted: that I assumed too great a similarity of opinion. But my research for this biography has led me to the opposite conclusion.

To say that Lenihan improved on acquaintance is hopelessly to understate the case. Many who did not know him at all took him for a clown; those who did come to know him were more and more impressed the better they knew him. The mask concealed one of the sharpest political brains of his generation, and an unexcelled depth and breadth of reading and understanding. But more: among Irish politicians he was extraordinarily, I would almost venture to say uniquely, cultivated and sophisticated. In that he differed strikingly from his nemesis Charles J. Haughey, whose cultivation and sophistication were no more than a veneer. But he differed almost equally from his friend and critic John Maurice Kelly, who had a massive intellect, fine appreciation and great human qualities but could not remotely approach Lenihan as a political operator or a political mind.

It never occurred to me that I might write Lenihan's biography until his son Conor suggested the project in May 1996. My reactions were in the following order surprise, pleasure, and dismay, with the last predominating. I realised that I had spent hour upon hour discussing the ifs and buts of European history with Brian Lenihan and had scarcely ever asked him such questions as, "what really happened on such-and-such a date, and why?" The sole exception of any importance was that I had listened to him expounding at length his theories regarding the "secret history" of the 1990 presidential election.

On beginning my research, I soon found that my feeling of dismay was well justified. Lenihan's political career spanned his entire adult life. The available documentation, as customary in Ireland, is inadequate. Some incidents in his early career are difficult to verify because too many of those involved are dead; at the other end, too many are still alive and one has to beware of giving offence, especially the kind of offence which attracts the attention of lawyers and with which journalists are all too familiar. I had exceptional, and time-consuming, difficulty in finding out (or working out) the truth of the controversy over the proposed university merger in the 1960s and have been obliged, in the end, to rely, not on precise information, but on plausible theories which I believe to be correct.

There were few enough surprises. The research confirmed my already high opinion of my subject, as well as my belief in our coincidence of views; and it further confirmed in the majority of instances my pre-existing opinions, good or bad, of most of the major players. It takes very little research, and very little reflection on twentieth-century Irish history, to conclude, for example, that Sean Lemass was a giant. Much less well known is the extent of the services rendered to the Fianna Fail Party and the country by Dr James Ryan and his son Senator Eoin Ryan. More significantly, the nobility and self-sacrifice, as well as the abilities and depth, of President P. J. Hillery are often underestimated.

But from a personal viewpoint the great surprise was the discovery of remarkable, almost uncanny, similarities in Lenihan's family background and mine. I had known vaguely that during World War Two his father and mine had served together in the Local Defence Force, under the same Command, but that would have produced little more than a casual acquaintance. (In our small country, it is not really an extraordinary coincidence that my father also served with a Regular Army officer, Jack McQuillan, later Brian Lenihan's adversary in Roscommon politics. Sadly, McQuillan died while the present work was in progress.) More piquant was my discovery of the similarities of his earlier ancestry and mine, both featuring Bible-reading teachers who admired the work of Milton and Bunyan.

One notable feature of such a cultural background is that it makes ignorant Anglophobia all but impossible. Oscar Wilde, referring to the English, quoted Goethe on the French: "How could I, to whom culture and barbarism are alone of importance, hate a nation which is among the most cultivated of the earth, and to which I owe so great a part of my own cultivation?"

To love English culture, however, is not to approve of Britain's countless Irish "crimes, follies and misfortunes", or to find fault with the Irish insistence on achieving, maintaining and enhancing independence. Here again I found an uncanny similarity between Lenihan's background and mine. We could both claim a republican ancestry on the maternal side, but his grandfather Patrick Lenihan, like most of my ancestors of that generation, was a Parnellite and later a Redmondite. I find no oddity in persons with such a background switching sides to Michael Collins, or indeed making the further switch to Fianna Fail (as Brian Lenihan's father did) or to Labour, any more than in their continuing to support Fine Gael, the successor party to the pro-Treaty side in the civil war, like the Lenihan family friend John B. Keane. Charles Stewart Parnell wanted the maximum (in his case rather ill-thought-out) available degree of independence for Ireland. So did Michael Collins. It fell to later generations to put flesh on the bones. Brian Lenihan played a large, and usually underrated, part in that enterprise, in three respects. The first was his achievements as a minister; the second, his capacity as a political thinker, illustrated here in quotations from him, especially in the last chapter; the third, the subtlety he employed in his efforts to persuade intransigents of the futility of violence and in the redefinition of the so-called "pan-nationalist front" as a nationalist consensus of quite another kind, which accepted the principle of consent in relation to Northern Ireland, and sought to draw Sinn Fein into that consensus.

I knew from the beginning that documentation would present difficulties. Lenihan left his own papers in relatively poor shape. Doubtless he expected to have the time to sort them out in preparation for the literary work he planned for the years that, alas, would be denied him. Doubtless, too, he knew where to find papers of interest, just as he and his father knew where to find any book in his father's library. It would have been almost literally impossible, and of doubtful value, to trawl back through all his Dail contributions. Thankfully a vast amount of material was available in the shape of his newspaper interviews, articles and book reviews. The family were tremendously helpful, and the Department of Foreign Affairs supplied me with all his major speeches as minister, as well as insights into his style and achievements. In recent years much useful material has emerged from the National Archives under the thirty-year rule.

Although the Lenihan family have been immensely generous with their time and co-operation, this is not an "official" biography. Not even the lightest restrictions were placed upon me. I was given only two injunctions: "tell the truth" and "not too much about the presidential election". The first I have attempted to the best of my ability. The second was easy enough because the 1990 election campaign was, although a climactic event, only one incident in a long career marked by more successes than failures. Nevertheless, I owe the warmest thanks to members of the family: Ann, Brian, Conor, Niall, Paul and Anita Lenihan, and Mary O'Rourke. I also owe a debt of gratitude to the Department of Foreign Affairs; to the staff at Fianna Fail headquarters, in particular the former secretary, Pat Farrell, and the archivist, Philip Hannon; to the editor of the *Irish Independent*, Vinny Doyle, and the staff of the Independent House library; and to Independent Newspapers, *Business and Finance* magazine, and my former employers, the *Irish Times*, for the opportunities they have afforded me of observing Irish politics at close quarters over very many years. I thank wholeheartedly the politicians, journalists and others who have given me valuable help, interviews, documents and insights: Bertie Ahern, Bruce Arnold, Sylvester Barrett, Ray Burke, Richard Burke, Mike Burns, Lord Carrington, Stephen Collins, John Cooney, Maire Cosgrave, Caitriona Crowe, Austin Currie, Sean Donlon, Sean Duignan, Fergus Finlay, Sheila Fitzgerald, Peg Fogarty, Maire Geoghegan-Quinn, Dermot Gleeson, Niall Greene, Brendan Halligan, Des Hanafin, Mona Hanafin, David Harman, Charles J. Haughey, Michael Herbert, Dr P. J. Hillery, John Horgan, John B. Keane, James Kelly, Geraldine Kennedy, Tom King, Liam Lawlor, Miriam Lord, David McKittrick, General Gerry McMahon, Seamus McKenna, Patrick McKernan,

Kevin McNamara, Vinny Mahon, Seamus Mallon, Martin Mansergh, P. J. Mara, Michael Mills, Mark O'Connell, Ulick O'Connor, Tony O Dalaigh, Professor Martin O'Donoghue, Nuala O'Faolain, Brendan O'Kelly, Michael O'Kennedy, Olivia O'Leary, Emily O'Reilly, Des O'Malley, Tommy O'Sullivan, Sean Power, Pat Rabbitte, Arthur Reynolds, Bride Rosney, Lean Scully, Raymond Smith, John Stephenson, Dick Walsh, and Commandant Peter Young. If I have inadvertently omitted any others, I hope they will accept my apologies. Any errors, like the opinions expressed in this book, are my own.

James Downey
Dublin, August 1998.

One

What is bred in the bone comes out in the flesh.
LATIN PROVERB

Since legendary times one of the main strategic Shannon crossings has been just below Lough Ree. In the early middle ages the calm waters south of the lake made a link rather than a barrier between the allied provincial kingdoms of Meath and Connacht. On the left bank of the river there arose the chief among Irish monastic cities, Clonmacnois, a place of enormous economic and strategic as well as religious significance in a culture that built no towns.

Modern Athlone was built and fortified a few miles upriver, just below the lake. In 1691, during the Williamite war, it was the scene of a heroic defence by James II's Irish army when besieged by the forces of William of Orange.

Brian Lenihan was born in Dundalk on 17 November 1930, but he was brought up in Athlone and maintained all his life a close association with the town. Town, monastery, location, legend and history ought to have provided sufficient sentimental and romantic associations for any taste, but in his whimsical or romantic moments Lenihan liked to point to his deeper roots farther west. He would maintain that "the real Irish", the pre-Celtic inhabitants of the island or, quite contrariwise, those driven across the Shannon by Oliver Cromwell's commissioners in the 1650s, came from the west. Among them was his grandfather Patrick Lenihan, a schoolmaster in a little village in North Clare.

His grandfather was indeed a major influence, but not in any romantic or whimsical sense. For Brian Lenihan was a recognisable Irish "type", the son and grandson of teachers and imbued with the traditions of families of that kind.

1

In the late nineteenth century the village schoolmaster, especially if a considerable man like Patrick Lenihan, was a figure in a small community second only to the parish priest. Teachers did not see their role in community and national life as confined to imparting to their pupils the limited education of the national schools and fighting for scholarships for the few fortunate enough to go farther. Of these they were intensely proud: they would boast that "we educated bishops." But they educated, in another sense, the adults who remained behind. Through them were mediated to the people the views and ambitions of the Dublin nationalist intelligentsia, as expressed in the pages of the *Nation*. They were mostly constitutional nationalists, content with the modest version of Home Rule which their heroes, Charles Stewart Parnell and William Ewart Gladstone, came close to achieving. In later generations they would want more; they would want the maximum degree of independence possible for Ireland to attain. In this regard the history of the Lenihan family for a century and more has been the history of Ireland.

Their relationship with the people they thus educated was close, if only because most of the schoolmasters, like most of the clergy, had sprung from the ranks of the upper peasantry. They might regard themselves as egalitarians, but if they acknowledged no superiors and did not share the English obsession with rank and class and if their views were liberal or "advanced" by the standards of the age they could be authoritarian and peremptory in their personal dealings. And the political condition of the peasantry was paradoxical. They had been politicised by Daniel O'Connell in the first half of the century, but politicisation had its limits. It did not reach those on the social and geographical margins. It did not reach the desperately poor, the illiterate, or the inhabitants of considerable swathes of the west of Ireland where faulty electoral registers effectively disfranchised a large proportion of the adult male population until some considerable time after independence. And along with poverty and ignorance went the extreme conservatism induced, or certainly aggravated, by the shock of

2

the Great Famine. The schoolmasters might consider these unsophisticated, priest-ridden people their equals in theory, but seldom in practice.

Teachers organised the Gaelic League, the Gaelic Athletic Association, the co-operative movement, and their own trade union, the Irish National Teachers' Organisation. If they usually worked hand in glove with the clergy, their endeavours to assert greater independence through the INTO and otherwise frequently brought them into conflict with them. They might admire the austere intellectuals who then occupied episcopal palaces, but found themselves obliged to confront the petty tyrants in the parishes. Patrick Lenihan played a minor but honourable part on the side of justice in the "Fanore affair" when the parish priest of Fanore on Galway Bay ordered a schoolmaster to marry his assistant teacher and, when he refused, tried to move him to Connemara. The priest had falsely denigrated the man as a drinker, but wanted to send him to a parish where, as Breandan O hEithir wrote in *The Begrudger's Guide*, "poteen was as plentiful as tea." As chance would have it, Lenihan had married his own assistant teacher and, after her death, the woman who replaced her, but in neither case at clerical dictation.

These men loved words, and many, Lenihan among them, The Word. A fashion for Bible reading had grown up among educated Catholics, who felt that it both enhanced their understanding of religion and brought them closer to their Bible-reading Protestant acquaintances. It seldom disturbed their own Catholic orthodoxy: unsurprisingly, since it was commonly confined to the Douai version of the New Testament. In Lenihan's case it went hand in hand with a fervour for English, and especially English Protestant and Puritan, classics. In addition to the inevitable Shakespeare, he force-fed his son Paddy on a diet of Milton and Bunyan. Paddy would go on to feed his own children from a much wider literary menu, but Milton and Bunyan would remain part of it. And here one sees another characteristic of the Lenihan family through the generations: a person with such a literary background could fight for the highest degree of Irish freedom from Britain, but without any taint of Anglophobia or sectarianism.

Patrick Lenihan maintained his political loyalty to Parnell and subsequently to John Redmond, who eventually reunited the Irish parliamentary party at Westminster. But by cleaving to the latter allegiance he left the political mainstream, for Irish nationalism shifted radically and permanently in the second decade of the twentieth century.

Redmond, having reunited the nationalist movement, split it again in 1914 when, without having achieved Home Rule except on paper, he committed his Volunteer force to fight in France for Britain in World War One. The minority who rejected him fell under the influence of the secret Irish Republican Brotherhood, committed to obtaining independence by military force. A handful of Volunteers under Patrick Pearse, along with another handful from the Irish Citizen Army under James Connolly, mounted the Easter Rising in Dublin in 1916. German help failed to arrive, and the insurgents surrendered after five days' heavy fighting. Public opinion was massively opposed to them, but swung in their favour when the British executed their leaders — and, vindictively, Willie Pearse for no better reason than that he was their commander's brother.

Among the prisoners taken by the British were three men who figure prominently in twentieth-century Irish history, and in this story. Eamon de Valera, commander of one of the insurgents' posts, escaped execution because of his American citizenship. Michael Collins, who had fought in the General Post Office under Pearse and Connolly, went briefly into captivity. A small, sallow schoolboy, often described as "foreign-looking" or "Jewish-looking", was given the proverbial kick in the backside and told to go back to his lessons. His name was Sean Lemass.

Lemass did not go back to his lessons; nor did de Valera or Collins return to normal life after their release. Those who believed that freedom could be obtained only by force, and who now had the people with them, took over the Sinn Fein party as their political arm and used the Volunteers, soon renamed the Irish Republican Army, as their military arm. Sinn Fein scored a conclusive victory in the Westminster general election which followed the end of the world war in 1918. Their MPs refused to take their seats in the House of Commons, and at the beginning of 1919 they established their own legislature, the first Dail Eireann. Simultaneously a guerrilla war broke out. It was of course never possible for them to defeat the British in the field, but it was possible to make the country ungovernable. Sinn Fein set up their own courts and their own bank, and controlled local government. Collins, amazingly, raised a national loan while directing the war of independence and eluding British death squads, while at the same time organising his own death squads to kill informers and British agents. Civil disobedience, the blatant lack of legitimacy of British rule following the foundation of the Dail, and the revulsion of American opinion and liberal British opinion at the atrocities committed by the "Black and Tans", worked at least as strongly as the guerrilla war to persuade Whitehall to come to terms.

But now came the worst split of all. De Valera opposed the Anglo-Irish Treaty of 1921 which gave effective independence to twenty-six of Ireland's thirty-two counties and was made the nominal leader of the IRA factions who plunged the country into the civil war of 1922-23. Lacking clear war aims, and lacking public support or credibility, they were easily defeated by the new Free State Army. The causes and course of the conflict have been too well rehearsed elsewhere to need elaboration here, except in so far as they relate to the then activities and subsequent career of Paddy Lenihan and the views he passed on to his children.

Lenihan, as a student at University College Galway, had joined the IRA and taken part in minor engagements in the war of independence. In the split of 1922, he took the pro-Treaty side. In most instances such decisions came about essentially from chance, for the men simply followed their unit commanders on to one side or the other, but Paddy Lenihan evidently made his own decision as an admirer of Collins.

Lenihan fought in at least one civil war engagement, was wounded, recovered, and after the end of hostilities in 1923 returned to his studies. Many years later he applied to the military authorities for a medal, but not for the pension to which he would have been entitled. He wrote, quaintly, in his application that he had "sufficient competence" to forgo the pension. It was not the end of his military service: during World War Two he became an officer in the Local Defence Force (LDF), the wartime volunteer reserve. Many who had fought on both sides in the civil war, and their sons, joined this force, making it an agent of reconciliation.

That reconciliation had been slow to come in the immediate aftermath of the civil war. The execution of seventy-seven Republican prisoners — by no means a large number but seen as vindictive and, as to the notorious first four executions, illegal — caused bitterness that in some cases lasted for generations. After the conflict ended Republicans suffered discrimination in employment, another source of grievance. But discontent was by no means confined to their side. Had Collins lived, men like Lenihan might have been better disposed to maintain their allegiance to the pro-Treaty side and their Cumann na nGael party, but Collins was killed in the civil war and many of his followers soon fell victim to a variety of disillusionments in addition to that already caused by the executions. One sprang from the "army mutiny", a crisis which put paid to the influence of senior officers who had originated in the IRA. The boundary settlement of 1925 appeared to copperfasten the partition of the country with the agreement of the infant Irish government. In fact the Cumann na nGael premier, W. T. Cosgrave, had no option whatever but to accept it, and he ever afterwards felt betrayed by the British, but his opponents used it against him.

The playwright John B. Keane, who would become Lenihan's close friend, always stayed loyal to Cumann na nGael's successor party Fine Gael, but he concedes "the general harshness of the regime". Besides issues like the executions and treatment of prisoners, that included social and economic conservatism. Although Cosgrave did a fine (if until recent times too often unacknowledged) job of reconstruction, the country was run on rigid and unimaginative lines. When

Cumann na nGael went out of office after ten years' rule in 1932, ninety-six per cent of all exports still went to Britain. Ireland was an agricultural country, with more than half the population dependent on that underdeveloped industry, and in the more backward regions a very poor country. Modernisation and mass urbanisation had barely begun. It was not for this, men like Lenihan felt, that they had fought.

Lenihan had been Collins's man. He would come to be Sean Lemass's man. Collins and Lemass were in some ways strikingly similar types, who in less tragic times might have made a great team. Lemass had taken the Republican side in the civil war and his brother Noel had been murdered, but he wasted little time in reproaches: one of his finest characteristics, shared with the Lenihan family, was magnanimity. This, and his extraordinary capacity for hard work and organisation, appealed to the disaffected Paddy. So did the prospects for social and economic development, seen as neglected by Cumann na nGael but held out by Fianna Fail, the new party founded, largely at the instigation of Lemass, in 1926.

Lenihan had taken a job as a teacher in Belfast, where his pupils included the future Cardinal William Conway and the future doyen of Irish journalists, James Kelly. He was immensely popular with the boys, not least because of his frequent use of pungent language. In Kelly's words, "he taught us Latin with sundry curses." He played hurling with his pupils in the Falls Park and took part in athletic competitions, organised and unorganised. He had an excess of physical as well as mental vigour. Kelly recalls that if he saw some large object, like a hurdle, in the then virtually traffic-free back streets, he could not resist the challenge of jumping over it. He drank in a pub whose owner admired de Valera, but that hardly counted for much as a political influence. A greater influence may have been his wife, Ann Scanlon, a prizewinning scholar who came, in the words of one of his grandsons, from "a more orthodox republican background". Her family lived in Sligo, not far from the foot of Ben Bulben, and after one civil war engagement the bodies of Republicans killed in the fight were laid out in their house.

When de Valera broke from the Sinn Fein rump in 1926 and founded Fianna Fail, Lemass wanted to call the new party simply the Republican Party, but de Valera had at least two reasons for choosing the strange name. He allegedly said it had the advantage of being untranslatable, though it has customarily, and often mockingly, been rendered into English as Soldiers (or Warriors) of Destiny. The second reason was more practical. De Valera wanted to attract people like Lenihan who had fought on the pro-Treaty side and might dislike the term "republican" because "republicans" had killed their comrades.

Des Hanafin, best known in another generation as a campaigner against divorce and abortion, came from a staunch republican background in Tipperary. The Hanafin family folklore recalls fierce arguments over Cumann na nGael defectors, some of whom disliked de Valera too intensely to make a straight switch to Fianna Fail and formed their own, ephemeral, half-way-house party before settling for the pragmatic option. Individuals might be said to have committed atrocities in the civil war (they may merely have been the victims of personal prejudice) or to be insufficiently republican, corrupted by the accession to Cumann na nGael of former adherents of Redmond's party and former unionists. Lenihan, in Belfast and later in Dundalk where he worked for the Revenue Commissioners, was far removed from these disputes, but he would certainly have been counted among those whom some in Fianna Fail call to this day "Cumann na nGael republicans" or "Fine Gael republicans".

Lemass looked out for talent while organising Fianna Fail in almost every parish. He spotted Lenihan, they became firm friends, and after the party first came to office in 1932 he persuaded him to leave the public service and go to Athlone to build up General Textiles (Gentex), one of the industries that flourished under the policy of protection introduced by Lemass as Minister for Industry and Commerce. Lenihan not only carried off this operation successfully, he showed himself a man of the most extraordinarily varied parts.

He bought the Hodson Bay Hotel on the western shore of Lough Ree, along with a farm, much of which he donated to be made into a golf course. He founded the all-Ireland drama festival, based in Athlone. He wrote radio plays. He read every newspaper, Irish and British, that he could lay his hands on. At all-night drinking sessions, he quoted W. B. Yeats. Glass in hand, he declaimed Yeats's "Come Gather Round Me, Parnellites" and sang Jacobite songs. He sat on the lakeshore in the early hours of the morning and told Ulick O'Connor, barrister, sportsman, playwright and critic, that he preferred Yeats's later work because the flesh had been stripped away and the bare bones shone through.

His friendship with John B. Keane began when the playwright attended his first Athlone drama festival. He describes Lenihan making a semi-regal progress through the town, like some medieval or oriental prince. He describes, too, the drinking sessions and the virtual impossibility of extracting a bill from the hotel. Lenihan in his cups would address Keane as "you old Blueshirt" — inappropriately enough considering his own origins and the fact that Keane was a very much younger man.

The lakeshore and the hotel grounds played a considerable part in these festivities. Once Keane fell into the lake, but luckily into only three feet of water: he had to borrow ill-fitting clothes from the Lenihans, Paddy and Brian. On another occasion, as the revellers went to bed in the dawn, Lenihan spotted a courting couple from his bedroom window. He made no objection to the trespass, but only shouted advice to them in the explicit terms which his Belfast pupils had enjoyed.

Yet the roistering did not prevent him from running two successful businesses, from making numerous business trips abroad, or from engaging in local and afterwards national politics, though he did not enter the Dail until 1965, four years after his son Brian. Nor did it mean neglect of his family, least of all their intellectual nurturing. The parents read and discussed the newspapers over breakfast. The children were encouraged to read everything, and had the run of a vast library.

Michael O'Kennedy, a future Foreign Minister and European Commissioner, was a friend of both father and son. It impressed him that either of them could lay hands instantly on any book out of the thousands. Under the seeming chaos, rigorous minds were at work.

It was from this remarkable background that Brian Lenihan came, and in this remarkable milieu that he was brought up.

Two

A foolish consistency is the hobgoblin of little minds.
RALPH WALDO EMERSON

As in several other Irish towns, the British garrison had left among its legacies to Athlone the game of soccer. Before the Lenihan family moved to Hodson Bay, they lived in the Gentex factory compound, and there young Brian played football with the workers. He took a slightly self-conscious pride in his egalitarianism, but his egalitarianism, in this and all other contexts, was genuine and permanent. He soon surpassed his elders in skill. He went on to play the Beautiful Game as a member of the University College Dublin team and at amateur level for Ireland, and had he so chosen he could have made a career as a professional footballer as a centre-forward with one of the major English clubs. That, however, would have been a foolish career choice. In those days professional footballers did not become millionaires. They were paid artisans' wages, and not the highest artisans' wages. In London, there were cases in which boys took up apprenticeships to printing in preference to playing for famous clubs like Arsenal.

Besides, Lenihan did not take his football too seriously. According to one abiding legend, he once turned out for Ireland with a blinding hangover, and was careful not to head the ball. But he was a lifelong lover of the game, and had strong opinions on how it should be played —dashingly. He told Ulick O'Connor that the ideal was for a winger to run half the length of the field, fending off tackle after tackle, and pass the ball to the centre-forward, who would find the net. But that style of play only survived "until Alf Ramsey abolished wingers." Football and other sports had the double advantage for him that he enjoyed all sport, and that it made a convenient subject for

11

conversation with those who did not care about, or knew nothing of, his more intellectual interests. He did, however, insist that it meant more to him in a more profound sense, in that his love of sport increased his dislike of all forms of bigotry and exclusion. He early fell foul of the then GAA "ban on foreign games", being prohibited from playing Gaelic football when caught playing soccer by one of the infamous "vigilance committees" of the time. Long after, as Foreign Minister, he would vehemently oppose Irish rugby tours to South Africa in the apartheid era, and would have a difficult time when the United States boycotted the 1980 Moscow Olympics and the US administration put extreme pressure on other Western countries to do likewise. While the controversy was at its height, he was drinking one day in a pub with Dick Walsh, *Irish Times* political writer (later political editor) and author of a history of Fianna Fail, *The Party*. Lenihan went to the bar to buy drinks, and on returning to their table said suddenly: "I know what we'll do."

"Do about what, Brian?"

"Do about the Olympics. We'll go to Moscow but we won't take the shaggin' medals."

Walsh collapsed in laughter. The chances in those days of Ireland winning any gold were slight, and the ridiculous compromise a piece of pure Lenihan inventiveness. Lenihan never had any intention of yielding to the American pressure.

*

At school in St Mary's College Athlone, as subsequently at University College and the King's Inns and at the Bar, Lenihan made himself a name as the brightest but also the laziest. He was one of those enviable people who have instant absorption, combined with extraordinary retention. Examinations gave him, to use the phrase for which he would become notorious, no problem. More significant than his school and university work, however, was his reading.

Like his brother and two sisters, and like his own children later, he learned to read before he went to school. By the age of five he was reading children's comics; by ten, *Uncle Tom's Cabin* and *From Log Cabin to White House*. From these books, which made a tremendous impression on his young mind as on countless other young minds, he not only took in the sentimental and humanitarian connotations but developed an enormous admiration for Abraham Lincoln and for all leaders of countries who make epochal decisions and carry them out regardless of their costly consequences.

By his teens, he had graduated to Dickens and Dostoevsky, strong meat beloved of sensitive adolescents. Soon he discovered philosophy. In those days bright Catholic boys learned a smattering of philosophy at school. This typically consisted of no more than an introduction to Socrates, Plato and Aristotle and a quick jump to St Thomas Aquinas, where in the orthodox view the science came to a full stop. Commentaries on Aquinas were available, usually infantile and pietistic. They did not satisfy Lenihan, who went on to study the genuine article, Jacques Maritain. But he did not stop there. He developed an interest in Locke and Hobbes and later philosophers (and in particular their theories relating to politics). The preferences give a clue to his character and views. These were practical, commensensical writers. Metaphysics was not much in his line.

He kept up his reading all his life. Where did he find the time? One partial explanation is that he had the ability to read in a moving car while being driven from one political function to another. Whatever the explanation, he gobbled up Irish, British and especially European history and biography (and late in life expressed the unoriginal opinion that one learned more from biography than history). More uncommonly, he continued to read novels throughout his life. He by no means confined himself to the English and Russian classics, but discovered a variety of modern authors including the great Czechs Kafka and Kundera. He read, naturally enough, George Orwell and Arthur Koestler and late in life came to Albert Camus. He read poetry, too, in English and other languages: as Minister for Transport and Power he would be able to quote Baudelaire to a congress of French travel agents. But his forte was European history, in which his breadth and depth were unrivalled among Irish politicians. In his political dealings at home he generally concealed, indeed deliberately concealed, his erudition. Those who did not know him well were almost entirely unaware of it, and those who knew him best were often irritated by the damage the concealment did to his reputation. But his expertise would stand him in good stead in Europe when the time came.

His reading of European history was supplemented by personal experience of a most unusual, indeed almost certainly unique, nature. His father had business contacts in England, and took his son on business trips there when Brian was as young as thirteen or fourteen. Experience of wartime Britain, for one coming from neutral Ireland, inevitably made a deep impression. After the liberation of Belgium, Paddy also developed business contacts there, and shortly after World War Two ended the fifteen-year-old Brian made a trip through several countries of devastated Europe with the son of one of these contacts. His studies and reflections on the causes of the two world wars inspired a passionate commitment to European union (there were other reasons for that commitment, which will be examined later.) They also inspired a strong sympathy with defeated and divided Germany. Comparing him with another fervent Europhile, Garret FitzGerald, Brian Lenihan junior offers the intriguing view that his father's view of European history was "Germanocentric", that of FitzGerald "Francocentric". That comparison could lead down many delightful but probably blind alleys. Let it suffice that Lenihan was fascinated by Bismarck and the first reunification of Germany and never wavered in his belief that the country would be reunited a second time.

By the time he grew into adulthood, his striking physical characteristics were thoroughly fixed. He was not exceptionally tall — barely six feet — but he was well built and looked bigger than his height. He also looked more robust than his sometimes fragile health warranted. Despite his large bones, he was light on his feet and an excellent ballroom dancer. His most prominent features were his tier upon tier of "accordion-pleated" (the phrase of the Athlone novelist and critic John Broderick) black hair, his green eyes and his ready grin. When he was annoyed, a rare enough occurrence, the eyes would narrow and swivel from side to side but the grin would remain, often grow broader.

The smiling countenance would serve him well, sometimes too well, in politics, the only career he ever really wanted. His contemporaries say that he had a splendid legal mind and could have made a great barrister if he had had the temperament for it, but he did not have the temperament. Although he had an adequate capacity for hard work when necessary, it was not for the midnight-oil kind of work that makes barristers rich. In court, as in politics, he thought on his feet, quickly grasping the essentials of a brief that might have taken him only minutes to read, alert for angles, witnesses' mistakes, and what would nowadays be called plea bargains. For a man of his intelligence, it was easy work. But it was not the work he wanted.

Lenihan "devilled" for Tom Finlay, afterwards Chief Justice, and practised on the Midland Circuit. The conditions in which judges and lawyers travelled the circuits in the fifties were typical of an age in which more than one profession floated on a sea of alcohol, almost inevitably so in view of the terrible dearth of social and cultural opportunities. The relatively few who could afford it drank in the morning, drank in the afternoon, drank into the small hours (shades of Hodson Bay). Drink drove the rougher sort into violent and indecent behaviour, usually covered up. The more gentlemanly sang, recited poetry, played word games, argued current affairs. Those who did not drink could lead a rather lonely life.

Ulick O'Connor, a non-drinker at the time, practised on the Western Circuit, and his reminiscences give a flavour of the life. He was at his wits' end for amusement, especially in the winter when his sporting activities were curtailed. Even in Galway, the liveliest and most cultured city outside Dublin, things could be bleak. "You could go to the theatre and see a performance of *Charley's Aunt* in Irish!" Elsewhere, the opportunities for recreations other than drink and "crack" were even more limited.

Proceedings in the courts reflected the participants' extramural habits. On one occasion a barrister who rejoiced in a double-barrelled name confronted a judge with a hereditary title, both much the worse for wear — and by no means the only persons in the courtroom in that condition. The titled one told the double-barrelled one: "Your client is as drunk as a lord", earning the reply: "He isn't as sober as a judge." On a whim, a barrister bought a bull at a fair and grazed it in Eyre Square, the main square of Galway. (In those days, cattle fairs were held in the square.)   As well as can be ascertained, the city council did not charge any rent for the grazing.

From this ambience Lenihan escaped, but only into another, the political, in which alcohol figured heavily. Whether at the Bar, in the pubs of Westmeath and Roscommon, or in the more rarefied circles of Dublin and other European capitals, he would spend much of his life in the company of heavy drinkers, often of alcoholics. But since his drinking attracted much criticism all through his mature years, it is well to emphasise at the beginning that he himself was emphatically not an alcoholic.

Des Hanafin is an alcoholic, dry for a quarter of a century following a cure that saved his life but caused him intense and lengthy suffering. He speaks of it with great frankness and makes the essential difference with Lenihan: "Brian was not an alcoholic. He was a heavy social drinker." Heavy, and consistent, and for decades on end. He was never seen falling-down-drunk, but often seen much less than sober. The more important question is, did it affect his judgement? Not in any profound sense, for when it came to truly significant matters his judgement was usually impeccable; but there can be little doubt that hangovers and lack of sleep must have played a part, along with his irrepressible optimism, in the frequent verbal excesses and outright blunders from which he would extricate himself with great skill and some, but not complete, dignity. A second question: Did he use it to conceal the private, even shy man who lurked under the ebullience? Not really. Like so many of his contemporaries, he saw it as normal.

*

Although Paddy Lenihan did not enter the Dail until 1965, four years after Brian, he was a member of the Fianna Fail national executive and he played a prominent role in the local politics of Athlone and the county of Westmeath. The party in the county was "run" by a near-legendary figure, Joe Kennedy, an Old IRA chief and a bachelor, still remembered with affection in the locality, who dedicated his life to the party. Like the Lenihans father and son, he admired Lemass; he admired Paddy Lenihan for his work for Athlone; and he became in his turn an important influence on Brian, who liked his radical or "social-republican" opinions. He was pleased to find that Brian wanted a political career, and took him under his wing.

The first step was to get Brian a nomination as a candidate in the 1954 general election in the Longford-Westmeath constituency. Kennedy, who controlled the nominating convention, simply told him, "leave it to me," and Brian was duly nominated. He campaigned enthusiastically, and had an obvious appeal for those who relished the possibility of electing a twenty-three-year-old for a party rapidly drifting into gerontocracy under the septuagenarian de Valera. But unfortunately for him, one of the outgoing Fianna Fail deputies was Erskine Childers, whose father, the author of *The Riddle of The Sands*, had been a friend of de Valera and one of the republicans vindictively executed during the civil war. Word reached de Valera that the upstart might unseat the son of his friend of long ago. Orders went down, directly or indirectly, to Kennedy that "Erskine must be looked after." Such were the discipline and self-sacrifice of the day that Kennedy not only obeyed but asked electors in his own town, Castlepollard, to give Childers their first preferences. Childers was elected, Lenihan rejected. Characteristically, Lenihan bore no grudge but always insisted that he liked Childers

Oddly, it remains unclear whether the Lenihan pro-Treaty background entered into the reckoning. Notwithstanding the process of partial reconciliation described by Hanafin, the joint service in the LDF, and the Fianna Fail distinction between "republicans" and others among their opponents, Fianna Fail exclusivity took a long time to die: Paddy Lenihan's daughter Mary O'Rourke had her father's record held against her as late as 1982. Local meetings were attended not only by members of the town or constituency establishments but by "men with their caps back to front", to borrow a phrase from Sylvester Barrett. These had fought, or claimed to have fought, in the war of independence and/or the civil war, and were hugely prejudiced against anyone who could not claim a pure-blooded republican background. In the 1954 election, however, Kennedy's impeccable republican credentials must have offset any such feelings.

Lenihan's attitude to de Valera was ambivalent. In his early days he was impatient, and an enthusiast for the modernising Lemass wing of the party. Reflecting on the events of the period in later life, he told the present writer that it was unconscionable that the old man clung on to office until 1959 and that the only merit of his staying in power so long was that it ensured the succession of Lemass and not of a much older candidate, Sean MacEntee. Yet, according to Charles J. Haughey, "he revered de Valera as an icon"; and the Chief's portrait hung in his drawingroom.

This first election campaign gave birth to one of the most enduring Lenihan stories. The editor of the *Longford Leader*, Tom Rennick, arrived to stay at Hodson Bay, accompanied by two persons variously described as photographers or "acolytes". They took ample advantage of Paddy Lenihan's copious hospitality.

De Valera was to address a rally in Longford within a few days. The proprietor of the newspaper, a formidable lady, telephoned with instructions for the editor to write a leading article on the subject. Rennick, in no condition to undertake the task, was dismayed. Brian volunteered to take on the job. He asked him what were the difficulties and demands of Longford and what was de Valera's record. He then wrote an editorial consisting of a list of pointed questions. When de Valera addressed the rally, he roundly denounced the newspaper as "a scurrilous Blueshirt rag" while Lenihan sat, grinned, nodded, and applauded. The proprietor thought the piece the best editorial the paper had ever carried. If she was not aware of the authorship, de Valera almost certainly was: his administration might have been out of date, but his sources of information were excellent.

Earlier and later, Lenihan engaged in more demanding journalistic work than the *Longford Leader* editorial. He wrote editorials for the *Irish Press*, and as a law student he had contributed articles to the *Leader*, a much-respected journal of opinion at the time. These included a two-part article on proportional representation, in which he advocated the introduction of the "straight vote" and a Fianna Fail–Fine Gael alliance. This latter was highly inconsistent with his lengthy advocacy of an alliance between Fianna Fail and Labour, but his opposition to PR, as we shall see below, was both understandable and consistent.

Following his defeat in Longford-Westmeath, he was obliged to retire behind the Shannon into Roscommon, to get himself elected to the county council, and to prepare to fight the next general election if he could get a nomination. Meanwhile he threw himself with his customary fervour into the process of organisational reform led by Lemass. It was typical of Lemass's amazing energy and dedication that in the fifties, in his later middle age, he worked all over again at the same task that he had performed so successfully in the twenties and thirties.

This time he had a band of young men to help him, among them Lenihan, Haughey and Eoin Ryan (senator, businessman, son of one of the party's founders, Dr James Ryan, and father of Eoin junior, Fianna Fail deputy for Dublin South East). Their task did not consist merely of organisation. They also spread the gospel of Keynesianism and economic planning, the Lemass formula for taking the country out of the economic and social trough in which it languished.

Paddy Lenihan, a self-made man who despised inherited wealth, always called himself a social democrat. So did Brian. In addition Brian, much less plausibly, insisted that Fianna Fail was a social democratic party. Although he sometimes contradicted himself and moved, rather like his party, hither and yon with the wind, his view of his own politics was undoubtedly accurate. One of the countless Lenihan legends has his sister Mary O'Rourke asserting that he was a conservative who thought himself a liberal whereas she was a conservative who would like to be a liberal. Alas, like so many Lenihan stories it is apocryphal. Another description of him, accurate and not altogether incongruent, came half a lifetime on from Professor Richard Sinnott in his magisterial book *Irish Voters Decide*. Sinnott called him and his sister "centrists". This was entirely true in so far as it related to Lenihan's normally unerring instinct for the centre in national policy and in internal party controversies, but unquestionably Lenihan never ceased to regard himself as a social democrat. As late as 1989, in an introduction to *Nealon's Guide to the 26th Dail and Seanad*, he wrote, in quixotic opposition to the prevailing wisdom, that "we are all social democrats now."

But in the fifties the prevailing wisdom was very different. It was, for one thing, widely believed by political and economic thinkers in Western Europe that state direction of industrial and economic affairs was desirable and that the failures of the communist system, which would be so devastatingly disclosed in the eighties and nineties, applied only to the lack of democracy and human rights and not to calamitous economic and industrial policies. For another, it was natural that their Irish counterparts, contemplating the wretched condition of the country, should feel that only radical new departures could save us from the abyss. As to Lenihan's mentor Lemass, he remained what was known at the time as a *dirigiste*, and as late as the mid-sixties, close to the end of his premiership, said that he wanted the banks to lend money in accordance with national needs and priorities.

In the areas at first most familiar to Lenihan, much of Westmeath and parts of Roscommon enjoyed a modest prosperity. Not so the poorer parts of Roscommon (or the section of Leitrim joined with it for a time in one constituency). There, in the fifties, many lived in conditions which would have been instantly recognisable to Lenihan's grandfather in Clare and almost wholly unrecognisable at the end of the twentieth century. They inhabited miserable houses, usually of three rooms; it was not at all uncommon for one of the rooms to fall down and for the owners to neglect, out of poverty and despair, to repair it. They had no electricity or running water. They had scarcely any cash income. Along with the smallholders there often lived a category of persons described in the census returns as "relatives assisting": bachelors and spinsters of all ages, without money, without quotidian pleasures, without the opportunity of marriage and a family, above all without hope.

The young had an escape route, but a painful one. The rate of emigration was an appalling 50,000 a year. On the border of Roscommon and Sligo, in the Curlew Mountains, stood a little railway station, Kilfree Junction. There in the early autumn, the emigration season, were witnessed the most heartrending scenes as boys and girls, often as young as fifteen, started on the first stage of the long journey by train, boat and another train to London or Birmingham. They wept helplessly on those trains and boats. And worse: owing to the practice of late marriages, associated with rural poverty, many of their fathers were as old as seventy. An old man weeping uncontrollably is a bitter sight, fit to move harder hearts than that of Brian Lenihan.

What was to be done? Provide jobs at home, said Lemass. While in opposition he promised to create 100,000 jobs. In time, Lenihan would conclude, wrongly as it turned out, that emigration would nevertheless remain a permanent feature, and got into trouble for saying so. But he also concluded that if our young people had to emigrate, they should emigrate with education and qualifications and that those sad boat and train journeys should not lead to dead-end jobs.

Meanwhile, Lenihan and his colleagues criss-crossed the country, assuring anyone who would listen that the power of amelioration lay in the hands of Lemass. Letters passed at least weekly between the Boss (a title freely conferred on Lemass and later appropriated by Haughey) and his young men. They were paternal on the one side, "Dear Brian", and respectful on the other, "Dear Mr Lemass", in a surprisingly small, crabbed hand. The Boss would arrive either by car or train at such and such a time. He would want Lenihan to address such and such a cumann or such and such a constituency organisation. Lenihan went everywhere, fitting in his Keynesian speeches and his visits to party notabilities with his Bar practice and his work in Roscommon politics. He made a great many friends, among them Hanafin and O'Kennedy. Most of all, he became literally a lifelong friend of Lemass. He saw himself as closer to the Boss than any others of the younger generation. Their association would continue to the end of Lemass's life. After his resignation as Taoiseach in 1966, he and Lenihan lunched together once a month and discussed current affairs. But whether the message of economic planning, or Lemass's jobs creation promise, made much impression in the fifties and sixties, is open to doubt.

O'Kennedy made his first foray into national politics several years after Lenihan. At a party meeting in the "back hills" of Tipperary he made a speech on economic planning. His audience listened politely, but when the meeting ended the local Fianna Fail chief took him aside and explained the nature of Tipperary politics: "I shout 'Up Dev' and my Fine Gael friend X shouts 'up Cosgrave' and then we go off and have a drink together."

Nobody enjoyed or understood that kind of thing better than Lenihan. The success of Lemass's young men was much less in putting across the economic message than in revitalising the organisation. Fianna Fail has often been described as a monolith, but the monolith has often shown cracks at all levels. No party can flourish without attention to unity, discipline and constant refreshment of the grassroots.

Three

Democracy substitutes election by the incompetent many for appointment by the corrupt few.
BERNARD SHAW

In 1946 Sean MacBride, a former IRA chief of staff and son of one of the executed 1916 leaders, founded the Clann na Poblachta party as a constitutional republican alternative to Fianna Fail. It attracted to its ranks socialists and republicans, particularly those who saw the two ideologies as interlinked, along with advocates of cranky causes — and two sections infinitely more significant in the Irish political spectrum, Fianna Fail activists disillusioned with de Valera and teachers in dispute with his government over pay.

The Clann won two sensational by-elections, and expected an equally spectacular success in the 1948 general election. In the event they won, disappointingly, only ten Dail seats, but their intervention sufficed to deprive Fianna Fail of their parliamentary majority. They thereupon formed an alliance with Fine Gael to give the country its first coalition government, a wonderful raggle-taggle. Along with Fine Gael and Clann na Poblachta, it took in Labour, National Labour (soon to be reunited with the mother party), Clann na Talmhan (farmers) and independents. Even the independents were represented in the cabinet, in their case by James Dillon, a figure of distinguished Westminster Irish Party background, who had been expelled from Fine Gael for opposing wartime neutrality. The formation of the coalition helped to reconcile him with Fine Gael, and he eventually became their leader.

At the election, Fine Gael fell below 20 per cent of the first-preference vote for the first time in their history, and returning to office gave them the kiss of life — a pattern with which the country would grow familiar. MacBride made them pay dearly for it. He vetoed the choice as Taoiseach of their leader, General Richard Mulcahy, because Mulcahy had played a major part on the pro-Treaty side in the civil war. The job went to John A. Costello, who had been attorney-general under W. T. Cosgrave two decades earlier.

Clann na Poblachta had two cabinet seats. MacBride took Foreign Affairs for himself and had a young doctor, Noel Browne, untried as a politician, appointed to Health.

In 1937 MacBride had accepted de Valera's constitution and split with the IRA, holding that the constitutional claim that the national territory comprised all thirty-two counties of Ireland should satisfy the remnants of the IRA and "take the gun out of Irish politics". It had not; and neither did the proposal now brought forward by the Clann leader, to declare the twenty-six-county state a republic. The declaration was followed by MacBride's muddying the waters on the issue of neutrality. He told the United States administration that Ireland could not join the North Atlantic Treaty Organisation because of partition, but offered the Americans a bilateral defence pact which, on British advice, they rejected. He thus both made nonsense of any claim of principled neutrality and set in train a debate which has lasted to the present day and has been conducted in a manner which would have been typical of the man himself, confused, self-serving and anti-intellectual. It would have strange echoes long afterwards when Brian Lenihan, eighteen years old at the time of these events, was Foreign Minister.

The coalition was fatally weakened by the controversy over the Mother and Child Scheme introduced by Browne. It fell from office on an entirely separate issue in 1951, but the real and poisonous legacy was not this long-forgotten issue: it had to do with church-state relations. For Browne, forced out of the government, caused his correspondence with the Catholic hierarchy to be published in the *Irish Times*. The correspondence devastatingly revealed the bishops' arrogance and their success in dictating to politicians on any matter which they held to be one of faith and morals. It was not the full story: other Irish governments handled their relations with the hierarchy more skilfully and frequently had the better of arguments with bishops, long before the decline in religious practice undermined the hierarchy's political power. But unquestionably on that occasion Irish politicians (not excluding Browne) crawled, and crawled publicly, at the sight of the crozier, and the Irish state looked uncomfortably like a theocracy.

Naturally Fianna Fail made full use, though not particularly principled use, of the coalition's shame. In their own relations with the church they favoured secret negotiations which often had considerable success, and after they returned to office following the 1951 debacle James Ryan as Health Minister brought in, with episcopal approval, a scheme not altogether dissimilar from that of Browne. But certainly, then and until very recent times, Christ and Caesar went hand in glove in Ireland.

All these events mattered much less to Fianna Fail stalwarts than the fact that real or supposed republicans, led by MacBride, had embraced the old enemy. It was a shock and a betrayal beyond their comprehension. Michael O'Kennedy's father was typical. He had defected from Fianna Fail and worked for Clann na Poblachta in the 1948 election and in one of the previous by-elections. The day after the coalition was formed, he went back to Fianna Fail.

The Mother and Child disaster helped to persuade such people, who needed little persuasion, that coalition governments did not work and that the country needed strong, single-party government. They maintained this view notwithstanding that de Valera's brief penultimate administration of 1951-54 was no model of effective or wise government. Indeed, Sean MacEntee's deflationary 1952 budget aggravated the country's economic ills. But the second Costello administration of 1954-57 was worse than the first; Fianna Fail underwent the Lemass-inspired revival; and in 1957 de Valera returned to office with a then-record Dail majority.

These developments affected Lenihan in a number of ways. He was one of those who needed little convincing of the merits of strong, single-party government. The Clann sank without trace, Fine Gael he correctly regarded as dilettantes, Labour were led by people memorably described by Conor Cruise O'Brien as "dismal poltroons". Democracy to flourish needed strong parties, and Fianna Fail was the only strong party available. He would go on to take his devotion to the principle and the party to too great lengths, and Hanafin, dwelling with some bitterness on the controversies of a later age, would sum up his attitude as "The Party! The Party! The Party!" In the fifties, however, and not only in the fifties, he had excellent grounds for his view.

Lenihan saw Browne in the mid-fifties as an ally and as someone who could influence Fianna Fail to move leftwards. Browne, in search of a second political home, joined the party against the objections of MacEntee, with whom he shared the Dublin South East constituency. Countless ordinary party members were delighted by the accession of so charismatic, if also so awkward, a personality. He was elected to the national executive and briefly became part of the Lemass modernising group along with Lenihan (who simultaneously succeeded his father on the executive), Haughey, Eoin Ryan and others.

They did not much enjoy the meetings. De Valera, in the chair as president of the party, had a foolproof method of getting his own way. Haughey recalls that the proceedings went on for hour after hour, sometimes half the night, until such time as de Valera had ground down any opposition or any attempts at innovation. At one meeting during Fianna Fail's period in opposition between 1954 and 1957 Lenihan, Haughey, Browne and Ryan succeeded in having a motion passed which called for access to higher education for all sections of the community. At the next meeting this was amended so heavily as to lose all meaning. The insertion in the minutes is in the secretary's handwriting, initialled by de Valera in the chair. It would take more than another decade to bring in free secondary education, and much longer still to ensure that most of those who could profit from it would have access to third-level education (and even today the proportion of students from working-class backgrounds in our universities is disgracefully low). When Lemass succeeded de Valera, business at executive meetings was conducted briskly and efficiently, and the meetings lasted an hour at most.

Again largely owing to MacEntee's enmity, Browne was denied a Fianna Fail nomination for the 1957 general election. He was elected as an independent and expelled from the party. It was by no means the last kick of the Old Guard, but thankfully their biggest attempted stroke failed. In 1959, when de Valera finally let go his grip on the reins of office and consented to run for the presidency, MacEntee and Frank Aiken tried to keep Lemass out of the succession. Lenihan always credited Ryan with ensuring a unanimous succession. It was well for the country that MacEntee and Aiken did not succeed. Even after becoming President, de Valera endeavoured to interfere in political affairs, until Lemass's astonishing patience finally wore out.

The rise and fall of Clann na Poblachta had intriguing repercussions in the second constituency in which Lenihan hoped to be elected.

A former Army officer and noted Gaelic footballer, Jack McQuillan, had been elected Clann na Poblachta deputy for Roscommon. He broke from the party over the Mother and Child Scheme but refused to follow Browne into Fianna Fail. He later joined him in the two-man National Progressive Democrats. When Labour moved leftward in the sixties and found a new vigour, while greatly improving their organisation, both men joined Labour. For McQuillan, however, that was an unwise move and almost certainly the main factor in the loss of his Dail seat in 1965.

In the fifties, rivalry and conflict between McQuillan and Lenihan, the two who stood head and shoulders above the other members of the Roscommon county council, were inevitable. Soon they would carry their rivalry further, into the Dail, where on one occasion Lenihan described McQuillan as "a professional agitator" and McQuillan in his turn called Lenihan "a professional chancer". McQuillan, who declined to canvass votes in public houses, affected to despise Lenihan for his practice of spending hours in pubs in the company of genuine supporters and mere hangers-on. As one of the few immune to his rival's charm and bonhomie, he discounted the fact that Lenihan, in Haughey's words, "simply liked people", all sorts of people.

Vinny Mahon, in his later career chief sub-editor of the *Irish Independent*, took a more benign view than McQuillan. Mahon, then a very young reporter on a local newspaper, was attracted to politics by the high hopes held out by Clann na Poblachta and by McQuillan's personality, and was for a time a staunch McQuillan supporter. But he soon came to form a deep affection and admiration for Lenihan, becoming one of his closest personal friends. He observed with acute interest and sympathy the conflict, but also the co-operation, between Lenihan and McQuillan on the county council. They collaborated in cleaning up the county, abolishing such demeaning practices as requiring candidates for jobs as teachers in vocational schools to canvass the votes of councillors for their appointments.

Lenihan's professed attachment to social democracy did not extend to any sort of liberalism or "political correctness", much less nicely, on the issue of local government powers. His experiences in Roscommon and afterwards on the Dublin county council were enough to disillusion anyone from the hard-baked to the most sensitive. The Dark Ages culture of Roscommon ("a heavily dependent constituency," in Mahon's words) and the planning scandals of the Greater Dublin area had their counterparts elsewhere, and Lenihan had plenty of opportunities to observe a variety of deplorable practices. In some counties, councillors' votes were all but openly bought by candidates for jobs as rate collectors. Certain independent councillors sold their Seanad votes. At least one fixed a price and held to it regardless of whether or not he got a better subsequent offer, thus proving himself an honest man by the celebrated definition by Boss Richard Croker of an honest man as one who "stays bought." Lenihan developed a profound contempt for Irish local government as no more than "an endemic nursery of corruption".

He was back in the Dark Ages in another sense when it came to his dealings with the local version of the Fianna Fail Old Guard, who were rampant in Roscommon. For all his work on the county council and within the party, he made an inadequate impression on the shambolic organisation and his enemies contrived to deny him a nomination for the 1957 general election. He was "added on" by the national executive but defeated at the polls. In a year of a national Fianna Fail electoral landslide, the party took only one of Roscommon's then four seats. Local worthies wrote pained letters to Lemass lamenting the decayed condition of the party in the constituency and begging him to see to it that Lenihan got a Seanad nomination. Lemass replied that he would do his best, and Lenihan duly obtained his nomination. He revelled in the tour of the country which the campaign involved, seeking the votes of councillors, refreshing existing networks which he had built up on his organisational tours, and making new contacts, many of which would endure for decades, some for his lifetime. He was elected, and immediately began to make his name in national politics; and he was close, if not quite close enough for his liking, to the centre of the scene when he rejoiced at Lemass's long-delayed succession to de Valera in 1959.

*

In the same year his first son, Brian junior, was born. The previous year he had married Ann Devine, six years younger, a student of dentistry who, however, had little love of the subject and abandoned her studies without regrets. (In middle age she returned to university to take an arts degree.)   There are, alas, no romantic tales to be told about their first encounter, for Ann came from Athlone and says of Brian, "sure I had known him all my life." As a teenager she had of course thought him immensely old, but when she reached her twenties the age gap looked less formidable.

They were to have five more children, Conor, Mark, Niall, Paul and Anita. Mark died in 1965. His illness and death coincided with the marriage of Michael O'Kennedy and his wife Breda, who held their wedding reception in the Hodson Bay Hotel. It was characteristic of Lenihan that in the midst of his and Ann's agony he went briefly to the hotel to wish them well.

His own marriage was, for an Irish politician, highly unusual. Ann considered herself entirely apolitical, and Brian was determined to guard her from intrigue and back-stabbing and to keep their family life as private as possible. He had no objection to competent and ambitious women like his sister making their own careers in politics, but he deplored "political wives" standing behind thrones, and these abounded, often to his distress, throughout his career. Although he would take Ann to the many unavoidable political and official receptions to which they were invited, they preferred first nights at the theatre and family gatherings at which literature made as much a subject of conversation as politics. At the time of their marriage he told her: "You're to have nobody in your house you don't like. You are to entertain only people you like."

As with himself in his own childhood, his children became voracious readers; and again as in his own childhood, no subject of conversation was forbidden. Family discussions were lively, not to say noisy, especially when his children grew old enough to put forward their own political viewpoints. He was, as one might expect, an indulgent if often necessarily an absentee father, except in two particulars. He told Ann: "Don't spoil the children. Don't give them too much pocket money — it's bad for them." The second was predictable enough from this son and grandson of teachers. He took a pressing interest in their school work and examination results, and this interest did not falter with the passing of the years. In the last weeks of his life he badgered his ewe lamb Anita over her exact results when she sat an MA degree at Cambridge. Any kind of Cambridge MA would be good enough for most, but not for him: he saw the Lenihan norm as firsts, or two-ones at a pinch.

In some ways, an ideal family; but in many ways a world removed from the idyllic picture it would be so easy but so misleading to paint, of a full family circle enjoying their comfort and privacy. For in addition to his real work, which took him away from home most of the time, he had to endure, especially at weekends, the persecution to which Irish public representatives are subjected — and to which they too willingly subject themselves. In Lenihan's case, this was aggravated by his good nature, his hatred of saying no to anybody, and the catchphrase "no problem" with which he answered every request. It was a double-edged sword. He gained a reputation for achieving extraordinary favours, often quite imaginary, for clients in politics and at the Bar; on the other hand, when he failed to deliver, either through carelessness or because the request was outrageous in the first place, the clients were not slow to complain and denigrate him.

Hordes of petitioners besieged the first house the family occupied in Athlone and the second, larger, "squireen's house" a short distance outside the town to which they soon moved. Mahon describes the queue, literally half a mile long. The siege was literal too, with petitioners making their way into the house, standing at the foot of the stairs and impeding Ann on her way to give the children their baths. Mahon and another eyewitness, O'Kennedy, were infuriated by these proceedings, especially since they were for the most part pointless. In Mahon's words, "ninety per cent of what they [the clients] wanted were their entitlements and the other ten per cent was impossible." O'Kennedy recalls that when Lenihan had an office built on to the second house, removing the need for clients to use the front door, some of them complained that "we're not good enough to go into the house!"

This insufferable annoyance was one of the reasons why the family moved to Dublin in 1971, buying a comfortable, spacious but far from ostentatious house hard by the Castleknock gate of the Phoenix Park. There were others, including easy access for the boys to Belvedere College, probably the best school in Ireland, and Brian's health. He had suffered, ominously, a liver infection at a very early age, and heart fibrillation in the 1960s; it was convenient for him to be close to one of the best hospitals, the Mater on Dublin's northside. Remarkably, he concealed the "warnings" with tremendous success, and most people, deceived by his appearance and manner, continued to think that he enjoyed robust health.

It is also reasonable to conclude that since the petition game owed much to the system of proportional representation in multi-seat constituencies, the sufferings other Irish politicians shared with him in some measure (though not in full measure) contributed to prompting him to work assiduously in the two doomed attempts to change the system in 1959 and 1968. And the encouragement of the petition game is not its only defect. In another country a young man of Lenihan's promise, destined to be a prominent figure in a powerful party, would have had a safe single-seat constituency found for him, or been placed in a comfortable position on a party list, depending on the prevailing system. In Ireland he had to take his chances. He had been mangled by the PR system twice before the 1959 referendum, in other words before he was thirty years old, and he would go through a much worse mangling five years after the 1968 referendum.

Nevertheless, there is undeniably some inconsistency between his imprudent advocacy of the British "straight vote" system and his enthusiasm, first expressed as early as 1963, for an alliance between Fianna Fail and Labour, a party that could have suffered severely from a change in the system; and his efforts to square the circle were not wholly plausible.

The attempts to bring in the British method of voting were a mistake to begin with. Irish voters in 1959 and again in 1968 knew virtually nothing about the continental list system, but they were familiar with the alternative vote (AV) in, for example, by-elections and presidential elections. A proposal to change to AV in single-seat constituencies was seriously considered in 1968, and might conceivably have succeeded. The straight vote proposal was seen on both occasions, and correctly, as a Fianna Fail power grab: it could have meant almost permanent power, and huge Dail majorities, for the biggest party.

In 1959, moreover, voters, including many Fianna Fail voters, saw the tactic as too clever by half, since the referendum was held on the same day as the presidential election and it was hoped to sneak it through on the "coat-tails" of de Valera's guaranteed sweeping victory. (The electorate have often been praised — perhaps over-praised — for the sophistication they displayed by electing de Valera and simultaneously rejecting the change in the electoral system. Their descendants displayed it again in 1998 by voting almost unanimously for the Good Friday peace agreement but endorsing the Amsterdam Treaty by a relatively small majority on the same day. In 1998, however, the turnout was very much lower and the voters complained loudly that they had not received sufficient information on the treaty.)

Meanwhile, Lenihan's relations with de Valera had continued strained. When the Chief met the young senator's bride, he discovered to his chagrin that neither she nor her husband had any interest in the Irish language, de Valera's greatest love. (Lemass similarly had no interest in Irish. De Valera counselled him to spend his time in opposition learning the language, but Lemass preferred to read J. M. Keynes.) Ann for her part found her social encounters with the party gerontocracy less than delightful. "What struck me was how old all the people were!" And how clannish! Grandees like MacEntee and Aiken would ask her such questions as "whose daughter are you?" They assumed that her father had to be one of their own.

Lenihan campaigned with his customary enthusiasm in the presidential election, more in the hope of the Lemass succession than for any other reason; and in the PR referendum. In the latter, and again in 1968, some opponents of Fianna Fail did vote for abolition. There was a cautious sniff in Fine Gael at the proposal, more pronounced on the second occasion than the first, since a minority in that party thought it might help them by wiping out smaller groupings and instituting a two-party system. Lenihan for his part argued long afterwards that Labour, not Fine Gael, would become the second party in a two-party system and eventually attain office on their own. But that sounds suspiciously like a rationalisation and an attempt to explain apparent inconsistencies in his views on relations between Fianna Fail and Labour.

In sum, however, the inconsistencies were minor; and it is a foolish politician indeed who refuses ever to bow to *force majeure*. Lenihan echoed Lemass, and frequently went somewhat ahead of him, in calling Fianna Fail "the real Labour party", "the party of practical socialism", and so forth. He meant this sincerely, and when the prevailing wind swayed him during the era of Jack Lynch to condemnation of "isms and ologies" the condemnation was as half-hearted as it was cliché-ridden. When the moment came at last in 1992 for a coalition between Fianna Fail and Labour he insisted, and undoubtedly believed, that the two parties were more compatible than any others. But he believed most firmly of all that representative democracy relied on strong parties and that Fianna Fail, social democratic or otherwise, were fundamental to the system in Ireland. If they enjoyed big majorities and lengthy periods in power, so much the better. And if other parties could not match them in commitment and organisation, so much the worse for them.

Four

It is a marvel of modern Irish history that Sean Lemass, sixty years old when he succeeded de Valera as Taoiseach in 1959, still retained so much of his youthful revolutionary vigour; and all the more marvellous in that he applied it to so conservative a country and so conservative an administration.

The roots of Irish rural conservatism are often sought in the shock of the Great Famine but the famine was only one, though a most important one, of the causes of a radical change in mores. Before, early marriages and a high marriage rate were normal. After, there was a frantic search for security. Late marriages or no marriages at all became the main means of birth control. Those who did marry often brought up large families, with husbands in their seventies fathering the last of their children on wives well into their forties, but of their numerous children only one could inherit and the options for the remainder were few and unappealing. Girls could "go into service", which frequently meant exploitation and misery. For the boys, few jobs were available in the cities and towns. Both sexes could settle for the wretched life of drudgery that was the lot of "relatives assisting" on smallholdings, or emigrate. For those with energy and initiative, emigration was usually the best course.

Most of those who stayed in the rural areas wanted social change only as a means to greater security. Far the most significant change occurred at the turn of the century with the sale to tenants on easy terms of their holdings and the creation of a large class of "peasant proprietors" Having a stake in the country naturally made them even more conservative. So did the opportunities to improve their status. The social attitudes of the Irish in the late nineteenth century are commonly ascribed to the influence of the Catholic church, but the influence of the growing class of moderately comfortable farmers was at least as strong. The clergy, the better-off farmers and the traders worked together in an unspoken alliance, which they would all have assuredly considered benign, to create the conditions which prevailed in the early twentieth century and in which the improbable Irish revolution occurred.

Improbable, yes; but not inexplicable or irrational, as sometimes argued on the wilder shores of the revisionist movement. In parallel with the moderate nationalism of O'Connell, Parnell and Redmond, to which Patrick Lenihan had been committed, and sometimes overlapping with it, had long gone the revolutionary and occasionally violent strand of nationalism. The Irish Republican Brotherhood, the secret inspirers of the 1916 Rising, traced their origins and ideology back through the previous risings of 1867, 1848 and 1798 to the French Revolution. However, before 1916 revolutionary ideas had little appeal to the bulk of the people, who were content to follow the constitutional leaders. And the Easter Rising itself was greeted at first with dismay and shock, and its leaders regarded as madmen.

But when public opinion swung in their favour after the 1916 executions the revolutionaries were ready to exploit it by using Sinn Fein as their electoral instrument in opposition to the decaying Irish Party. And the Great War had brought two other factors into the equation. First, it had conferred a grisly sort of normality and respectability on bloodshed on a far vaster scale than would ever be known in Ireland. Secondly, when recruitment for the British army dried up — partly because of the casualty rate in France, partly because of post-1916 alienation — Ireland was swamped with discontented, unemployed or under-employed young men, easily recruited for the revolution. Then in 1917 the British, with characteristic hamfistedness, attempted to impose conscription on Ireland. They failed, having provided Sinn Fein with fresh and widespread support.

It was always well understood by all but the most extreme revolutionary leaders that complete independence, in the sense of a thirty-two-county sovereign state without any ties with Britain, was not and could not be in question. The issue was (and would remain at the time of Brian Lenihan's birth and throughout his forty-year political career) the maximum degree of independence attainable. But when the Irish delegation went to London to negotiate the 1921 Treaty, and achieved more than their supporters abroad had thought possible, they knew that when they returned they would inevitably deliver less than the "pre-existing Republic" proclaimed in 1916 and that some would accept nothing inferior to that then impossible dream.

In addition to the impossible dream, the IRB and their successors had left another problematical legacy. They had always insisted that independence must come first and its nature be argued about afterwards. In 1916 James Connolly believed that he had converted Patrick Pearse to a form of socialism. In 1919 the first Dail adopted a radical economic and social programme. But Connolly may have been mistaken; the programme was more cosmetic than real; those executed in the civil war included at least one putative republican socialist leader, Liam Mellowes; and Collins, who notwithstanding a certain amount of de Valera-style rhetoric about rustic idylls saw independence as the prelude to social and economic progress, was killed. After the civil war the Irish state, under Cumann na nGael, reverted to its seemingly God-ordained conservatism.

And to speak of a God-ordained conservatism is not to exaggerate. A large and influential section of opinion in church and state viewed independence as a means of making the country more conservative, not less. They cheerfully set about prohibiting divorce and contraception, banning books and films, imposing stricter public house licensing laws and controlling dances. And when Fianna Fail came to power in 1932 they not only maintained these measures, they capped them. The worst excesses of book censorship occurred after their accession to office. The ban on divorce went into de Valera's 1937 constitution, and took nearly sixty years to remove.

Fianna Fail to their credit promoted industry and made — by the standards of the age, and during a world recession — enormous improvements in areas like housing and social welfare. But in time they fell victim to inertia and complacency. De Valera was himself a fervent Catholic. A couple of his ministers made the long journey from ideological left to right, ending, as so often happens, on the far right. Outside the parliamentary party, Fianna Fail radicals tried to associate with republican socialists in ventures like the Republican Congress in the thirties and Clann na Poblachta in the forties. Those who remained in the party were up against the unyielding de Valera, and also against the simple fact that Fianna Fail were in office too long and, like all parties too long in office, bound to run out of steam. They stayed in power continuously from 1932 to 1948, and after the two short interludes of 1948-51 and 1954-57 were to enjoy a second uninterrupted period of sixteen years' power from 1957 to 1973. In addition, they had grown old; and the senior civil servants, with whom they enjoyed an intimate relationship, had grown old along with them.

Leaving aside the republican socialists, always well outside the mainstream, Lemass was the last of the revolutionaries. That needs a little explaining. Like the Lenihans father and son, he could be regarded as a social democrat, but he was emphatically not a liberal in any sense in which the word is understood at the end of the twentieth century. When an Irish television service was established, he described it bluntly as an arm of the state. Under his regime, Haughey brought in an Official Secrets Act of which the most unreconstructed bureaucrat would have been proud. He was not given to philosophical speculation, and did not seek the company of artists or intellectuals: his recreations were the card table and the racecourse. But he was a superb politician, with depth of mind as well as his celebrated pragmatic bent. He believed in his country, and in the potential of its people. He wanted to revitalise Ireland, and he somehow managed to possess his soul in patience until his chance came to do it. When it came, he succeeded beyond the country's own expectations.

He had to proceed cautiously. He inherited from de Valera most of the Old Guard, as well as two of their sons, one being the same Erskine Childers who had bloodied Brian Lenihan's nose in 1954. He gradually brought in new men: Haughey, Donogh O'Malley, Dr P. J. Hillery and George Colley, son of another member of the Old Guard. Lenihan's failure to capture a Dail seat in 1954 and 1957 handicapped him, but when he reached the Dail in 1961 he became part of the Lemass modernising project.

This project rested on the firm foundation of industrialisation and urbanisation. Nothing remotely like the full consequences of either, much less the adverse consequences, could then be foreseen. In so far as they could foresee them, the modernisers rightly judged that they were preferable to gloom, depression and a falling population. They also knew that to carry the project to its conclusion required enormous changes, especially in education — as Lenihan, Haughey, Ryan and Browne had foreseen as early as 1955. But more: in several ways Lemass's young men, with his approval and to a considerable extent under his guidance, set about reversing mores and, it is hardly too much to say, overturning the existing society. Haughey set out to take away a man's supposedly inalienable right to dispose of his property as he pleased, however unjustly. His opponents thought it a monstrous intrusion on property rights. Lenihan liberalised the film and book censorship. O'Malley introduced free secondary education for all, ending a situation in which secondary and higher education were the preserve of a quite small minority.

And while they did it, they had a lot of fun.

*

Parnell, the Lenihan family hero, stands in bronze at the top of O'Connell Street, insisting that no man has the right to set a boundary to the march of a nation but pointing, according to the Dublin wags, towards Mooney's pub. Behind the monument, there once stood a yet more famous imbibing establishment. Groome's Hotel was not only the best known but the most respectable of Dublin late-night drinking resorts, and it was at the height of its popularity in the fifties and sixties. The customers were politicians, chiefly but not exclusively of the Fianna Fail persuasion; actors and directors from the Gate Theatre opposite; journalists, artists, intellectuals and writers, among them Peadar O'Donnell, Sean O'Faolain, and Kate O'Brien. Over the proceedings presided Mrs Patti Groome, sailing through the rooms, as Ulick O'Connor puts it, "like a great galleon", keeping strict order and ensuring that if arguments became heated, they became no more than that.

Her presence was decidedly necessary. Among the Fianna Fail Golden Boys who became known as the Three Musketeers, Lenihan and Haughey could be trusted to behave themselves regardless of the size of their intake. Not so Donogh O'Malley, brilliant and utterly charming when sober but what is sometimes called in Ireland "a serious alcoholic", truculent, violent and impossible, constantly barred for wild misconduct from pubs and hotels in Dublin, his native Limerick, and elsewhere. In the end he gave up drink. Abstinence increased his restless energy and caused Lenihan to issue the warning, "beware the dry alcoholic". He died, sadly, aged forty-six, to the great loss of Irish politics.

Dick Walsh in his book *The Party* describes Lenihan in Groome's as at once "bombastic and self-deprecating". Bombastic, perhaps, about how the new men in the party would change the world; certainly self-deprecating and self-mocking and concealing his great intelligence partly from his interior shyness and privacy, partly from a gentlemanly reluctance to parade his learning, and partly from a fear of seeming to affect an intellectual status above that of those less favoured. Walsh and Mahon were not the only ones to see the shyness and privacy. On Lenihan's forty-second birthday (17 November 1972) John Broderick would write in the *Irish Times*: "He has an innate diffidence; and like many another such, he tends to guard it with a boisterous gusto." Few observers have given a better clue to Lenihan's character and conduct.

Haughey could hardly have been more different. From his earliest days in politics he set out to impress all with whom he came in contact with his intellect and power.

Lenihan's friendship with Haughey would ultimately prove fatal, and even in those early times his association with Haughey and O'Malley harmed him perhaps more than he knew. He was regarded, both within the triumvirate and outside it, as the junior member, the butt of many jokes and the victim of the misattribution of many anecdotes. At the lowest level, one quip was and still is frequently attributed to him. The group supposedly were drinking, not in Groome's but in another late-night haunt, when the police raided it. One of them asked a policeman — in one version a raw young Garda, in another a sergeant — "would you like a pint or a transfer?" (meaning a transfer to some remote and undesirable location). O'Malley might have said it. So might a Fianna Fail minister of whom the story was told at least a decade earlier. It is utterly inconsistent with Lenihan's courtesy and kindness, but it stuck. If Ronald Reagan was the Teflon man, Lenihan was the Velcro man, for everything stuck to him, fairly or otherwise, and he would suffer from this phenomenon throughout most of his life.

Lenihan also suffered from his association with two men whose financial practices were dubious. Haughey's, the subject of endless rumour and speculation from the sixties onwards, were finally exposed, at least in part, by the McCracken Tribunal in 1997. O'Malley was involved in one of the earliest major forms of corruption. This worked very simply. A politician, possibly operating via a "front" company, would take an option to buy agricultural land close to an expanding city like Limerick. He might have had advance knowledge that the land would be rezoned for residential or industrial purposes, thus increasing its value tenfold or more; or he might have the power to have it rezoned subsequently. He would then exercise his option and take his profit, sometimes without having physically invested a penny. Lenihan, unlike the other two, had no interest in money, gained honestly or otherwise, and deplored, as we have seen, the "endemic corruption" in local government.

When, in the sixties, a rather absurd support group called Taca was set up, featuring £100-a-plate dinners, it was taken as the outward sign of Fianna Fail corruption and favouritism for their business friends. In fact it was an extraordinary and a foolish move to parade the party's business links in this manner. The expensive dinners at the very least signified an exceptional degree of arrogance and carelessness of scrupulous standards. At worst, they indicated that the diners regarded themselves as the new masters – and permanent masters, with no respect for the public or for propriety. Naturally, and quite rightly, opponents of Fianna Fail denounced Taca. Equally naturally, but not accurately, they attached the tag to the entire party, with the exception of those like George Colley who publicly complained of "low standards in high places".

Lenihan never let his friends down, and when another friend, Neil Blaney, defended the organisation in gross terms, he did not contradict him. Blaney lauded Fianna Fail as the party that had brought wealth to people who previously "did not have an arse in their pants." The chip on his shoulder almost rivalled that of Haughey, son of a family that had come down in the world and enormously resentful of his straitened boyhood. Lenihan had the confidence and self-assurance that came from his ancestry and his affluent and socially secure upbringing, but he was guilty of great carelessness and did his reputation enormous and lasting damage by letting himself be thought another in the same mould.

It would be a ludicrous mistake to suppose that the triumvirate spent most of their time roistering. On the contrary, they worked extremely hard, and they could not have done otherwise since Lemass required hard work of all his ministers. When they reached the cabinet, he expected them to be at their desks in their departments at nine o'clock every morning. In addition to their departmental work they had to attend the Dail, sometimes until midnight or beyond. They had to look after their constituencies, make speeches on behalf of the government all over the country, appear at meetings of the national executive and other bodies, and make occasional trips abroad — though foreign trips were then much less common than they became after our European accession, which imposed an ever-increasing and ultimately almost intolerable burden on ministers.

Some of the jollity they fitted in easily enough with their duties. Haughey explains that a vote on an issue of substance would commonly be taken in the Dail at 10 p.m. or 10.30 p.m., which gave the three plenty of time for a bibulous dinner. Two favourite resorts were the Shelbourne Hotel and the Russell Hotel, both on St Stephen's Green, always assuming that O'Malley was not banned from either or both. One could never tell what O'Malley might get up to on the way there or back. According to one story, on an occasion when the park in St Stephen's Green was closed, Lenihan climbed the railings, went in, and stole a duck from the pond. Long afterwards he told the journalist and novelist Deirdre Purcell, "ah no, that was O'Malley." Another yarn, which has the merit of being true, concerns the trumpeter, the lady and the dog. The Three Musketeers picked up a man playing the trumpet at the top of Grafton Street, as well as a lady with a large dog, versions of whose precise breed differ, and repaired ensemble to the Russell. Their arrival was well heralded, for the trumpeter kept on playing and every time the dog heard the trumpet, he barked. The staff would not let the dog into the diningroom, and found him quarters in the kitchen while the five dined well. When the dinner bill arrived, O'Malley was horrified to find that it came close to £200, an enormous sum for a meal for five persons in those days. On inquiry he was told that it was accurate, since the dog had eaten the entire contents of the dessert trolley. He was further told that they were banned from the hotel. But a silent diner at another table had witnessed the incident, and wrote about it in the *New York Times* as a delightful example of Irish mores. The ban was lifted.

Yet another Lenihan story of the period has him striding across O'Connell Bridge on a windy night, allowing masses of petitions to fly out of his overcoat pocket into the Liffey. That is most improbable. What he did with all the "impossible" petitions remains something of a mystery, but the wind on O'Connell Bridge is seldom wild enough to dislodge papers from overcoat pockets, and after 1961 he generally travelled about in an official car, freeing him from any need for such perambulations.

*

Meanwhile, there was important work to be done; and Lenihan expected to be given important work once he escaped in 1961 from the Limbo of the Seanad into the Heaven of the Dail. He — and Lemass, and the British Prime Minister, Harold Macmillan — had not reckoned with one of the most formidable personalities of the age, President Charles de Gaulle.

When Britain applied for membership of the EEC (European Economic Community; strictly speaking the European Communities or EC; now the European Union or EU) Ireland had no option but to attempt to join also, since such an enormous proportion of our trade was with Britain. But Lemass emphatically did not see the application as made on Britain's coat tails. Membership would have colossal economic advantages, in the first place for agriculture and secondly for trade, though it would create savage problems for Irish industry. More important, it would take us out of the British shadow, widen our political horizons, and provide us with far more genuine independence, as opposed to paper sovereignty, than had ever before been foreseeable: Irish European policy is far more political than economic, a point frequently overlooked but thoroughly understood by Lemass and Lenihan although, curiously, much less so by Haughey.

With advance knowledge of the British application, Lemass decided to steal a march on Whitehall and get the Irish application in first. The physical task was entrusted to the cabinet secretary, Dr Nicholas Nolan, known as "Meticulous Nicholas". Instead of sending the document through diplomatic channels, Nolan put the document in an envelope, had the envelope registered, and with his own hands popped it into the pillar box at the corner of Merrion Street and Merrion Square. A day or so later anxiety arose when it was found that the Irish embassy in Brussels did not have it in their possession. A very junior diplomat received a telephone call from his counterpart in the British embassy who had got wind of the Irish application. He knew nothing about it, but telephoned Dublin and found that it was safely in the mail. He did not tell the British, who might have taken the opportunity to speed up their own application in the time available. The junior diplomat, Eamonn Gallagher, went on to become a high official of the European Commission.

Five of the then six members of the Community were wholly in favour of British, Irish and Danish membership, and it was generally assumed that the applications would succeed. For Lenihan, the prospect was intensely exciting. Unlike those misled by his fondness for socialising, Lemass knew the worth of his intellect and his knowledge of European history and politics. Lenihan expected him to appoint him "minister for Europe", which would have meant control of the greater part of the Foreign Affairs brief. The Foreign Minister, Frank Aiken, had little or no interest in Europe but a deep interest in the United Nations, where he concerned himself, honourably and with some success, with issues like nuclear non-proliferation. Northern Ireland is chiefly the province of the Taoiseach, and Northern Ireland was not at the time an issue that engaged a great deal of the government's attention. As minister for Europe, Lenihan would at once have become one of the top figures in Irish politics.

There were two difficulties, one obvious and one barely foreseen. Did European entry mean abandonment of Irish neutrality? Specifically, was membership of Nato a precondition? Lemass tried desperately to find out. There were a handful of splendid officials in his office and in the Department of Foreign Affairs, but the Irish diplomatic service was tiny and sources of information were very limited. The file on the subject in the National Archives shows Lemass reduced at certain points to reliance on newspaper reports and interviews, one of the most significant being an interview with Professor Walter Hallstein conducted by Desmond Fisher for the *Irish Press*. Hallstein, one of the leading lights of the European enterprise, opined that Nato membership was indeed a precondition.

John Healy of the *Irish Times* always maintained that Lemass used the Haughey-O'Malley-Lenihan triumvirate to fly kites for policies on which he wanted to test the air. Haughey, who considered Healy "an incurable romantic", says that this notion is imaginary. "The only real kite was flown by O Morain." The reference is to Micheal O Morain, Minister for Lands, whom we will encounter in more than one guise in these pages.

As to the reality of that particular kite, there is no doubt whatever. O Morain was regarded as something of a buffoon, and Lemass may well have decided to employ him in preference to a more highly regarded figure or one who might appear more plausibly to speak with the Taoiseach's authority. The result was a characteristic Irish mixture of the serious and the comical. O Morain made a speech favouring Nato membership in his Mayo constituency. This led to noisy Dail exchanges in which doubts were cast on his sobriety on the occasion.

The real doubt, however, had little to do with the unimportant question of O Morain's sobriety and a great deal to do with the vexed issue of Irish neutrality. It is beyond question that for those at the heart of the establishment, then and since, neutrality has not been an issue of principle but one of policy. De Valera, who before World War Two argued for collective security and was disappointed, was not in principle a neutralist; and his wartime neutrality was heavily — and rightly, and necessarily, if in strict terms of international law illegally — biased in favour of Britain. Sean MacBride was not a neutralist; how could he be, when he offered the Americans a bilateral defence pact? In time, policy settled down to the proposition that we would join, not Nato but a European defence system under the European Union if such came to pass, and Lenihan in later life analysed the question thoroughly and persuasively. But in the early sixties Lemass was perfectly willing to bring Ireland into Nato if he thought it essential and if he could "sell" the policy to the public.

It turned out, however, to be no more than a hypothetical question for that generation. For de Gaulle vetoed British membership, and the Irish application went into cold storage. It is all but certain that de Gaulle, through his Prime Minister Couve de Murville, offered Lemass "association", but Lemass very properly rejected second-class citizenship — another demonstration of the primacy of politics.

For Lenihan, the event was a grave blow, and a worse blow than he then knew. In one way it would be easy to see his political career as one of almost uninterrupted advancement for a Golden Boy. The reality was, and would continue, otherwise. He had already suffered two electoral setbacks, and now, while the first of the new generation were reaching the cabinet, he found himself denied the glittering European prize and becalmed in one of the most obscure backwaters of the administration: the Department of Fisheries, to which Lemass appointed him parliamentary secretary in 1961.

Five

As long as there are bananas there will be banana skins.
WILLIAM WHITELAW

On the face of it, Lenihan's situation in 1961 was enviable. At the age of thirty, he was a member, albeit a junior member, of a dynamic administration, superbly led, in a country finding its running legs. And although not yet in the cabinet, he had in effect a department of state for himself, as was undoubtedly Lemass's intention. The Minister for Lands and Fisheries, Micheal O Morain, appeared to have written off fisheries as an industry of any potential, and devoted himself entirely to Lands. This meant in large part the consolidation of smallholdings, an activity which provided splendid openings for patronage and popularity, not least in his own Mayo West constituency. Lenihan must have expected great latitude and a chance to shine.

The reality was somewhat different. Ministers and senior civil servants generally came from similar backgrounds, shared very similar attitudes and life experiences, and had, literally, grown old together. Officials in Fisheries reported to more senior officials in Lands, who reported to the cabinet minister; and the methods so hilariously satirised in the *Yes, Minister* television series applied in Ireland as much as in Britain. A generation later, Lenihan would deny in print that there were any Sir Humphreys among the Irish mandarins, but privately he told the present writer that he found *Yes, Minister* terrifyingly accurate. The civil servants were dedicated and incorruptible, but in many cases narrow and conservative — as much so as the Fianna Fail Old Guard, most of whom were by then as conservative as Cumann na nGael had ever been. Dynamic as the Taoiseach might be, he had to concentrate on the broad thrust of his economic policy (as well as on party organisation, which he never ignored) and could not concern himself with every byway and alley, to whose occupants the message had not penetrated that "development" was the keyword of the Lemass administration. In fairness to them, few at the time could have envisaged the colossal demands that would soon be made on the administration in such areas as health and education, or that they would rise so successfully to the challenges posed to them. The culture as well as the structures of the department thus operated in Lenihan's disfavour. And as many other junior ministers have found to their cost, lack of access to the cabinet table is disastrous, especially when it comes to the struggle for resources. For all Lemass's friendship with the Lenihan family, he would not have welcomed constant approaches from a junior minister.

The condition of the industry was grim. Men fished within sight of the shore, from boats at most fifty-six feet long. Many were very much smaller: large numbers of currachs, virtually unchanged in design and construction since prehistoric times, were in use. They had no radios or safety equipment. There were few processing facilities, and distribution was often non-existent. Over most of Ireland it was all but impossible to buy fresh fish — and this in an overwhelmingly Catholic country, when eating meat on Fridays was forbidden to Catholics.

Lenihan was frustrated. As a rule throughout his career he liked lean, clean administration and deplored the multiplication of state boards and agencies. Lemass, too, would have preferred a tighter and more logical administration, but when he came up against the bureaucratic culture and saw departments as not fulfilling a developmental role, he set up state commercial and other companies, which came to be known by the very Irish and not very accurate tag of "semi-state". Needs must ... Lenihan head-hunted a successful young businessman, Brendan O'Kelly (like himself a footballer of some note), out of the private sector, made him executive chairman of the sea fisheries board, An Bord Iascaigh Mhara (BIM), and gave him independence and a mandate to build up the industry.

O'Kelly thought his own lack of a political affiliation an advantage. But he found political interference rampant in the industry. Politicians found fertile pickings in securing boat grants and loans for constituents and making representations on behalf of fishermen who defaulted on repayments to the state. The over-indulgence of deputies had contributed to the dire financial position of the board and the stagnant state of the industry. O'Kelly thought the politicians' place should be outside the door, and on at least one occasion literally put them outside the door. He saw his function, and that of others like him, brought in by Lemass from outside the official world, as making up for the defects of the civil service and providing impetus in key areas of economic development. But after Ireland's accession to the EEC in 1973 their role would diminish as new guidelines and administrative structures were put in place in Brussels. Meanwhile, political and official inertia would baffle O'Kelly and Lenihan.

Lenihan's new responsibilities were not welcomed by O Morain, who might have had little interest in fisheries but viewed Lenihan's appointment as a dilution of his own power. Initially the Sea Fisheries Division of the department were happy enough, seeing the change as an escape from the domination of the main department. But few of them were enthusiasts for the restructuring of BIM and the appointment of a chief executive from the private sector. Lenihan was very conscious of the pitfalls he would encounter if he took too radical an approach. It would take all his incipient political skills to avoid them and he would learn many lessons from his bruising early encounters: the need for "lateral thinking", for indirect approaches, for circumventing the bureaucracy where necessary and using it to full advantage where there was a meeting of minds. But it would be a long time before he would find that meeting of minds in the Department of Foreign Affairs, where the officials had minds, and subtlety, to equal his own. His troubles with the bureaucracy, like O'Kelly's, had only begun.

O'Kelly had come from an environment in which change, flexibility and communication, as well as profit, were essential. The status quo was anathema to him. So were the infighting and knifing in which, he found, the private sector with which he was familiar came a poor second to the public sector. Money alone, he believed, would not build up the industry: people had to be motivated to overturn the "social service" culture which prevailed in the industry. He brought in measures aimed at encouraging investment, enterprise and commercial initiatives. For the politicians, the negative side was his attempt to eliminate existing hire purchase debt and to take a strict approach to fishermen's repayment obligations.

Finance, however, was still important. One happy result of the new policies was increasing demand from young fishermen for larger vessels, but the board was starved of finance. It therefore raised money abroad in France, Poland, Norway and Holland. This and other initiatives displeased some of the bureaucrats. Relations between BIM and the department deteriorated almost into open warfare. Employing his own brand of "lateral thinking", O'Kelly embarked on a strategy which he believed would pull down some of the roadblocks. He had earlier done postgraduate work at the Harvard Business School, where he had become acquainted with the Kennedy Mafia (the coterie of intellectuals, advisers and political fixers, many from Boston, who accompanied John F. Kennedy to the White House in 1961). Through this connection he met James K. Carr, Under-Secretary to Stuart Udall, Secretary of the Department of the Interior. Udall's portfolio included responsibility for the Bureau of Commercial Fisheries. O'Kelly persuaded Carr that an objective outside appraisal of the potential of Irish fisheries would make a substantial contribution to Irish-US relations. Whether the Americans saw any strategic advantage in the proposal is not clear from the relevant documents, but in them there surfaces a strong and intriguing hint of "resource wars", a question that would soon arise in our relations with Europe and would have unfortunate implications for the fishing industry.

O'Kelly kept his plans a secret from the department and confided only in Lenihan, who in turn confided in Lemass. The subject was placed on the agenda, along with tourism and US investment in Ireland, for a meeting between Lemass and Kennedy in Washington in 1963. According to the rather quaint language of the official report,

> Turning next to the sea fishery resources of Ireland, Mr Lemass spoke of the immense possibilities for development. The Irish authorities, he mentioned, would be glad to have access to the research carried on by a deep-sea exploratory vessel. President Kennedy replied by referring to the visit to Dublin, quite recently, of Mr J. Carr, US Under-Secretary of the Interior. Arising out of the discussions which Mr Carr had in Dublin with Irish fisheries authorities, it was being arranged that the US official in charge of the Bureau of Commercial Fisheries would go to Dublin in November for further and more detailed discussions. Mr Lemass expressed his pleasure at this development. He commented that rapid increases in population throughout the world called for more intensive development of the fishing industry. President Kennedy remarked that Soviet Union [sic] had already been convinced of that fact, judging by the scale of their activities on some of the fishing grounds in easterly regions of the North Atlantic.

Donald McKernan, head of the Bureau of Commercial Fisheries, visited Dublin in November 1963. In January 1964 he and O'Kelly prepared a joint report which noted the Irish desire to train fishermen, skippers, technicians and scientists in modern methods.

> The Irish ... would like to send some of their people to the United States to further these objectives. They would also like to have American specialists come to Ireland to work with the Irish in training their fishermen and technicians ... If co-operation in

fishing oceanographic research is to develop between the two nations it is mutually advantageous to exchange experts to develop the maximum co-operation ... Ireland has no high seas research vessel. There is need for one if their ocean research programme is to be of maximum benefit either to them or to the United States.

A schedule of special recommendations included the establishment in Ireland of a research and development operation. Following that, the Americans would lend us one of their surplus research vessels. A co-operative programme of oceanographic research would "contribute to the accumulation of knowledge of the North Atlantic Ocean." A team of American experts arrived in April 1964 and completed their report in June. It was released in October, but by then Lenihan was no longer in Fisheries. He had been appointed Minister for Justice following Haughey's promotion to Agriculture, and George Colley had succeeded him.

Colley found himself perusing a report which criticised government policy for the industry and recommended increased autonomy for BIM. The department's reaction was hostile, while the new parliamentary secretary saw his job as very much a temporary one and a stepping stone to higher things and was in no mood for a confrontation with the bureaucracy. Only one of the recommendations of the McKernan-O'Kelly report, the "objective appraisal", was ever implemented. Plans for joint educational, research and technical programmes went by default. Later, worse would come. Plans for the development of the industry came up against an insuperable obstacle in the negotiations for EEC entry in 1972. Other countries wanted "equal access" to our vast waters, which would become EEC waters, with exclusive Irish fishing rights restricted variously to twelve, six and three miles from the shore — whereas elsewhere in the world countries conscious of the vast resources under the sea were pushing out their limits. Later still, Irish fisheries would be caught in a pincer movement, with quotas for varieties of fish added to the problem of access, a phenomenon that would continue to the present. But that is to get ahead of our story, the story of Lenihan. He had now reached the cabinet, but his troubles with the bureaucracy had only begun.

*

Lenihan arrived at the cabinet table in 1964, aged thirty-three, as Minister for Justice. In 1968 he moved to Education after the sudden death of O'Malley.

In both departments, his troubles with civil servants continued, this time for a specific and rather extraordinary reason. Peter Berry, the legendary Secretary in Justice, and Sean O'Connor, Assistant Secretary and afterwards Secretary of the Department of Education, were magnificent public servants, but infatuated with Haughey and O'Malley respectively and severely prejudiced against Lenihan. Berry told the broadcasters Mike Burns and Sean Duignan that Haughey was the best minister he had ever served, and Lenihan the worst. An absurd judgement, and immensely ironic in view of what would eventually happen in the Haughey-Berry relationship.

When Lenihan undertook his first task in Justice, however, he encountered no difficulties with Berry. This task was to complete the legislative process for the enactment of Haughey's justly famous Succession Bill. It might have been thought that a rigid conservative like Berry would have taken the view that a man should be able to make whatever disposition of his property he pleased, no matter how "unjust and cruel" (Haughey's words). That certainly was the view of substantial sections of the Fianna Fail and Fine Gael parties, whose opposition continued after Lenihan took over from Haughey. And opposition was by no means confined to the more obviously rustic and unenlightened. Long after Haughey's departure from the department, the *Irish Times* sniped at him for leaving it to Lenihan to "patch and prune" what it called a "misbegotten" measure, "unleashed without a word of advice from any legal body ... the pipedream of a member of [Haughey's] department". But as to Berry, again to quote Haughey, he devoted himself to matters of state security —

there is another irony here — and the Minister, along with a small group of officials and legal advisers, had a free hand with the Succession Bill.

It has to be admitted that Berry did have some cause for annoyance. Although, as noted acidly by Vinny Mahon, ninety per cent of the petitions Lenihan received were the petitioners' legal entitlements and the other ten per cent impossible, he could not refrain from trying to find chinks in the system. And he was — then, before, and later — not above dropping hints that his powers of manipulation were greater than the very restricted reality. Occasionally the sardonic and Delphic side of his otherwise sunny nature showed through, leaving his auditors to wonder what exactly he meant. He told Arthur Reynolds, editor of the *Irish Skipper*, that he would do him a favour if he could but "I can't get you off a drunken driving charge!" (He knew of course that Reynolds was literally a sober citizen.) His attempts to spare people the consequences of minor, and some not so minor, offences led to many a difficult Monday morning with Berry. Nor was his habit of over-relying on his quick wit at all palatable to the Secretary. Though usually capable of glossing over verbal gaffes, he was too often caught "with his foot on the floor and his mind in neutral", the jibe of Frank Cluskey, afterwards leader of the Labour Party. And he found himself getting the blame for incidents when neither he, nor his officials, nor yet the police, were blameworthy. A dispute between the government and the National Farmers' Association (later renamed the Irish Farmers' Association) led to the brief imprisonment of a number of activists. A crowd of NFA supporters took exception to the sight of two men being taken into a prison in handcuffs, and questions were asked in the Dail. Lenihan explained that the two handcuffed men had nothing to do with the NFA prisoners, who had gone into the prison "freely". It was a singularly ill-chosen word.

But this was trifling stuff compared with his main work of reform. In addition to completing Haughey's work on the Succession Bill — for which he could have claimed almost as much credit as its author — he set about liberalising the censorship laws to such effect that he would deserve an honoured place in modern Irish history if he had never done anything else in his long career.

The climate favoured him. The papacy of John XXIII and the second Vatican Council had evoked enthusiasm in Ireland. Liberal Catholics, including many liberal clergy, prematurely hailed a new departure for the church. When the formidable Archbishop John Charles McQuaid of Dublin told his flock that the Council had changed nothing, he was widely and publicly contradicted, an experience to which he was not accustomed and which he did not relish. For the most part, the conservatives bided their time, knowing it would come again. But for the moment, although reform inevitably attracted some episcopal condemnation (chiefly from McQuaid and Bishop Cornelius Lucey of Cork, who wanted the laws made stricter, not easier) the liberals were in the ascendant, respected clerical thinkers supported Lenihan, and he said that his main opposition came not from the church but from the civil service. By that he meant, mainly, Berry.

First he tackled film censorship. This was so strict in those days that masterpieces of the cinema were abominably mauled. Sometimes the cuts were so savage as to make the plots impossible to follow. Lenihan employed the simple expedient of licensing films for viewing by persons above a certain age. The even worse censorship of books was said to make us a world laughing stock: a ridiculous exaggeration, since most of the world seldom takes any notice of Ireland. André Gide might have raised a Gallic eyebrow on learning that English translations of his work were banned here, but in all probability ninety-nine per cent of his fellow-countrymen neither knew nor cared; and among the many grotesqueries of the system, anybody able to read his work in French was free to do so. Indeed, the censorship did not apply to books in Irish, a language which, in theory at any rate, a large proportion of the population could read. An English translation of Brian Merriman's classic eighteenth-century poem *The Midnight Court* was banned; not so the original.

While the prohibition of much of the great literature of the twentieth century was bad enough, the main burden of the censorship fell on Irish authors. Almost all the best contemporary Irish authors had their work banned — and for ever, and on the flimsiest grounds. The law provided for the prohibition of a work on the grounds of its being in its general tendency indecent or obscene. By no stretch of the most prurient imagination, one might have thought, could this description have applied to *The Land of Spices*, a novel of the utmost delicacy and refinement of feeling by Kate O'Brien. In a climactic scene, a girl glimpses her father and a young man "in the embrace of love". For that phrase, the book was banned. And there can be no doubt of the prurience, or the vulgarity, of certain censors. One, a university professor, would carry books into the senior common room and gloatingly inform his colleagues that he might read them and they might not.

A publishing sensation occurred in 1965 with the appearance of *The Dark*, by John McGahern. McGahern, then living in Dublin, had been born in Leitrim and brought up in Lenihan's Roscommon constituency, and eventually returned to settle in Leitrim. His book entranced critics with its meticulous and painstaking style, and its content. It was a searing, and a totally accurate, account of provincial lower-middle-class life, with its terrible sexual deprivation, its petty snobbery, and its narrow horizons. It was of course promptly banned. But whereas Kate O'Brien merely expressed polite puzzlement at the prohibition of her books, the banning of *The Dark* caused a tremendous furore for several reasons. First, McGahern had put on paper what everybody knew and few dared say. Secondly, since influential foreign critics praised the work, the event really did come close, this once, to making us a laughing stock. Thirdly, the prevailing if ephemeral atmosphere in Catholicism was opposed to the suppression of serious literature. And fourthly, there was a young and liberal minister in office who admired McGahern's work and who knew the realities of Roscommon life better than most.

His drinking companions in Groome's shook their heads. A young journalist called Bruce Arnold (whose path would cross Lenihan's again, as so many paths do in this story) was Dublin correspondent of the *Guardian* and secretary of the tiny Censorship Reform Group. He approached Lenihan and found himself pushing the proverbial open door.

Another door, however, was open: that of Berry's office, in which he had a cabinet full of pornographic books. In kindness to his memory, one must suppose that he kept them as horrible examples, not for pleasure. In the manner of the censor with his university colleagues, he told his Minister that he might not read them. Lenihan replied, sharply enough, that he had no interest in pornography but did not want the Irish public deprived of the opportunity to read masterpieces. He called in aid the Grand Old Man of Irish letters, Sean O'Faolain, who had been a civil servant and knew the art of drafting legislation. O'Faolain helped in the drafting of, and may have actually written, Lenihan's reform bill. Again, this was a very simple measure, providing for the "unbanning" of any book after a period of years. The legislation went through with little difficulty in 1967. Thousands of books were immediately "unbanned" and have remained so ever since. Nowadays the few books prohibited tend to have whips, leather and so forth in their titles.

Lenihan was enormously and rightly proud of his achievement, and he would have been either more or less than human had he not rejoiced in his triumph over Berry. Soon after, however, he had to deal with another formidable official.

*

In March 1968 Donogh O'Malley collapsed while campaigning for Sylvester Barrett, the successful Fianna Fail candidate, at a by-election in Clare. He was dead on arrival at a hospital in Limerick.

Not long before his death, he had enjoyed a triumph greater than that of Lenihan's on censorship, the introduction of free secondary education more than a decade after de Valera had put paid to the ambitions of Lenihan and others on this subject. As with the Succession Bill, it fell to Lenihan to complete the work. He did so with such enthusiasm as to inspire another friend, Michael Herbert, to say that the Department of Education was his natural home. This opinion is not shared by those who believe that his natural home was the Department of Foreign Affairs. It was not shared, for very different reasons, by Sean O'Connor.

O'Connor had been for O'Malley at all times a fervent and most important ally, and at some times a chiding, cautious counsellor in his quarrels with the Catholic church. These should not be given undue importance. The clergy at all levels were of course concerned to maintain as much influence as possible under the educational revolution, but that is not to say that they were necessarily opposed. On the contrary, the best thinkers among them, like Cahal Daly, who would go on to become Cardinal Archbishop of Armagh, were wholly in favour, seeing the departure as necessary and benign, while the most astute politicians among them saw it as an opportunity to extend their empires. McQuaid encouraged priests, nuns and brothers running schools in his Dublin archdiocese to participate. O'Connor wrote in his memoirs that "I was informed by a member of one of the orders of nuns that the archbishop had issued what was tantamount to a directive to the convents to join the scheme and that therefore all the schools of that order would participate. What reason the archbishop gave I do not know, but one would surmise that he wanted the convent schools to attract to themselves the newcomers to secondary education." Quite so. But certain consequences of the education reforms, envisaged by O'Malley, would be very much less favourable to McQuaid.

Rows, however, there were, with religious orders which wanted to keep their schools exclusive. This led to one notorious outburst by O'Malley, who threatened in apocalyptic terms to expose those who were trying to impede his work. It was less an example of a church-state confrontation than of "the dry alcoholic" seeking an outlet for his energy. O'Connor, greatly distressed, worked to mend fences; O'Malley realised that he had been foolish; the row blew over.

Lenihan inherited the practical problems associated with the introduction of free education. In his dealings with the church at all levels, as also with his studies of the church, he saw it for all his Catholic conformism as a political institution, with which one negotiated and made deals. But he also inherited a more tangled problem.

O'Malley had proposed a merger of the University of Dublin (Trinity College) and University College Dublin, a constituent college of the National University. With characteristic hyperbole, he declared that "apartheid" between Protestants and Catholics — the latter forbidden by McQuaid to attend Trinity without special dispensation — existed in the capital and he meant to end it.

Strangely, three decades on nobody can say for certain why O'Malley, stoutly backed by O'Connor, wanted the merger. Even Tony O Dalaigh, private secretary to several education ministers including O'Malley and Lenihan, says he does not know. It is, however, possible to make a very good guess.

It is stranger still that O'Connor, as is clear from his memoirs, did not know that the enterprise was literally impossible. It is a fundamental principle of the Irish state and establishment that one never tramples on Protestant privileges in health and education; and to force Trinity into a merger with UCD would have amounted to trampling on Protestant privileges. Certainly O'Malley was furious with the Trinity authorities, and with good cause. Back in 1961 they had told the Commission on Higher Education that a figure of three thousand students was their upper limit, but in 1965 they decided to raise the number to four thousand, of whom only 1,344 would come from the Republic. In other words, they expected the government to subsidise places for large numbers of students from Northern Ireland, Britain and farther afield. O'Malley railed against the Trinity "enclave", but he must have known that forcing the merger through would be condemned as a sectarian move. His true intention appears to have been founded on the knowledge that free secondary education would inevitably bring an enormous increase in the numbers seeking university entrance; that places would have to be found for them; that in addition to expansion, this could be done by replacing British and foreign Trinity students with Irish students; and that a debate on the merger would bring about the ending of the ban on Catholics entering Trinity, as indeed it did.

O'Connor, however, remained a lifelong supporter of the merger, and in his memoirs he disparaged, at least by implication, the sceptic Lenihan. He seems to have believed that Lenihan wanted the merger as much as himself and O'Malley, and abandoned it only out of weakness. He also, in his anxiety to vindicate O'Malley, muddled up his dates, an amazing thing for a senior civil servant. But he deserves to be remembered for his dedication to improving Irish education, not for minor faults.

Lenihan for his part proposed autonomy for the National University colleges, a project which proceeded at the usual Irish glacial pace for the next three decades. As a small step towards greater equality of opportunity, he quadrupled the number of university scholarships to one thousand, a figure that looks derisory now but was significant then. As a sort of compensation for the abandonment of the merger, a rationalisation of Trinity and UCD faculties was set in train, though this took several years to complete. More significant was the proposal to set up two "institutes of higher education", in Limerick and at Glasnevin in Dublin, now the University of Limerick and Dublin City University. Fathership of the latter, initially the Dublin Institute of Higher Education, was claimed both by Lenihan and by Richard Burke, who became Fine Gael Minister for Education in 1973; the credit for Limerick is certainly Lenihan's. He was derided at the time for promising to give Limerick "something better than a university", but the eventual outstanding success of the project proved that he spoke no more than the truth.

*

These were very substantial achievements for a minister who held the portfolio of Education for little more than a year. It is typical, but enormously unfair, that when his contemporaries recall his tenure of the office they are more apt to bring up one silly incident than to laud him for his work.

To call the Irish student revolts of the sixties idiotic would be to over-praise them. They were pale copies of events in France and the United States. The participants came almost by definition from the privileged classes, to which they soon returned without shame or apology. The causes for which they agitated have been forgotten. But Lenihan got himself caught up in them. Besieged at a meeting in Trinity, he escaped through a lavatory window. "That's Brian for you," people said when they saw in the newspapers the picture of him clambering through the window.

It has, however, to be said that during this period (and most periods) of his career he continued to contribute to the comical side of the Lenihan legend. Friday afternoons, for example, he liked to spend with one of his senior officials in a pub close to the Department of Education in Marlborough Street. It was part of O Dalaigh's duties to extricate him, often under protest. "Minister, you have to be in [such and such a location in his constituency or elsewhere] at eight o'clock." He gained a reputation for gross unpunctuality and for keeping people waiting, often for hours, for him to arrive and, as he would hope, charm them out of their irritation. A delegation wishing to discuss state support for the arts waited for him in Buswell's Hotel until midnight. So did, much later, a group concerned about an industrial problem in his second constituency, Dublin West. One of its members said: "He finally arrived, the worse for wear, and told us that he knew all about it. We knew he was bluffing. He knew nothing about it."

Very likely Lenihan was indeed bluffing, but the delegation member may have been unaware of his sagacity and his skill in damage limitation. If there was something he did not know, he had excellent means of finding out, and quickly. More than half the battle is to know who knows, and Lenihan always knew who knew.

But the legend survived, and grew, and he did nothing to discourage it. While he still lived in Athlone, one of his drivers could take him home in a little over an hour, even on the dreadful roads of the era, because official drivers are brilliant. But he could not forbear to stop on the way, somewhere he could find good company. A favourite was Harry's Bar in Kinnegad, where the Athlone and Mullingar roads diverge. A classic Lenihan story has him receiving an urgent telephone call from his department late one night. A popular version has a junior official poring over an Ordnance Survey map, identifying each village on the way to Athlone and deciding which one to try. Finally, "is that Harry's Bar?" "Yes." "May I speak to Minister Lenihan?" "Speaking!"

The incident in fact occurred in the morning, not at night. The civil servant was no junior official, but Tony O Dalaigh. The "map" was a telephone directory. The location was Byrne's of Kilcock, not Harry's of Kinnegad. But yes, an official did call a pub to say that Lenihan could not postpone an engagement; and yes, the Minister did answer the telephone.

Six

This we can call a constitutional principality, to become the ruler of which one needs neither prowess alone nor fortune, but rather a lucky astuteness.
    NICCOLO MACHIAVELLI, The Prince

Lemass was an astonishingly young sixty when he became Taoiseach in 1959, and a very old sixty-seven when he resigned in 1966. He had worn himself out, but he could contemplate his work with satisfaction. Now someone must carry it on. But the question of the succession was difficult, and the consequences of the succession race ultimately disastrous.

Colley was the candidate of the Old Guard, who pointed, and whose apologists still point, to his total integrity. That, however, was in large part less an argument for Colley than an argument against Haughey, whom they regarded with suspicion; and Lenihan for one thought that integrity was not enough and that Colley was a man of severely limited ability.

Supporters of both Colley and Haughey tried to spread an impression that their man was the favoured successor, but Lemass was careful to give no hint of any preference. His only overt action was to alert Colley to his retirement, so that he could return early from a foreign trip and contest the party leadership should he choose. That was only fair. As to Haughey, the circumstance that he was married to Lemass's daughter assuredly did not weigh with his father-in-law.

On one thing, all factions in the Fianna Fail establishment were agreed: Neil Blaney must not have the leadership. Blaney, described by Haughey as "a Donegal tribal chief, hewn out of granite", was a highly competent minister but a vehement irredentist on the Northern Ireland issue. That moves towards conciliation would fail calamitously and that the North would soon descend into a generation of violence could not then be foreseen. But undoubtedly Blaney could not be trusted to continue the rapprochement with unionism first set in train at a meeting between Lemass and the Northern Ireland Prime Minister, Terence O'Neill, in 1965. Lemass was said to have "gone ballistic" at the thought of Blaney as his successor.

It was therefore essential to prevent either of two outcomes, the accession of Blaney or a divisive contest between Colley and Haughey. In fine, a compromise candidate had to be found, and one was ready to hand in the Finance Minister, Jack Lynch. There can be no doubt that Lemass gave Lynch his blessing, and the outgoing Taoiseach's dismay at Lynch's expressed unwillingness to stand is on the record. It is also probable that Paddy Lenihan, who had followed his son into the Dail in 1965, played a minor part in persuading Lynch to declare his candidature, although he soon grew disillusioned with him. Haughey withdrew from the contest and he and his faction, including Brian Lenihan, supported Lynch. Colley, however, insisted on standing and polled respectably in an election confined to Fianna Fail deputies, but Lynch won conclusively. So much for the events on the surface. The underlying reality was that both Colley and Haughey considered the real contest to have been merely postponed, and both had every intention of fighting it out another time, as they would indeed come to do.

Lynch loved the tag "the reluctant Taoiseach", and permitted his intimates to assert *ad nauseam* that he had accepted the premiership under duress. Seeing that he held the party leadership for thirteen years in government and opposition, this claim may be described in all kindness as implausible.

His great strengths were his guile and his public appeal, the latter much more obvious than the former. Some called him the most popular Irish leader since Daniel O'Connell. Michael McInerney, political correspondent of the *Irish Times*, dubbed him the Lord Mayor of Ireland. More hard-bitten observers likened him to a bank manager or the man from the St Vincent de Paul Society, and saw that whereas he might have succeeded admirably in such roles as these, the most striking aspects of the early years of his premiership were conservatism, lack of control over the cabinet, and the loss of the momentum that had characterised the Lemass era.

This profoundly disturbed the modernisers, who saw the new mood as both wrong in itself and politically dangerous. Sean O'Connor wrote in his memoirs that if Lynch instead of Lemass had been Taoiseach at the time the free education scheme was announced he would not have permitted O'Malley to proceed. (Lynch as Finance Minister had entered a strong protest. That may have been *pro forma* and the scheme in fact went ahead under his premiership, but by then he could not have stopped it.) Paddy Lenihan resolved to set up a left-wing ginger group in the hope of reviving the former momentum.

Brian bowed, in public at any rate, to the prevailing wind, but in his heart he believed that Fianna Fail under Lynch was out of tune with the times and that conservatism would cost them the next general election. The student protests might have been trivial, but they signified that Ireland was not immune from the stirrings of the sixties. The swing to liberalism and the left, in the church, in politics, and in society at large, appeared unstoppable. As in the rest of the developed world, a sexual revolution was in progress, which faltered only slightly when Pope Paul VI in the encyclical *Humanae Vitae* condemned artificial contraception. The Labour Party, revitalised by a dynamic young secretary — Brendan Halligan, who would grow close to Lenihan through their shared enthusiasm for European union and their shared belief in strong, united political parties — published a set of radical policies; and Fine Gael, in the document *The Just Society*, embraced economic planning and social reform. Fianna Fail, once in important respects the most radical party, were in danger of looking like the most out of date.

The main author of *The Just Society* was Declan Costello, who a few years later abandoned politics for the High Court bench, but the outstanding figure on the liberal wing of the party was Dr Garret FitzGerald. FitzGerald wanted to turn Fine Gael into a social democratic party, and conceived the daring idea of a merger with Labour. Labour, however, not only turned him down but adopted a policy of refusing to enter another coalition with Fine Gael.

It was this decision that swung the 1969 general election. Most of the Fianna Fail leadership, including Lenihan, thought they would lose notwithstanding, but Fine Gael and Labour voters did not transfer preferences to one another's candidates in sufficient numbers, Labour suffered a severe setback, and Fianna Fail won a Dail majority. The election campaign was also influenced by Fianna Fail rhetoric to the effect that Labour intended to introduce "Cuban communism" into Ireland and by Lynch's extraordinary campaigning methods, notably touring convents and singing *The Banks of My Own Lovely Lee* at election meetings in Cork. But it was the transfers, or the lack of them, that decided the issue.

When it came to cabinet portfolios, Lenihan drew one of the shorter straws. Lynch made him Minister for Transport and Power, a technocratic job ill-suited to his abilities and a most unglamorous job for a man who had held the high-profile portfolios of Justice and Education and entertained hopes of higher things: specifically, Iveagh House. Lenihan was deeply disappointed by the demotion, but put the best face possible on it, saying that a job was a job and membership of the cabinet was what counted. As minister, he scored some little-acknowledged successes. He supported — as did his father — the campaign to keep the Shannon navigable, against the wishes of councils that wanted to build bridges which would have prevented navigation. He pushed for the reopening of the Shannon-Erne canal, a project that did not come to fruition until the 1990s. And he showed himself farsighted by seeking, albeit unsuccessfully, what later came to be known as a "strategic alliance" between Aer Lingus and a major foreign airline.

Haughey became Finance Minister, a fact that would assume enormous importance in the crisis of the following year.

The disgruntled Paddy Lenihan had made slow, if any, progress in his efforts to invigorate the party. He now decided to work on the 1969 intake of new deputies, with Michael

Herbert, deputy for Limerick East, as his chief ally. Herbert, a man of great veracity and honour — and also an impatient man who despised the Lynch regime and compared it with "the USSR under Brezhnev" — found, as he says, that some of the deputies were no better than the "messenger boys" and "parish pump politicians" who notoriously throng the corridors of powerlessness. Nevertheless, he and Lenihan decided to go ahead and set up a committee with himself as secretary and Lenihan as chairman. They agreed to meet in Buswell's Hotel one evening early in 1970. Lenihan never turned up. He had died suddenly. He was sixty- seven years old.

Shortly afterwards, Lynch addressed a parliamentary party meeting. He apologised for having neglected, the previous summer, to brief the "new boys" on such basic matters as how to find their way around Leinster House. By now, he assumed, they would have found out for themselves the whereabouts of their offices, the bars, the lavatories and so forth. He went on to say that he wanted to emphasise one point: there must be no factions, no cabals, no backbench groups.

"My heart stopped," says Herbert. "Someone had grassed!"

For an honourable man like Herbert, the discovery that one has to watch out for sneaks was painful. But for Lynch to deplore factions and cabals on the back benches was profoundly ironic. For his own cabinet was riven by factions and cabals, as would soon become obvious. And the crisis was already upon him.

*

Nobody had ever quite known what to do about Northern Ireland.

The 1920 Government of Ireland Act provided for two Home Rule parliaments in Dublin and Belfast, and a Council of Ireland in which the two bodies could co-operate. The Liberal Prime Minister, David Lloyd George, envisaged that under these arrangements Ireland would eventually be reunited as a semi-autonomous part of the United Kingdom. The war of independence put paid to his plans. The new Free State got

Commonwealth status and the Northern Ireland unionists a form of Home Rule for which they had never bargained but which they implemented with zeal.

They had claimed the right to stay out of the Irish state in which Catholics were a majority. Ultimately nationalists would concede that right. But within the six counties they ruled the unionists claimed more, the rights of a majority. Their institutions mimicked those of Westminster, where power changed hands from time to time; in Northern Ireland power never changed hands. They had control of the security forces. They gerrymandered local government areas and discriminated in a multitude of ways against Catholics.

The Catholics' plight, however, was not in the early decades the chief concern of the Free State. Indeed, it was hardly a concern at all, for two reasons. First, it was hoped that the 1925 Boundary Commission would cede large swathes of territory to the Free State, making Northern Ireland unviable. Nothing of the sort happened, but even after the Dublin government accepted the existing frontier in 1925 the opinion that the North was ultimately unviable continued to prevail very widely. Secondly, the injustice was felt, not so much as an injustice to the Northern Catholics as to the country at large. This perception was reinforced by the spectacle of the remnants of the Anglo-Irish "ascendancy" ruling the North before a "Presbyterian meritocracy", to borrow a felicitous phrase from Maurice Hayes, gained their place in the sun. And it was compounded by nationalist failure to understand the Protestant view of church-state relations. Most Catholics could not see that Northern Protestants viewed the Free State as a theocracy. When they heard that view expressed, they thought it perverse.

They also felt that Britain's true purpose in imposing partition and giving the unionists a free hand in the North was not to assert the rights of the Northern Protestant community but to maintain a British foothold in Ireland. Here they had considerable justification. A British post-World War Two cabinet memorandum declared bluntly that even if a majority in the North voted to become part of a united Ireland, Britain would still need the territory for strategic reasons. Not until 1990, after the Cold War ended, did a British cabinet minister say that Britain no longer had any "selfish strategic or economic interest" in Ireland, an assertion repeated in the Downing Street Declaration of 1993. That of course constituted an admission that Britain had previously had such an interest; and it was followed by a statement by a senior official that it was now possible to seek "a democratic solution for Ireland", in effect an admission that the former arrangements were not democratic.

It is only right to note that the policies consistently pursued by Irish governments increased the divisions between the two parts of the island. Crucially, neutrality in 1939 would have been impossible without partition. All Irish governments have put the perceived interests of the state first and last, often to the anger of Northern nationalists. But that is what governments are for. The North could wait. Historical determinism, an increase in the Northern Catholic population, the British sense of fair play, something or other would solve the problem. Meanwhile, we had our own lives to live.

One course of action, it was accepted by all but a handful of irredentists, would solve nothing. We did not have the means, if we had the will, to invade the North and take over the territory by force; and while most of us believed that we had a moral right to the territory we did not believe that we had a right to use force to subdue it. In a curiously phrased assertion, de Valera said that it would be as wrong to coerce "that section" (the unionists) as for the British to coerce Ireland. Sporadic outbreaks of terrorism and guerrilla warfare, ill-conceived and poorly organised and equipped, petered out or were crushed, with the co-operation of the Free State's, later the Republic's, governments and security forces.

Constitutional agitation for a united Ireland continued. This chiefly took the form of working on the British Labour Party and on American opinion. Lemass in the early 1960s cautiously attempted a rapprochement with the Northern unionists. He did not resile from the traditional demand for reunification, and continued to refer to the unionists as a "national minority", but made a step in their direction by accepting their status as a majority within the North — a concession understood only by the sophisticated. The British and American routes led to very little, notwithstanding the election of the Irish-American John F. Kennedy as President of the United States in 1960 and that of the supposedly sympathetic Harold Wilson as British Prime Minister in 1964. In the light of the hysterical hatred of the Kennedy family widely prevalent in Britain, it is intriguing to recall that John F. Kennedy was an Anglophile and took relatively little interest in the land of his forefathers, though he did take an intense interest in Irish-American votes. His visit to Ireland in 1963 was, as normal, preceded by a briefing session between the President and the Irish ambassador in Washington. Lemass seems to have been greatly taken aback to learn that Kennedy ruled out any reference to reunification.

*

Austin Currie first met Brian Lenihan in 1961 when he was a member of a moderate nationalist student group at Queen's University Belfast and Lenihan was Parliamentary Secretary for Fisheries. Currie would soon become a member of the Stormont parliament representing the old, ineffective Nationalist Party, which he left in 1970 to found the Social Democratic and Labour Party (SDLP) with Gerry Fitt, John Hume, Paddy Devlin, Paddy O'Hanlon and Ivan Cooper.

The student group found it far from easy to entice politicians of any consequence to their meetings, and were delighted that a parliamentary secretary from Dublin accepted an invitation to speak to them. They were even more delighted when, after the meeting, Lenihan bought them drinks at a hotel near the university.

Currie takes the usual Northern nationalist view of Southern lack of interest, but makes an exception for Lenihan. This is not entirely fair to the Dublin establishment. As we have seen, the establishment always put the interests of the twenty-six-county state above all other considerations; but as we have also seen, Lemass wanted to raise the issue with Kennedy in 1963. In serious Dublin political conversations, the subject continually came up, if only to be abandoned with bafflement. Irish ambassadors abroad would devote a spare weekend to putting their reflections on paper, to be read with interest by the Secretary of the Department of Foreign Affairs, circulated to a few chosen thinkers, and filed away in the National Archives for thirty years.

As to Lenihan, he always had contacts in the North, varying from unionists to moderate nationalists like Currie to the most extreme republicans. In that he differed from the great majority of his Fianna Fail colleagues, who either had no interest in the subject or whose contacts were only with republicans and republican sympathisers, a fact which would assume importance in the crisis of 1969-70. To all Lenihan's Northern contacts he would listen carefully: as his son Conor says, he was a very good listener. To few of them did he make any commitments. One of his enormous strengths was his ability to form relationships with the oddest people, and one of the more unusual was Frank Maguire, who came from Lenihan's town of Athlone. In the following decade, Maguire was elected Westminster MP for Fermanagh-South Tyrone as a "unity" candidate (i.e. a candidate acceptable to Sinn Fein) and is remembered for his decision to attend the House of Commons in order to "abstain in person" on the vote that brought down the Labour government of James Callaghan in 1979 and initiated eighteen years of Conservative rule.

Like the ambassadors putting their musings on paper for the delectation of a few colleagues, Lenihan occasionally mulled over ideas that might help, if not to open the road to a united Ireland, at least to improve relations with the North. In 1964 he suggested that we might rejoin the Commonwealth. He dismayed a nationalist Scots audience by telling them that formal independence wasn't all that it was cracked up to be, a statement too easily misunderstood. The dilution of independence involved in rejoining the Commonwealth would be negligible compared with the pooling of sovereignty inherent in our membership of the European Union — which gives us more, not less, effective independence. His next contact with Currie showed another aspect of his pragmatic side; and it showed his dedication to organisation and the minutiae of politics. He counselled him to apply for the job of assistant secretary of the Fianna Fail Party, telling him that he would thus learn the ropes and fit himself to reorganise the chaotic Nationalist Party. Currie on reflection declined. The job went to Gerry Collins, while Currie took one of the leading roles in an epochal new departure.

*

If force was both immoral and unfeasible, if no real aid was forthcoming from the Republic or Britain, and if Terence O'Neill's feeble reform efforts were certain to fail, as they did conclusively with his toppling from power in 1969, what were Northern nationalists to do? They looked across the Atlantic and derived inspiration from the black civil rights movement in the United States. The Northern Catholic middle class, and especially those who owed their status to the educational opportunities opened up by the British Education Act of 1944, admired and identified with Martin Luther King. They would make moderate and reasonable demands, like his. They would reject violence, as he did. They would campaign peacefully against discrimination in housing, employment, and a voting system in local government loaded against them. "One man, one vote" is a powerful slogan.

They had allies, not always the most comfortable allies. The failure of the last pitiful armed campaign in 1956-61, and the left-wing fever of the sixties, had prompted the IRA and their political wing, Sinn Fein, to profess the abandonment of violence, adopt Marxist policies, and engage in a range of non-violent tactics, such as "fish-ins" in the Republic to protest against plutocratic or foreign ownership of fishing rights. Their renunciation of violence was, to say the least, questionable. In the interval between 1962 and the crisis of 1969 they continued to arm, recruit, and train; the IRA had an active membership of over one thousand; and one of their leaders drew up a bizarre plan to assassinate RUC men by using poison darts. Unionists, however, were mistaken or self-serving when they claimed that the IRA were the driving force behind the civil rights movement. The biggest contribution of Sinn Fein and the IRA was their dedication, their organisational abilities, and their quasi-military discipline, which they deployed in their competent stewardship of civil rights marches.

It is important to remember that, chiefly because of the events that would occur in 1969-70, but more important to remember that the civil rights movement based itself essentially on the general rights taken for granted in a normal modern society — and on the normal aspirations of the middle class in any such society. Its origins were complex, but it may suffice to identify four elements: the Campaign for Social Justice, founded by Dr Conn McCluskey and his wife Patricia, to whom Lenihan grew close after McCluskey wrote to him, praising him as one of the few Dublin politicians who understood the North; agitation by a significant number of British Labour members of parliament; a personal initiative by Currie in protest against outrageous housing policies; and the foundation of the Northern Ireland Civil Rights Movement (NICRA).

It soon became common to predict a Protestant backlash, analogous to the white backlash in the United States, and to present extreme unionist activities as a reaction to the civil rights movement. That was less than accurate, since opposition to equality for Catholics actually predated the birth of the civil rights movement. The Rev Ian Paisley led his first march in protest against O'Neill's tentative efforts at rapprochement with Catholics in 1963. Paisley also mounted a protest against the meeting between O'Neill and Lemass in 1965. The first murders of Catholics were committed in 1966 by the Ulster Volunteer Force on the pretext that the celebrations of the fiftieth anniversary of the Easter Rising had provoked a resurgence of republican feeling. Early in 1969 a march from Belfast to Derry by the People's Democracy, conducted against the wishes of the mainstream movement, was ambushed by Loyalists at Burntollet, near Derry, with the blatant complicity of the Royal

Ulster Constabulary. In the spring of that year, the unionist extremists brought down O'Neill. In August, opposition to a provocative march on the walls of Derry by the Orange "Apprentice Boys" set off days and nights of riots. In Belfast, Catholic areas were attacked by Loyalists, not so much helped as led by the RUC. Whole streets were burned to the ground. Thousands fled south. Wilson and his Home Secretary, James Callaghan, sent in the British army in the hope of controlling a situation of which the Northern security forces, and the unionist government, had plainly lost control. In Dublin, what would be the reaction? Horror? Dismay? Or to seize a perceived opportunity?

Seven

Political history is far too criminal a subject to be a fit thing to teach children.

W.H. AUDEN

In August 1969 the inhabitants of the Belfast Catholic ghettoes thought they were about to be massacred. In addition to those who fled south for safety were those who came for a different purpose, to seek arms from the Dublin government for the defence of the ghettoes. These people, the representatives of the "citizens' defence committees", included pillars of the local Catholic society and had to have at the very least a courteous hearing.

Such was the atmosphere in which a divided and panicky government had to consider its response to the crisis. And it had to do so in the light of several of the most basic facts of domestic and Anglo-Irish political life.

Can one trust the British? At one level the answer to that question is: of course not. Perfidious Albion would lie and swindle, would trick you over a boundary commission, would try to bully you out of neutrality after her own defence chiefs made a reckoning that Irish neutrality in World War Two was advantageous to Britain rather than otherwise. But at another and infinitely more significant level the answer is emphatically yes. A British government may conclude that, in a notorious phrase, "an acceptable level of violence" prevails in a region of the United Kingdom, but no British government will permit mass pogroms of its own subjects on a part of its own sovereign territory.

Secondly, rejection of force is an absolute; and that comprises actions a long way short of military intervention. The latter merits very little discussion. It has often been alleged that at most the Irish army in 1969 could have crossed the border and occupied and held the town of Newry. Holders of this opinion must be sadly lacking in knowledge of either military matters or topography. Newry lies in a hollow, and occupying troops — ill-armed, to boot — would have been sitting ducks. It might have been possible to occupy for a time the major part of the city of Derry, on the left bank of the Foyle, but everybody knows that such a thing exists as aerial bombardment. Much more to the point, crossing the border would have been a gross breach of international law and would have attracted British anger and rapid and severe punishment.

What of supplying arms to the citizens' defence committees? The Lynch government made a contingency plan for such a move in the event of Doomsday while hoping and believing that Doomsday would never arrive. Meanwhile, to fend off those in favour of immediate action, the government sailed as close to the wind as it dared. Lynch sent his Foreign Minister, P. J. Hillery, to the United Nations to complain of the injustice of partition. Troops were stationed near the border, field hospitals set up, a consignment of rifles despatched to Dundalk barracks, and a handful of men from Derry given rudimentary military training in Donegal. Public funds allocated for "the relief of distress" were the responsibility of a cabinet sub-committee, effectively controlled by the Finance Minister, Haughey. A ragbag of worthies ranging from Northern nationalist politicians to public relations men went to foreign capitals to "put the Irish case", meaning, to counter to the best of their ability the British propaganda machine. Going any farther was out of the question: Hillery presciently derided the proposition that guns could be used for defensive purposes only. And the deployment of British troops on the streets of Belfast and Derry calmed the situation, at any rate initially.

Another absolute was the protection of the state itself and its institutions. So far as humanly possible, the Northern violence must not be permitted to spill over the border. Sympathy for the predicament of the Northern Catholics did not extend, in the view of the political establishment, to any action that might worsen the existing violence in the North, still less to any action that might destabilise the system in the Republic. Lynch might echo the slogans fashionable in the sixties — on one occasion he denounced "institutional violence", strange words coming from so conservative a leader — but he was much more concerned for calm in the Republic than in the North. Michael McInerney maintained that he would earn his place in history on the grounds that "Lynch kept us out of the North" just as "Dev kept us out of the war." Only a tiny minority, then or since, would disagree.

But if the minority is tiny now and was small even in 1969, it was powerful, and dangerous.

The IRA and Sinn Fein split into the "official" and "provisional" factions. The emergence of the Provisional IRA, in time to become the world's most sophisticated terrorist movement, had as its proximate cause the failure of the then IRA remnants to defend the Belfast Catholic ghettoes. But, strangely in view of their subsequent attachment to the aim of a united socialist republic, another stated cause at the time was that the movement from which they split had embraced Marxism. Some suspected, or affected to suspect, that the politicians in the Republic who had a hand in the split were motivated by a desire to replace a Marxist subversive organisation by a right-wing subversive organisation, less threatening to the system in the Republic, but this was a mistaken view. The Marxist faction never posed any significant threat to the state; and the motivation of the Provisionals' supporters on this side of the border was to initiate an all-out "war of liberation", forcing British withdrawal from Northern Ireland and the creation of an all-Ireland state.

At a distance of nearly three decades, that kind of thinking appears crazy; and even in the midst of the emotional fever of August 1969 it appeared crazy to most people. It would have implied the effective defeat of immensely superior forces, British and local, and could have been achieved, if at all, only at the cost of colossal violence and destruction. The analogy with the guerrilla war of 1919-21 was obviously flawed: the independence movement of the earlier period had an undeniable democratic mandate, whereas it was preposterous to suppose that the Irish people would have given a mandate to their legitimate armed forces, much less to a terrorist organisation, to subdue the North by force. And whatever the sins of unionist governments, there was unquestionably a unionist majority within the North whose rights must not be taken from them by violence.

Yet a number of politicians in the Republic, all the way up to the cabinet, involved themselves in this crazy exercise. Neil Blaney afterwards boasted that he had helped to create the Provisional IRA. He and others, including a Belgian-born businessman, Albert Luykx, set about finding ways of purchasing and supplying arms from the continent, ostensibly for defence, in reality for the IRA. Meanwhile, he made inflammatory public speeches, openly contradicting the line taken by Lynch. Throughout that autumn and winter Dublin pulsated with rumours of attempts to obtain arms and of contacts between ministers and both wings of the IRA.

One night, in a rare demonstration of the sardonic side of his nature, Brian Lenihan called to Luykx in a crowded room in Groome's Hotel: "I hear you're doing great work for Ireland, Albert!" Detractors have sometimes used the incident as evidence that because he knew something, he must have been involved. That is absurd. It may have been an indiscretion; more likely, he meant it as a warning to the plotters that their activities were well known. One of the most extraordinary aspects of the affair is that they went ahead when not only Lenihan, but hundreds of others, perhaps thousands, knew something, or thought they knew something. Certainly the Special Branch knew. British intelligence knew. Is it conceivable that Jack Lynch did not know? Is it conceivable that the conspirators thought they had his tacit approval for trying illegally to import arms for transfer to the North, and for misappropriating public funds for the enterprise? Or did they rely on his lack of control over his cabinet and party, thinking he would not dare to act against them?

Lynch's actions — and periods of inaction — have caused puzzlement ever since. Did he believe that the reports he received from intelligence sources and from Peter Berry personally simply could not be true? Did he bide his time, waiting for a suitable opportunity to suppress the dissidents in his cabinet? If the latter, he was unable to pick his own time. In the end, his hand was forced in the spring of 1970 when the Fine Gael leader, Liam Cosgrave, presented him with evidence of a conspiracy to import arms. Then he moved decisively. He demanded the resignations of Blaney and Haughey. When they refused, he dismissed them. He sought and obtained the resignation of the Minister for Justice, our old friend Micheal O Morain. And he decided that Blaney and Haughey must stand trial in the Central Criminal Court.

Here Lenihan comes back into the picture. He remained completely loyal to Lynch: towards the end of his life he would claim that he served, uniquely, in the Oireachtas under every leader of Fianna Fail and was loyal to all of them. But he refused to give up his friendships with Haughey and Blaney, thus becoming "the X in OXO", a phrase he often used mockingly against himself. He thus harmed his reputation doubly. He damaged his credibility by taking a "crisis? what crisis?" line in support of Lynch — and of a party that did not know what it was doing — while maintaining unwise associations. His friendship with Haughey was fatal in more ways than one. However, he gave Lynch good advice when he urged him not to have Haughey and Blaney prosecuted. As with so much good advice proffered by Lenihan, it was disregarded. Proceedings were issued against Haughey, Blaney, Luykx, Captain James Kelly of Military Intelligence and John Kelly, a Belfast republican (not to be confused with Lenihan's UCD classmate John Maurice Kelly, Fine Gael minister, expert on constitutional law, a constant critic of Lenihan but one who had warm feelings for him). A district court found no case for Blaney to answer. The other four went on trial in the Central Criminal Court. The trial collapsed. At a second trial, the jury returned a verdict of not guilty against the four defendants. The proceedings were bizarre in the extreme. Haughey denied all knowledge of a plot to import arms and his account, as the judge noted, was in total conflict with that of the Defence Minister, James Gibbons. Captain Kelly's case, by contrast, rested on the proposition that he had acted under authority. Confidants of Haughey were assiduous in putting it about that his own real but unstated case was similar, and Haughey on his acquittal addressed the crowd outside the courthouse as "fellow patriots" and called for Lynch's resignation.

Lynch, as Lenihan had foreseen, had made a mistake by insisting on the trial. But Haughey made a much bigger mistake by attacking Lynch head-on. Lynch asserted his authority by arranging that almost the entire Fianna Fail parliamentary party went to Dublin Airport to greet him on his return from a foreign trip. He then forced the dissidents to vote confidence, not merely in his new cabinet as a whole but personally in Gibbons. Blaney gagged at that, left the party and founded his own "Independent Fianna Fail" organisation. But Haughey saw himself as having no future outside the party and was willing to swallow any humiliation in the interest of his political career.

For the Lenihan family, this was a terrible time. Anybody associated with Haughey and Blaney came under suspicion; and suspicion of more than one kind. Leading opposition figures asserted, and evidently believed, that the purpose of the arms importation was not to despatch the guns to the North but to stage a coup. Telephones were tapped (this practice was common long before Haughey would come to power, but it was exceptionally prevalent at the time of the Arms Crisis. According to a senior official of the Department of Justice, the Special Branch filled an entire room in Dublin Castle with tapes of tapped conversations, mostly involving ministers.)   Men, presumably from the intelligence services, lurked outside Lenihan's house. He was "shadowed" on his way to work and social functions. Ministers would appear suddenly at the house late at night and disappear as quickly and mysteriously as they had come. Their movements were undoubtedly logged, thus bringing Lenihan under unfounded suspicion. The atmosphere at Leinster House was thick with fear and accusation, and Lenihan's good-natured efforts to make peace were unavailing. The natural result was that the Lynch coterie, from which Lenihan was excluded, drew closer together, insisting that Lynch had always behaved impeccably and had been betrayed by Haughey.

Among the chief members of this coterie were George Colley, now fully reconciled with Lynch, whom he had opposed for the party leadership in 1966; Erskine Childers, Lenihan's rival in Longford-Westmeath in 1954; and the new Minister for Justice, Des O'Malley.

O'Malley had won the Limerick East by-election which followed the death of his uncle Donogh in 1968. He and Lenihan first met at Donogh's funeral. Lenihan was delighted to meet this extremely intelligent and articulate young man, and immediately saw him as future cabinet material. Blaney, however, took no pleasure in observing their lively conversation. He took Lenihan aside and told him that O'Malley was "not one of ours" and "not a real Fianna Failer". O'Malley, thirty-one years old when Lynch appointed him Justice Minister, became one of the Taoiseach's closest friends and most vocal defenders.

It was none of these, however, but P. J. Hillery, who performed the most important public service for Lynch (important, also, for the Fianna Fail Party and the country). He told delegates to the annual ard-fheis, who wanted to express noisily their emotional "republican" feelings, that they must choose between Fianna Fail and traditional icons. They chose Fianna Fail. But another struggle was about to begin, this time an underground instead of an open confrontation, and Lynch would lose it.

*

The turmoil within the opposition parties, though not comparable with the convulsions in Fianna Fail, was considerable.

The Labour leadership launched "Operation Houdini" to reverse the policy of refusing to enter any coalition with Fine Gael. It succeeded, but not without hectic scenes at party conferences. The left wing of the party found allies in the North, like Bernadette Devlin, Westminster MP for Mid-Ulster, but the left was itself divided between those who sought a united socialist republic and splinter groups which embraced the "two nations" theory. The party at large was also divided, like Fianna Fail and Fine Gael, on such issues as legalising contraception, and on EEC entry. This last question it resolved by bowing to the wishes of the grassroots and opposing entry in the 1972 referendum campaign although most of the party leadership was wholly in favour. Brendan Halligan in particular was always a fervent European. But Halligan made no bones about the importance of party unity.

The Fine Gael front bench decided to oppose an anti-subversive measure introduced in the Dail by O'Malley. Cosgrave was determined to support it, if necessary at the price of his leadership. Lynch, seeing both main opposition parties divided, was ready to call a snap general election at the end of 1972. On 1 December, while the Dail debate on the measure was in progress, bombs went off in Dublin, killing two people. Like the much more destructive bombs of 1974, they were planted by Loyalist terrorists, almost certainly with the collusion of British intelligence, but this was not immediately known. Fine Gael caved in, and Lynch postponed the election. The decision would cost him dearly.

*

On Ireland's accession to the EEC on 1 January 1973, Hillery became European Commissioner for Social Affairs and Lynch appointed Lenihan Foreign Minister in his place. Lenihan now had his heart's desire. Unfortunately, he would have it for only a couple of months. During that short period he enunciated the core of Irish European policy: that we were wholly in favour of complete European integration — a couple of years earlier he had spoken of a "Republic of Europe" — but would demand

Paddy Lenihan (left) with General Sean MacEoin and Brother John Peter Flood at a Marist past pupils' dinner in Athlone, 1957.

Lenihan (kneeling, left) on the UCD soccer team, 1952.

Brian Lenihan (middle) with Charlie Doyle and Seamus Sorahan, call to Irish bar, March 1952.

SENATOR'S WEDDING

Brian's and Ann's wedding, St Michael's Church, Dun Laoghaire, 1958.

Political apprecticeship: Lenihan with his mentor Sean Lemass on Lough Ree. Even in a boat, Lemass's pipe remained between his lips.

The young minister receives his first cabinet seal of office from President de Valera.

Ann and Brian putting on the style for a film premiere, 1965.

Campaigning with Erskine Childers in the 1973 presidential election.

With President de Valera and the long-serving Papal Nuncio Monsignor Gaetano Alibrandi.

Celebrating his return to the Dail in 1977, Lenihan holds the hand of his fellow Fianna Fail deputy for Dublin West, Liam Lawlor.

Ann congratulates Brian on his return
to the Dail for Dublin West at the 1977
general election.

With his closest political ally in Europe, German Foreign
Minister Hans-Dietrich Genscher.

Two faces whose expressions hint at the enigmatic nature of the relationship between Lenihan and Haughey.

At the famous Dublin Castle Summit in 1980 (from left) Lord Carrington, Sir Geoffrey Howe, Thatcher, Haughey and a semi-detached Lenihan; behind Haughey (partly hidden) is Humphrey Atkins, Northern Ireland Secretary.

compensation for the economic effects of the "centripetal" tendencies that accompanied it. In Brussels on 15 January 1973 he set out what would remain among the fundamental tenets of Irish European policy for decades to come:

> My government are deeply aware that the centripetal forces making for further economic integration will need to be balanced by measures which cater adequately for the special economic, social and cultural needs of the outer regions. As the shaping of the economic environment directly affects the social and cultural development of societies, we must have due regard to the personalities of these regions so as to allow them to sustain their individual identities and thereby make their varied contributions to the social and cultural fabric of the Communities. As a member of the Communities Ireland will promote and support measures designed to achieve this objective, in particular the development of a comprehensive and effective regional policy.

It is needless to question the concern of Lenihan or his successors for the cultural identities of the regions, or his assurance that we would "play our part in the peaceful and democratic construction of tomorrow's Europe", but the chief message sent out by that speech (and well understood by Europe's German paymasters) was that Ireland would demand financial compensation for the economic disadvantages of peripherality. At the time, Lenihan could not have known that the compensation would eventually prove to be so generous and so important a factor in the creation of the "Celtic Tiger" of the 1990s. However, his view, and the establishment view, on the need for measures to protect the weaker countries and regions against "centripetal forces" would not change in the next twenty years. In 1993, as chairman of the Irish Council of the European Movement, he would speak in favour of monetary union but insist that it "cannot occur without economic union and social cohesion". He did not live to see the virtual completion of the first in 1998. The second aim is still very far from achievement.

*

Lenihan, and other objective members of the Fianna Fail establishment, had fully expected the party to lose the 1969 general election, as we know they would have done if Fine Gael and Labour candidates had transferred more votes to one another. Now, by contrast, they expected to win the 1973 general election. The country had calmed down, largely thanks to Lynch. The British Conservative government under Edward Heath had suspended the Stormont parliament in 1972, imposed direct rule from Westminster, and published proposals for the future governance of Northern Ireland in which Dublin would have a say: a substantial success for Irish nationalism. Europe promised both tangible and psychological benefits.

But just as Fianna Fail had been wrong in 1969, they were wrong in 1973. Labour, having completed Operation Houdini, did not rest on their oars. They entered into a pact with Fine Gael to fight the election on what was dubbed a fourteen-point plan (in fact this was a curious piece of miscounting, but at any rate it constituted a joint policy) and at the polls their candidates' second and lower preferences transferred so solidly that although the Fianna Fail share of the first-preference vote actually rose, Fine Gael and Labour between them won sufficient seats for a Dail majority.

During the election campaign, Lenihan had to forsake the delights of Europe for the travails of Roscommon. He was engaged in a delicate vote management exercise, hoping to secure the election in the constituency of a second Fianna Fail candidate, Dr Hugh Gibbons, as well as his own. Like his mentor Joe Kennedy in 1954, he asked electors to give their first preferences to his running mate. The exercise went wrong. It was not the only thing that went wrong.

In those days, domestic rates were a very unpopular tax, and the Fine Gael-Labour alliance decided to alleviate the (much exaggerated) burden by removing the element of health charges from them. Colley, now Finance Minister, panicked.

Lenihan arrived late one night at the Athlone house of his sister Mary O'Rourke and went to bed. Some time after 2 a.m. he was woken up and called to the telephone. It was Colley, who told him what Fine Gael and Labour proposed and said, "we'll have to cap that." Lenihan told him that auction politics was bad politics and went back to bed.

The following day, the Labour leader, Brendan Corish, was being driven around the Limerick-Tipperary area by a prominent Labour activist, Niall Greene, when they heard on the car radio that Fianna Fáil had indeed capped their proposal by promising to abolish domestic rates entirely. Greene told Corish that he had better telephone Cosgrave and decide a response. Corish was reluctant: he had not yet grown close to Cosgrave as he would do in office, and found personal contact with him awkward. In the end Greene persuaded him to make the call, and Cosgrave and Corish sensibly agreed to ignore the Fianna Fáil proposal.

Lenihan's reaction was very different. He was in Greally's Hotel in Roscommon town, not entirely sober, when Vinny Mahon entered and told him the news. "Jesus Christ!" he said. "They haven't done it!"

He had been right when he told Colley to keep calm. The promise to abolish rates, so blatantly made in the hope of catching votes, evidently did Fianna Fáil no good in the election. It assuredly did them no good in Roscommon.

A couple of days before the poll Mike Burns's father, who lived in the constituency, telephoned his son and said: "You're not going to believe this, but Brian Lenihan is going to lose his seat."

He explained. Lenihan, who was drinking heavily all through that campaign, had visited a village so small that it contained only one pub. As always, the customers made countless requests for favours, to all of which he replied with his customary bonhomie and nonchalance. A job for a son? No problem. A job for a daughter? No problem. As he was leaving, he took one of the petitioners by the arm and said, "I'll see your daughter all right." He should have said "your son". Nowhere was note of, and exception to, the gaffe more certain than Roscommon.

At the election count he was accompanied by one of his little sons, there to see Daddy's triumph. From an early point in the count, Lenihan knew he was done for. He admitted this in conversations with his tallymen and knowledgeable journalists, but in public, and with the child, maintained an air of confidence. The boy, sensing that something was wrong, began to cry.

When it was all over, those who remember it say, it was like a death in a family. Late that night, Sean Duignan came across two Special Branch men in the hotel, weeping into their beer.

For anyone less resilient than Lenihan, it would have been devastating. From one of the most desirable jobs in the country, he had fallen to ... nothing, or less than nothing. He did not even have a parliamentary seat. He had no other source of income. At forty-two, and with a young family, he would have to decide whether to abandon the political life he loved and go back to the Bar, competing with much younger men, studying briefs late into the night.

And almost anybody else would have engaged in some self-pity. It could hardly be considered self-indulgent or uncaring for someone in his dreadful situation to think only of himself and his family. Not Lenihan. He thought of those who had worked for his election, and needed consolation. He thought of his official drivers, and arranged that they should work for an amiable and sociable minister in the incoming government. And he thought, as too often, of the party, for which he had another job to do.

Eight

If you can't ride two horses at once, you shouldn't be in the bloody circus.

ANEURIN BEVAN

Erskine Childers held a variety of offices between 1944 and 1973. His career thus rivalled that of Lenihan for length, though emphatically not for distinction. The *Magill Book of Irish Politics* asserts that "throughout his ministerial career he was spectacularly unsuccessful. He was in Transport and Power when the Harcourt Street railway line was closed. He presided over the disintegration of the telephone service ... He took a very partisan line during the 1970 arms crisis, alleging, entirely without foundation, that there had been a conspiracy to commit treason on the part of some former government ministers ... "

These and other criticisms by the contributors to the *Magill Book*, while undoubtedly harsh, somewhat understate the case. Childers was tardy, incompetent, vacillating and pedantic, and held in contempt by several of his colleagues, notably Haughey. He did, however, have a number of fine personal qualities of which the most outstanding was magnanimity. His father before his execution forgave those who had ordered it and told Erskine, then a schoolboy, to seek them out and shake their hands. Erskine complied. For this, much should be pardoned.

Magnanimity was perhaps the only virtue he shared with Lenihan. In many ways they were polar opposites. Those who knew Lenihan best loved and admired him and would eagerly seek his company while, to his great cost, those who knew him least utterly failed to appreciate him. With Childers it was exactly the other way round. Those who knew him best found him boring and parsimonious and would literally flee his company, but many of the public loved his flowery phrases and his "beautiful Oxford accent" (in point of fact he went to Cambridge, not Oxford, but the difference is insignificant).

He was not, however, known as a great vote-getter. In 1961 he moved from Longford-Westmeath to Monaghan for the crude reason that Fianna Fail hoped the substantial Protestant population in that county would vote for a fellow-Protestant. Fianna Fail did not, therefore, hold the highest expectations of him when they chose him as their candidate in the 1973 presidential election which followed de Valera's retirement after fourteen years in Aras an Uachtarain — and which came in the immediate wake of a lost general election. Haughey for one was dismissive when Lenihan told him that Childers could succeed. Haughey had always disliked Childers, but all the more so in the previous couple of years, during which Childers liked to spit out the word "conspirators". Aside from their own candidate's apparent deficiencies, Fianna Fail were up against an impressive Fine Gael candidate, Tom O'Higgins, who had come within 11,000 votes of beating the great de Valera seven years previously. Had O'Higgins won on his second outing Lenihan, as personal campaign manager for Childers, could hardly have been blamed.

Lenihan, however, had other ideas. He liked Childers, but then, he liked almost everybody. His own election defeat had not quelled his optimism. More to the point, he discovered on the campaign trail that Childers was immensely popular, for reasons that baffled the cynical but could be exploited. At one level Childers was an appalling candidate. As his battle bus, dubbed "the Wanderly Wagon" after a children's television programme, passed through towns, he would rehearse his awful speeches ("I love every blade of grass of this dear land") instead of acknowledging the cheers of the populace. When Lenihan told him, "wave to the people, Erskine", he would raise a hand slightly and faintly move his fingers on the model of the Queen of England. A classic story of Sean Duignan's describes him addressing a crowd in a downpour at a dismal crossroads. He told them that he had seen the wonders of the western world but they were better off where they were. Duignan no less than

Lenihan marvelled at how the voters swallowed it. On polling day Childers was elected President by a handsome margin.

During the eighteen months in which he held office, he was an exceedingly energetic and popular but unhappy President. The Cosgrave government put paid to his proposal to set up a "think-tank" at Aras an Uachtarain (the dear Lord knows that the country could do with more political thinking, but it is not the President's job). Childers contemplated resignation but was talked out of it — could de Valera have had a hand in that? — and he had to content himself with the usual round of engagements, which he performed admirably. When he died suddenly in December 1974, the mourning was general and genuine and his state funeral in Dublin a fine piece of theatre, though not without the mandatory Irish comic moments. The cortege was dreadfully late in arriving at St Patrick's Cathedral, and Duignan, one of the radio commentators for the occasion, was desperate for something to say to fill the time. His eye fell on the immortal words inscribed in memory of Jonathan Swift: "Here he lies where fierce indignation can no longer rend his breast." With considerable presence of mind, Duignan avoided by a hair's breadth the temptation to liken Childers to Swift. Few men could have been less alike.

Fierce indignation was never much in Brian Lenihan's line, and in 1973 he had even less time or use for it than usual. Having done his job for the party and secured the election of Childers, he now had a political career to repair.

*

He had no difficulty getting himself elected to the Seanad; and he enjoyed the campaign. This and the presidential campaign afforded him an opportunity to renew and extend his remarkable national network. (He would soon create another network on a grander scale.) He was appointed Fianna Fail leader in the Seanad, a light enough task, and he made the acquaintance of a very young senator called Mary Robinson.

He did some Bar practice, but did not seek high-profile or challenging cases. Far more important than the Seanad or the

Bar was to find another Dail constituency. P. J. Burke had just retired as deputy for Dublin North and been succeeded by his son Ray. The Burkes helped Lenihan to establish himself in the new Dublin West constituency, and there began a lifelong friendship between Lenihan and Ray Burke. They would spend hour after hour together, drinking, discussing political ins and outs, and European history, Lenihan's favourite topic.

As they went on to approach the 1977 general election, there were three Fianna Fail candidates in Dublin West: Lenihan, Liam Lawlor, and Terry Boylan. Tension between Lenihan and Lawlor would become notorious, but it is questionable whether it was very much worse than the norm, for the multi-seat constituency system makes intense rivalry, and worse, common. Lawlor says that they left it to their supporters to play "dirty tricks" on one another while the candidates maintained at least formal relations and, in public, excellent relations. This they did in part by walking around the area, all three together, in peregrinations which as a matter of course ended in public houses. After Boylan's disappearance from the scene, Lenihan and Lawlor continued the practice whenever Lenihan was free on Saturday mornings. Some years later, when Lenihan was Foreign Minister, they found themselves in a pub in Lucan one day at lunchtime. News came through of the death of President Josip Broz Tito of Yugoslavia. Lenihan said, half to himself, half to a puzzled Lawlor, "I wonder what's the drill on Tito." He meant the protocol regarding messages of condolence, attendance at the funeral, and so forth. After a little reflection and agitation, he went to the telephone and asked the duty officer at Iveagh House: "What's the drill on Tito?" According to Lawlor, interested punters looked up at him from their pints and their racing pages, thinking Tito might be a hot tip for Leopardstown or Sandown.

Ann Lenihan remembers the period 1973-77 as "a happy time" for the family, since Brian spent more time at home than before or after. But that is, to put it mildly, relative. For in addition to his Seanad work, his Bar practice, and his cultivation of his new constituency, Brian spent a week of each month out of the country.

The first Irish members of the European Parliament were appointed, not elected: the first direct elections were not held until 1979. Lenihan was appointed a member of an impressive Fianna Fail delegation which, however, found itself in a decidedly embarrassing position. Michael Herbert, a member of the delegation before and after Lenihan's arrival and as we know a sharer of the views of the Lenihans father and son, was far from pleased to be seated to the right of the Fascists.

This absurd situation arose because of Fianna Fail's failure to ally themselves with any recognised group in the parliament. Their predicament derived from their failure to make up their minds on the subject. As Herbert recalls, he and Lenihan predictably wanted to join the Socialist group. Lynch, equally predictably, preferred the Christian Democrats. Someone else favoured the Liberals. "Haughey didn't know what he wanted" (a foretaste of Haughey's indecisiveness in the highest office, despite his having what Herbert calls "the most incisive mind I have known"). The Socialist and Christian Democrat options did not really exist, since these groups were allied with Irish parties, Labour and Fine Gael respectively. Herbert decided that the French Gaullists were the only real option and persuaded Lenihan of the necessity to make a choice, and after some fancy footwork between Europe and Ireland the Gaullist-Fianna Fail alliance, sometimes known as Fianna Gaul, was born.

Lenihan was not entirely happy, but with his dauntless optimism quickly persuaded himself of the merits of the alliance. He claimed, with some justification but also with some exaggeration, a fellow-feeling between his party, chiefly meaning himself, and the Gaullist left wing, represented by Christian de La Malene, to whom he grew close. He also claimed compatibility between Fianna Fail and the left wing of the Italian Christian Democrats, and formed a warm friendship with Giulio Andreotti, whom he characteristically never deserted despite his subsequent disgrace. A less likely friendship was with the leader of the British Conservative delegation, Sir Peter

Kirk. Kirk was a pillar of the Church of England, Lenihan a practising Roman Catholic but interested in the Protestant Reformation and the Protestant emphasis on individual conscience. On the floor of the parliament they would oppose each other fiercely on the issue of the Common Agricultural Policy, then adjourn to have a convivial drink (and perhaps to discuss Jacques Maritain). But Lenihan's greatest friend in Europe was undoubtedly the long-serving German Foreign Minister, Hans-Dietrich Genscher.

It is worth pausing a moment to look at both the variety and the consistency of these friendships. Lenihan liked thoughtful politicians, pragmatic politicians, politicians of the centre, preferably leaning, like himself, a little to the left, but devoted to process, not dogma. After Genscher, his favourite German politician was Helmut Schmidt. He admired leaders of the right wing of the British Labour Party, like Denis Healey and Anthony Crosland. (He thought the party erred badly by not choosing Healey as leader, but virtually all subsequent students of these matters would see that as a mistaken view. British Labour needed a leader who "came from the left" to reform it, and it found one in Neil Kinnock, whose brilliant party management led in time to Tony Blair's stunning electoral victory in 1997.) Among American leaders Lenihan liked to praise Harry Truman, a man, as he said, unafraid to take tough decisions. Among British Tories, his favourite was the suave and worldly Lord Carrington, a man of fine judgement. These are the choices of a very serious man who, regrettably, did not take himself seriously enough and was not taken seriously enough by others.

He made a doubly grand entry into Luxembourg, first earning the respect of the media, then of the parliament itself.

Herbert remembers the arrival at their hotel late on Lenihan's first night of the *Irish Times* correspondent, Fergus Pyle, accompanied by a squad of correspondents from the British "heavies". They expected, essentially, to meet a second-rate Irish provincial politician. They discovered a man with a first-class mind, who knew more about European history and politics than they, and who had no difficulty in answering the most searching questions about current affairs across the entire European and world range. Next day, Pyle told him how much he had impressed the English journalists.

That would not have surprised the relatively few journalists who already knew him well, such as Mike Burns, Sean Duignan, and Raymond Smith of Independent Newspapers. They loved his company, as he loved theirs, but they also understood the depth and breadth of his knowledge. As time went by, more and more media people came to share their feelings; and in later years a whole new generation of young journalists joined the throng. They were enchanted by his bonhomie and amiability, but not all of them came to an appreciation of his intellect and political sagacity. One who saw every aspect was Olivia O'Leary, of whom more later.

His first speech in the parliament was a triumph, which he immediately celebrated in the bar with Michael Herbert. As Lenihan took a glass of gin in his hand, Herbert looked at the monitor signalling the business under discussion and said with dismay: "You're on again, Brian." Luckily the debate signalled by the monitor was on a subject related to the one on which he had already spoken. He went back into the chamber and made a second speech, equally well received, without notes or preparation. On his return to the bar, an amazed Herbert asked him how he had managed. He snapped his fingers and said: "I played it by ear."

He showed the same capacity for retention and recall, and his ability to manage without notes, in an incident which occurred in the Dail at this time.

O'Kennedy, as the Fianna Fail spokesman on foreign affairs in opposition, had to reply to a major speech by the Foreign Minister, Garret FitzGerald, who notoriously spoke at up to three hundred words a minute. O'Kennedy arranged that Lenihan should sit behind him in the lobby which runs round the chamber and pass him notes. After a little while Lenihan handed him a note saying: "This is all bull. We were doing it anyway."

Afterwards I reproached him. He said, "it's true." I got annoyed: "So tell me what he said about the conference on apartheid in Lagos." He trotted it all out. Then I asked him about the Helsinki process. I thought those two a bit off the beaten track, not like European policy where there was no substantial difference. He had absorbed everything in the speech.

Why was he such a success in Europe? Because he had not only read, and continued to read, so much European history and politics, but considered these subjects profoundly. Because he knew so much about the culture, as well as the history, of every country, not only France and Germany, and delighted representatives of every country with this knowledge. Because he understood the essentially political nature of Ireland-in-Europe. Because, from his reading and his experiences during and immediately after World War Two, he fervently believed in European union. Because he had enormous sympathy for German fears of Russia and favoured German reunification: he had studied Bismarck and saw reunification as right and inevitable, thus pleasing his German colleagues. Because, notwithstanding his support for German unity in the long term and in the interim for defence of Germany, he looked forward, even through the more dismal episodes of the Brezhnev era, to reform in the Soviet Union and the re-entry of Russia into the "European family of nations". All this he could expound with clarity and fervour. But perhaps most of all because in the inner circles of Europe he did not conceal his intelligence and the subtlety of his mind, as he too often did at home.

In addition, he had an exceptional flair for finding the levers of power and for exploiting the system. He might discuss Bismarck with the Germans, but he never lost sight of Irish interests, as seen by the Fianna Fail Party. Irish MEPs, scattered among various groups, are all but lost in the vast parliament. On the European Commission and the Council of Ministers, Ireland has representation far beyond what her wealth and size would dictate. European union, the whole hog, certainly; in the fullness of time, enlargement to the East despite its implications for Irish agriculture; meanwhile, no advantage to Ireland must be missed, no threat to Irish interests ignored.

*

A few years on, Olivia O'Leary would spend two weeks constantly in Lenihan's company in order to write precisely how a minister spends his time. She found him absolutely frank and open in all circumstances but one. When in his constituency office, receiving petitioners or discussing local matters with the constituency officers, she was firmly excluded.

She already knew him well from Leinster House, and what impressed her most about him was his kindness and old-world courtliness. In the seventies, women writing on politics were a very new phenomenon, and political correctness had not yet made its appearance in the Leinster House visitors' bar. Women were subjected to a variety of unpleasantness from stares to winks to outright sexual harassment, and the politicians had not come to take women political writers seriously. Lenihan, the true gentleman, was always at pains to protect her.

She noted above all his fondness for the game of politics: "Watching the game ... loving the game." And Lenihan had a bigger game to play at home than in Brussels, Luxembourg or Strasbourg. Unfortunately, his absence from the Dail between 1973 and 1977 made him more a spectator than a player.

Jack Lynch wrote, or tried to write, the rules of the game. He set about modernising Fianna Fail, and at the same time copperfastening his authority. He chose three bright young men, Seamus Brennan, Frank Dunlop, and Esmonde Smyth, and appointed them respectively party general secretary, press secretary, and head of research. Within the shadow cabinet, with Childers and Hillery out of the picture, he relied heavily on Colley and O'Malley.

Dick Walsh called the process "Jack Lynch's Cultural Revolution". This subtle phrase needs explaining. Walsh meant that the Maoist Cultural Revolution in China was not an attempt to develop a new kind of communism but a device to ensure total personal power for Mao Tse-tung. Similarly, Lynch's actions had much more to do with enhancing his own power than with modernising the party. They failed, for very simple reasons. He had not succeeded in driving Haughey out of the party, and he had not reckoned with the strategy that Haughey now employed.

If the reasons were simple, so was the strategy. Haughey decided to appeal to the grassroots over the heads of the leadership and the parliamentary party. He went on the "rubber chicken" circuit. Usually accompanied by P. J. Mara, who would gain fame (and achieve the ultimate accolade by becoming the subject of satire) as his press secretary when in office, he drove all around the country, eating countless unpalatable dinners in countless unattractive locations. The nature of the conversation can be readily guessed. It was not necessary for him to pose as the hero of the Arms Trial, the man who had done his bit for Ireland and been betrayed like so many other great men; a nod and a wink would suffice; indeed, not even a nod or a wink; enough to listen, imply sympathy, tolerate nonsense. The grassroots had made the choice demanded by Hillery: they had chosen Fianna Fail and pragmatism. They did not want to send arms to the North. But they wanted to wallow in what John Healy of the *Irish Times* denounced as "verbal republicanism"; and they wanted a charismatic leader. Others might wish to set up Erskine Childers as a little tin god to worship, they preferred Haughey. Fondness for little tin gods seems to be an ineradicable human characteristic. The little tin god to whom they now devoted themselves, once a moderniser, thus allied himself with some of the most backward elements of the party.

One may be sure that the more intelligent and level-headed elements were appalled. One may be sure that they informed Lynch, begged him to stop the Haughey surge. If he responded, he responded inadequately. Once he had said, patronisingly, that Haughey was "working well within the party"; now he gave in to the grassroots and brought Haughey back on to the front bench. He put him in the humble position of spokesman on health, but nobody could doubt that Haughey was on his way back. Nor could anybody doubt that he would use his position on the front bench, and his certain membership of the next Lynch cabinet, to make another shot for the leadership.

The complacent Old Guard failed to see the extent of the danger. They assumed that when the time came for the next leadership contest Colley would win easily. That was still a reasonable view, but they also failed to see that a contest between Colley and Haughey, whatever the result, must be dreadfully divisive, and they made no endeavour to find a compromise candidate, another Lynch. That is the real criticism — though their successors may resent it — of these honourable but shortsighted men.

Many were so shortsighted as to see the result of the 1977 general election, at which Lynch won a record twenty-seat Dail majority, as a setback for Haughey. Not Lynch himself, who said that the majority was too large and would cause difficulties. And not Haughey, who was asked by a journalist why he rejoiced at the size of the victory. He replied: "They're all mine!" Not all the new Fianna Fail backbenchers were in fact his supporters, but he was not far wrong.

Could the coming showdown have been averted? Yes, it could. Too few people have accepted the idea that Lenihan could have been the compromise candidate, but unquestionably Haughey thought it a real option at the time. Among those with whom he discussed the question were the present writer, and Lenihan himself. Lenihan for his part refused to canvass, regarding an open campaign as disloyalty to Lynch; talked about the subject only to his intimates; and said that he was interested only if the party wanted him. There was, or could have been, a more plausible compromise candidate, but he was out of the reckoning for extraordinary reasons which had their origin in mistakes made by the Cosgrave government.

Nine

Nothing appears more surprising to those who consider human affairs with a philosophical eye than the easiness with which the many are governed by the few.

DAVID HUME, Of The First Principles of Government

In December 1973 representatives of the British and Irish governments and of an embryo Northern Ireland executive containing both unionist and nationalist members met at Sunningdale in Berkshire and, after three days of negotiations, signed the Sunningdale Agreement. The agreement provided that the power-sharing executive would take office formally at Stormont on 1 January 1974, and for the establishment of a Council of Ireland, with cross-border executive powers to be decided in due course. The Irish government formally acknowledged that the constitutional status of Northern Ireland could not change without the consent of a majority in the North. The British government in turn declared that should a majority vote to join a united Ireland, it would support the decision.

The settlement lasted less than five months. Sunningdale was overthrown by the following factors: the stepping up of the IRA campaign of murder and destruction; a constitutional action in Dublin in which the courts ruled that the agreement did not contravene Articles 2 and 3 of the Irish constitution (the so-called "territorial claim"); a strike called by the Ulster Workers' Council, a body effectively controlled by Loyalist terrorists, which paralysed the region; and, most importantly, the loss of legitimacy by the unionist chief minister, Brian Faulkner, when unionist candidates hostile to him won eleven out of the then twelve Northern Ireland House of Commons seats at the Westminster general election of February 1974. The twelfth seat was that of the SDLP leader, Gerry Fitt. Whether this desperate situation could have been overcome by firmness on the part of the British Labour government under Harold Wilson which took office after Heath's defeat in the Westminster election remains a matter of debate, but certainly firmness in relation to Northern Ireland was not a feature of that unhappy administration.

Lynch and the Fianna Fail front bench, of which Lenihan as party leader in the Seanad was a member, supported Sunningdale; and Lynch asserted, accurately, that by his previous dealings with Heath he had paved the road to the agreement. Lynch wanted to maintain bipartisanship on Northern Ireland in the Dail — although, mysteriously, he disliked the word bipartisanship, preferring the term "joint approach". He failed, for party-political reasons on both sides. Elements in his own party were eager to exploit the Cosgrave government's embarrassment and powerlessness in the face of the British government's refusal to meet its obligations. Certain coalition ministers, for their part, wished to exploit the internal difficulties which they saw looming for him in Fianna Fail. Much against his wishes, his party adopted a policy of demanding British withdrawal from Northern Ireland, with a fixed timetable. This was of course viewed as an undermining of his authority and a victory for the Haughey faction.

When Childers died, the ruling Fine Gael and Labour parties knew they had no candidate capable of winning a presidential election. They therefore accepted the candidate imposed on them by Lynch and he became President without an election. This was Cearbhall O Dalaigh, onetime attorney-general, a liberal Chief Justice, a judge of the European Court, and a man of considerable charm and erudition, but gravely lacking in political expertise.

In 1976 the British ambassador in Dublin, Christopher Ewart-Biggs, was assassinated by the IRA. In response, the government introduced emergency legislation which O Dalaigh referred to the Supreme Court for a judgement on its constitutionality or otherwise. For this perfectly correct exercise of his powers as President he was condemned by the Fine Gael Defence Minister,

Patrick Sarsfield Donegan, as "a thundering disgrace" (actually a bowdlerisation of the minister's exact words, but the phrase on which the world agreed). To compound the insult and the impropriety, the words were spoken, about their Commander in Chief, to a gathering of Army officers. Donegan repented, apologised, and tendered his resignation, which Cosgrave refused to accept. O Dalaigh continued to demand his resignation, and when it was not forthcoming he himself resigned.

Having provoked the crisis, the government now found itself in a similar quandary to that of 1974. It dared not face a presidential election at which it would assuredly suffer a decisive and humiliating defeat. Contacts took place between Cosgrave and Lynch with a view to finding an agreed candidate. Contrary to the popular wisdom of the time, relations between the two men were far from warm, and Lynch refused to put forward some harmless, non-political figure in order to save Cosgrave's face. He chose P. J. Hillery, who very reluctantly agreed to leave his comfortable berth in Europe for the constraints and miseries of the Phoenix Park. He did so, admirably, in the national and party interest; and seven years later he took on, again very reluctantly, a second term. But he gave up much more than a comfortable berth. He gave up his chance of succeeding Lynch as Taoiseach.

Hillery was an excellent President, but one greatly underrated and misunderstood. His low profile has often been compared to his disfavour, unfairly, with the glamour of Mary Robinson. Only after leaving the Phoenix Park after fourteen years did he admit publicly that it was adopted deliberately, with a view to restoring stability and normal relations between the presidency and the executive, rocked by Childers's unavailing attempts to achieve some independence and by the O Dalaigh debacle. He did the country a considerable service — and himself a considerable disservice. He could have been Taoiseach, and had he become Lynch's successor the country might have been spared enormous trouble. His acceptance of the presidency removed from the active political scene the most plausible compromise candidate to avert an open clash between Colley and Haughey in the eventual leadership contest, and set the scene for far worse divisions in the Fianna Fail party than those of 1966.

What of another possible compromise candidate, Lenihan? He was handicapped by being out of the Dail from 1973 to 1977, by his absences in Europe, and by the necessity to devote himself to a new constituency. He was even more greatly handicapped by his habit of "selling himself short", to quote Tommy O'Sullivan, a Land Commissioner and a friend of both Lenihan and his father.

That was certainly nothing new. As early as 1965 the widow of a Fianna Fail deputy had complained, with a wealth of alliteration, that she could not understand "how a young man bursting with brains could behave like a buffoon." Michael O'Kennedy's brother angrily told him that he should ask Lenihan "to stop defending the indefensible". He was trotted out on television to defend the most impossible decisions and actions of his party. John Kelly, another lover of alliteration, knew his intellect and his character. He said that "I like Deputy Lenihan — I can't help it" and that it made him feel better to be alive on "the same planet as Brian Lenihan", but constantly accused him of "blather, bluster and reckless bluffing". He was distressed when deputies from all parties laughed at Lenihan's unconvincing if lively television performances. When Fianna Fail returned to office, it was Lenihan who had to stand up publicly for the appalling decision to destroy Wood Quay in Dublin, the oldest Viking site in Europe, to make room for a hideous office building. His admirers were all the more annoyed because they knew his private opinion. He made a quiet if sardonic criticism of another dreadful new building, the Electricity Supply Board headquarters in Fitzwilliam Street, colourfully described by Kelly:

> Deputy Lenihan when he was minister for power or whatever the thing was then called — one has to grasp at the title of the department quickly these days before it is changed — paid an official visit to the

building. Even he stood appalled by it and, humble though his contribution in aesthetic terms may have been in trying to ameliorate the situation, at least he made it. He said, "would you think of putting a lick of whitewash on it? Would you think of taking a bucket of whitewash and see could you brighten it up that way?"

One of the protestors against the Wood Quay vandalism was Mary Robinson, another Dr Pat Wallace, director of the National Museum. Wallace lamented that "the most scholarly man in the Dail" should defend this indefensible action. As Tommy O'Sullivan puts it, "I was often puzzled why he did not demonstrate his intelligence. Nobody took him very seriously. He would not say no to anything no matter how bloody impossible it was. He did himself and the governments he served a disservice by selling himself short." Michael Herbert watched him making a name for himself in Europe and was anguished by the way he was disparaged at home.

Yet the better educated and more politically conscious elements of the Fianna Fail grassroots were as well aware of his abilities as his colleagues in the European Parliament. Had he mounted a campaign for the leadership, he would have had some support and might even had made an impression on the Old Guard — if they could have been persuaded of the need for compromise. But the reality was that neither side had much interest in compromise, and the confrontation would not be long delayed.

*

At the time, the sweeping Fianna Fail general election victory in 1977 was generally attributed to the spectacular package of bribes they offered to the electorate. These included our old acquaintance the abolition of domestic rates, along with the abolition of wealth tax and motor tax, and subsidies for house buyers. This view did not survive for very long among the more astute, and has certainly not survived the ensuing two decades. The manifesto was not only economically disastrous, but electorally unnecessary. The Fine Gael-Labour coalition would have fallen on the issues of Northern Ireland and style of government, exemplified by the deplorable treatment of O Dalaigh.

Privately (and not all that privately) Haughey derided the manifesto, as did Lenihan. "Blessed are the young," he commented, "for they shall inherit the national debt." He had two other reasons for disliking the manifesto. As we have seen from his curt reply to Colley in 1973, he deplored auction politics; and if he were to have any hope of the leadership, it did not suit him for Colley, the chief author of the manifesto, to enhance his own popularity. Unhappy about the renewal of the contest between Haughey and Colley, and not fancying his own chances at the time, he urged Lynch to stay on as Taoiseach past his planned retirement date, 1980.

Lemass had laid it down as a maxim that electoral promises become invalid the day after the election count. Disregarding this useful if cynical principle, the Lynch government went ahead and implemented all their promises. For them to have the remotest chance of success, they needed two things: economic growth and wage restraint, especially in the public sector. But the economy, then recovering, was soon hit by the second oil crisis of the seventies; and the trade unions did not co-operate. The public finances, in tolerably good condition when the Fine Gael-Labour coalition left office, went out of control.

Haughey was the great beneficiary of the troubles of Lynch, Colley, and their coterie. The 1977 tide swept into the Dail not only the representatives of the unlettered, but men with a background in business and accountancy, such as Albert Reynolds and Charlie McCreevy. These were as derisive of the Colley policies as Haughey himself. He profited from their discontents, and from the fact that a large part of the business and financial community, and of the media, shared his views and believed him to be the man to restore fiscal order.

Moreover, Lynch was dreadfully handicapped by the lack of progress on the Northern question. Harold Wilson's proconsul, Merlyn Rees, who had shown himself impotent in the face of the

UWC strike, had set up a unionist-dominated "constitutional convention" which came to nothing. His successor, Roy Mason, engaged in no political innovations but concentrated on security measures. He put down firmly a feeble attempt to repeat the UWC strike but got, and deserved, no thanks in the Republic, where it was seen that the British government had acted decisively against a threat to its own authority whereas it had allowed the power-sharing executive to fall in 1974. The Dublin establishment looked forward with more hope than confidence to the accession of the Conservative government under Margaret Thatcher. Meanwhile, a row blew up over overflights of the Republic's territory by British military aircraft. An attempt was made to discipline a Fianna Fail backbencher who had criticised Lynch. Colley, in charge of the shop during a foreign trip by Lynch, hopelessly mishandled the exercise.

Fianna Fail suffered a setback in the 1979 European elections. Their cause was not advanced by their Gaullist ally Jacques Chirac, who came from Paris supposedly to help them but succeeded in doing the opposite. To Lenihan's anger and amazement, Chirac said that he did not want direct elections to be held at all. Why, then, should anyone bother to vote for his Fianna Fail allies? Worse still for Lynch, he lost two Dail by-elections in his Cork back yard. What had become of his colossal popularity?

Since Lynch had intended to retire early in 1980, the endeavours of the Haughey faction to hasten his departure were inconsequential. It was the Colley faction, rather than the Haughey faction, who persuaded him to bring forward his retirement, assuring him that Colley would certainly succeed him in the leadership. He disregarded the advice of Lenihan, who with his unerring nose for trouble urged him to stay on, and the contest was held in December 1979. Haughey won narrowly.

The assertion that not a single member of the Lynch cabinet voted for Haughey has appeared in print many times. It is incorrect. Lenihan and Ray Burke had agonised, through many hours and many drinks, over their decisions. Burke declines to disclose how he voted, but it has always been believed that he voted for Colley. Lenihan said within his family circle that he was obliged to choose between a fool and a knave. It is quite certain that in the end he voted for Haughey. The voting was by ballot. He wrote the name diagonally across his ballot paper, making it possible for anybody to check with the teller that such a vote was cast.

Many Haughey supporters believed that he had voted for Colley, and he was jostled and intimidated by ruffians who, fired up by drink in neighbouring hostelries, had invaded the precincts of Leinster House. Who were these louts? A founder member of the party said with distaste that they had to have people like that, but they should never be seen in public. The first proposition is highly questionable, the second unchallengeable. A member of the national executive, who would in time defect to the Progressive Democrats, noted that one never saw them at any other time and hazarded a guess that they were "members of the black economy". Wherever they came from, their activities were to become a feature associated with subsequent critical events: in 1982 one of them kicked James Gibbons and another pulled John Feeney of the *Evening Herald* by the beard. Feeney identified his assailant wrongly, with the result that a very respectable backbencher brought a successful libel action against Independent Newspapers, the owners of the *Evening Herald*.

Haughey initially sought to unite the party and achieve a reconciliation with the Colley faction. He was rebuffed by Colley, who declared merely a conditional loyalty to the new Taoiseach and insisted on what amounted to a veto over appointments to Justice and Defence. Haughey did gain a certain amount of support and sympathy, in Fianna Fail and more widely, when Garret FitzGerald said that he had a "flawed pedigree". FitzGerald was felt to have gone too far, but he had drawn attention to a question constantly on Irish political lips: where had Haughey made the money that enabled him to live an extravagant lifestyle, with a mansion and estate in North Dublin, a private island off the Kerry coast, racehorses, an art collection, and an enviable wine cellar? It would take a very long time for the country to find a partial answer to the question at the judicial inquiry under Mr Justice Brian McCracken into payments to politicians by the supermarket tycoon Ben Dunne in 1997.

*

Lenihan had been very disappointed when Lynch consigned him to the Department of Fisheries in 1977. He tried to conceal his feelings even within the family, saying, as with his appointment to Transport and Power in 1969, that a job was a job. But it was frustrating work, and ultimately doomed, and he knew it. By then, the industry was effectively regulated from Brussels.

The insurmountable obstacle mentioned in Chapter 5, against which the Irish negotiators came up in the EEC entry negotiations in 1972, was the demand of their interlocutors for "equal access" to our vast waters. These would, and did, become Community waters.

In the period between Lenihan's departure from Fisheries in 1964 and our EEC entry in 1973, the industry had made considerable progress. The Department of Fisheries had been amalgamated for a time with Agriculture under Haughey as Minister, and while Haughey remained in the department he worked constructively with Brendan O'Kelly in BIM. An increasing number of young skippers invested in larger vessels, which fished farther from the shore and opened up new grounds. Domestic consumption increased, and larger quantities of fish were exported. But O'Kelly saw himself as engaged in a race against time unless satisfactory arrangements for Irish fisheries could be achieved in the European negotiations. Hillery, as Foreign Minister and chief Irish negotiator, held consultations with the industry and BIM. Two BIM executives were seconded to serve on the negotiating team. Shortly before the deadline for the conclusion of the talks, O'Kelly went to Brussels to participate. Before leaving Dublin, he gave an interview to a *Sunday Press* journalist which reflected the industry's opposition to the EEC "equal access" proposals. Whether because of the outspoken nature of the interview or for some other reason, the Irish ambassador, Sean Gaynor, arrived at O'Kelly's hotel room late at night and told him that he was *persona non grata* and should have no contact with the negotiating team. Suppressing his anger, he decided to return home immediately. When the final terms were announced, they fulfilled his worst fears.

By the time Lenihan arrived back in Fisheries in 1977, the industry had suffered a further blow in the shape of national quotas. These, ostensibly introduced as conservation measures, were based on historical performance and because Ireland had been so late in development this basis was hopelessly unfavourable to us. The combination of access and quotas constituted a pincer movement or "double whammy" and the latter remains a subject of pain and controversy to the present day. At the end of 1997 the Irish minister walked out of a meeting which imposed a new quota, on catches of horse mackerel.

Nevertheless, Lenihan did his best, and in typical style. For as long as possible, he used his friendships with the Germans to obtain concessions on the quotas issue. On this question, just for once, Britain was not completely isolated in Europe, since her interests and ours coincided; and Lenihan made friends with the British Minister for Agriculture and Fisheries, John Silkin, like himself a cultivated man. The time, however, soon came to ditch Silkin. Lenihan went into a room with his German counterpart and a bottle of whiskey, surrendered on the main issue but obtained in return from Europe's paymasters a handout of £36 million, a substantial sum at the time. The incident gave rise to a legend which will be dealt with below.

Few as the votes were on the fisheries issue by comparison with that of agriculture, there were sufficient votes in it to put him under severe pressure and cause him difficulties with Fianna Fail representatives from constituencies with fishing ports. Their anxieties came to the surface at the annual ard-fheis. Lenihan made one of his notorious "no problem" speeches, assuring the restive delegates that despite the twin difficulties over limits and quotas everything would be all right on the night. As he attempted to leave the hall, he was buttonholed again and again by delegates seeking further assurance. To all of them he replied in the same vein.

Dick Walsh walked out of the hall with him. He was greatly puzzled by the minister's apparent confidence, which contradicted all the information available on the subject. When they were alone at last, he asked: "What's the truth, Brian?"

"The truth, Dick," said Brian, "is that we're shagged!"

And we were.

*

On Haughey's accession as Taoiseach in 1979, Lenihan was appointed Foreign Minister and plunged into a new Anglo-Irish rapprochement in which Haughey wished, as he said, to raise the Northern Ireland issue to "a higher plane". This meant, in essence, seeking a solution between the Irish and British governments over the heads of the Northern communities, specifically over those of the unionists.

Vast quantities of nonsense have been talked and written on this subject, generally based on the proposition that the approaches of Haughey — and his successor as Taoiseach, FitzGerald — trampled on unionist rights. That ignores the indisputable fact that every attempted settlement had been destroyed by unionist obduracy. A true settlement was not reached until the Good Friday Agreement of 1998, when nationalists made substantial concessions and a small majority of unionist voters, in the referendum which approved the agreement, acknowledged nationalist rights. A more reasoned criticism of Haughey would hold that he aimed too high, that he reposed excessive hopes in his relationship with Thatcher, and that he ultimately ruined that relationship for reasons that cannot possibly command objective support.

He can also be criticised for approaching Thatcher with what he considered style and others might call vulgarity. At his first meeting with her in London, he brought with him a gift of a

Georgian silver teapot, giving birth to the phrase "teapot diplomacy". What became of the teapot is unknown.

Before that event, Lenihan had engaged in a demarche of his own, conducted in a manner as characteristic of him as the teapot was of Haughey.

John Stephenson organised the highly successful Sense of Ireland festival in London in 1980. It had been in danger of collapse through lack of resources. Lenihan squeezed extra funds out of the Department of Finance to avoid what would have been a grave embarrassment.

At a dinner to mark the conclusion of the festival, Lenihan was the guest of honour. Stephenson recalls that "significant British politicians and officials" were present and describes the conversation:

> I believe the [1985] Anglo-Irish Agreement was initiated on that night. It could only have been done by the sheer charm and intelligence of Brian Lenihan.
>
> I watched him charm the British with his bonhomie and clever wit, then begin to manifest his knowledge and intelligence. He began to challenge them. They had to play. It was like watching tennis. Back and forth. I sat spellbound. All those very superior types asking themselves, who's this buffoon, then seeing how quickly they were wrongfooted. They had to show that they also knew their history and philosophy. Then he defused it again and everyone relaxed over coffee and brandy. Then: What are we going to do about this situation, lads? How do we deal with these recalcitrant Northerners? I could see them thinking, these are civilised people, we can do business with them, the problem is sorting out all those Northerners.

The high point of the Haughey-Thatcher relationship came in December 1980 at a summit meeting in Dublin Castle to which the Prime Minister brought a huge delegation including, naturally, her Foreign Secretary, Lord Carrington, but more surprisingly her Chancellor of the Exchequer, Sir Geoffrey Howe (afterwards Foreign Secretary, a Thatcher opponent on European issues, and an instrument in her final downfall). Nothing was spared to impress the guests. Howe relates in his memoirs that he sat at dinner beside an Irish Finance Department official who asked him how he liked the wine. When he replied "very much," the official said "so you should" and told him the staggering price.

While Howe, seemingly to his own puzzlement, was present, the British cabinet secretary, Robert (later Lord) Armstrong, was absent. On Thatcher's return to London he asked her how Haughey struck her. She replied, "he's a romantic idealist." That description cannot but prompt reflection on the lady's deficiencies as a judge of personality.

This summit gave birth to the phrase "totality of relationships" and may also be said to have given birth to the closely related "three-stranded approach" or axis: an internal settlement in the North, involving power-sharing under some other name, North-South institutions, and a new Anglo-Irish relationship. This last has never been thoroughly teased out, though an outline of sorts exists in the Good Friday Agreement. A possibility often mentioned was that Ireland could rejoin the Commonwealth, out of which Sean MacBride had taken us in 1949. A more significant issue was defence.

It has often been asserted that Haughey offered Thatcher a bilateral defence pact. Lenihan vigorously denied that, and the probability is that his denial was correct. Associates of Haughey planted the story in British "heavy" newspapers in the hope that it would arouse the Prime Minister's interest, as indeed it did. She consulted defence experts, who told her that the issue was irrelevant. In the event of a major crisis, the Irish would do as they were told. Much later, Lenihan strenuously asserted in print that Haughey and Thatcher never discussed the question *tête-à-tête*. It should be noted that he told Olivia O'Leary that they did, but that may have been just one of many examples of his talent for spreading confusion and his careless acceptance of misleading hypotheses for the sake of keeping the conversation and the "crack" going. A worthier though associated talent was his ability to warn against unpopular and dangerous departures, and that became necessary when the Dail debated neutrality and the alleged discussion of a defence pact between Haughey and Thatcher. Bruce Arnold in his biography of Haughey offers this intriguing insight:

> There was only one way out of the chaos and that was to introduce more chaos. This was admirably achieved by Lenihan, who, in a brilliant piece of knockabout music-hall virtuosity, at the very end of the debate, managed to confuse and block discussion, and even to block the division at the end. There was this visible purpose, and a hidden purpose as well — namely, to warn Haughey, on behalf of the Fianna Fail Party, that he was moving too fast and committing himself and them to too much. Lenihan, who had himself been closer to the talks than anyone, came as near as he could to contradicting Haughey's claim that defence issues had formed part of his second summit meeting with Thatcher. "Defence arrangements would be the last matter to be discussed," Lenihan said, and Anglo-Irish relations were a long way from that.

According to another version, Lenihan discussed the issue with Carrington, both keeping their chiefs in ignorance. A colourful story has it that Lenihan went into a room with Carrington carrying a bottle of whiskey and leaving their officials outside the door, and that one of these officials was Padraig O hAnnrachain, a formidable civil servant and, piquantly, an intimate of Haughey's. Lord Carrington has informed this author that he has no recollection of any such incident. The explanation must be that it has been confused with Lenihan's meeting on fisheries with the German minister, at which privacy and a bottle of whiskey did indeed figure.

Nevertheless, it appeared at the end of 1980 that "everything was on the table" and that a new era in Anglo-Irish relations was about to be inaugurated. But almost immediately the new relationship went horribly wrong. For that, Lenihan shares a small part of the blame.

*

Both Haughey and Lenihan were criticised for "over-selling" the summit, in Haughey's case for describing it as "a historic breakthrough". In point of fact Raymond Smith asked him at a press conference whether he would so describe it, and he had little choice but to answer yes.

Lenihan for his part talked about a reference in the communiqué to "institutional change" and confused it with "constitutional change", thereby reading too much into the document. Many thought he had done so at Haughey's instigation, but Ann Lenihan puts it down to his irrepressible optimism. Thatcher, however, blamed Haughey, and at a European summit meeting shortly afterwards at Maastricht, a location later to gain notoriety for other reasons, subjected him to one of her celebrated handbaggings. Their meeting lasted only a few minutes, during which time she simply bawled at him. Haughey passed it on to Lenihan, with interest. Late that night the journalist John Cooney found him in the bar of the hotel where they were staying, plunged uncharacteristically in gloom and fearing for his career. Cooney joined a diplomat friend in trying to console him. There is another of many ironies here. While Haughey blamed his mauling at Thatcher's hands on Lenihan's "over-selling" of the Dublin summit, Lenihan felt that Haughey had oversold it and thereby endangered the gains.

Lenihan's role, and the over-selling of the summit more generally, contributed only in part to the failure of the Haughey-Thatcher relationship. It foundered for at least three reasons: differences over the H-Blocks hunger strikes and the Falklands war, and deep suspicions of Haughey in the British establishment, by no means confined to Thatcher or her party.

One valid cause of these suspicions was Haughey's attempt, at the very beginning of his reign, to shift Sean Donlon from his post as ambassador in Washington. This was an appalling piece of misjudgement which showed that although Neil Blaney had long been out of the Fianna Fail Party Haughey remained to some extent under his influence.

Donlon was an immensely impressive diplomat, with an astonishing network of contacts. A book purporting to list those with the greatest influence in Washington placed the President (first Jimmy Carter, then Ronald Reagan) at No. 1 and Donlon at No. 12, a barely believable position for the representative of a country the size of Ireland. He was on intimate terms with the chief Irish-American politicians, led by the "Four Horsemen": Senator Edward Kennedy, Senator Daniel Patrick Moynihan, Representative Tip O'Neill, and Governor Hugh Carey of New York. Along with John Hume, Garret FitzGerald and Jack Lynch — who, whatever turns his party might take, had not forsaken his own attachment to bipartisanship — Donlon devised and implemented a policy consisting on the one hand of rejection of the IRA and Sinn Fein and on the other of American pressure on Britain in the interests of a Northern Ireland settlement approved by Dublin and by the SDLP. The first leg of the policy was extremely urgent, since thousands of Irish-Americans regarded the conflict in the North as a war of liberation and contributed funds to the republican movement, supposedly for humanitarian purposes but likely to find their way into the hands of purchasers of arms. Irish-Americans were also engaged in running guns, either purchased (so easily done in the United States) or stolen from arsenals. More threatening in its own way was the establishment of an "ad hoc committee" by Representative Mario Biaggi of New York, seen in Dublin as Sinn Fein-leaning and believed to have links with Blaney. Donlon considered it essential that Dublin should maintain the axis with the "Four Horsemen" and reject Biaggi.

The proposal to move him from Washington to New York as ambassador to the United Nations, therefore, inspired dismay. Donlon enlisted the "Four Horsemen" to press Haughey to reverse his decision. Meanwhile, Mike Burns and Raymond Smith literally cornered Lenihan at an Iveagh House reception, pushing him up against a table ("we had him half-sitting among the canapes," says Burns) and telling him, at some length and with some force, that the move would be disastrous. Lenihan promised that he would see the Taoiseach first thing the following morning. The pressure from the Irish-American leaders probably counted for much more than Lenihan's influence; in any event, Haughey backed down and Donlon stayed in Washington.

The hunger strikes and the Falklands war will be discussed below. First we must follow Lenihan in the other direction, to the Middle East.

Ten

The truth is rarely pure and never simple.
OSCAR WILDE

Lenihan and a number of others in his party, notably Senator Michael Lanigan, had a profound interest in the Arab world. The reasons were twofold. Arab countries, mostly but not exclusively those that had grown rich from oil revenues, like Iraq and Libya, were an important market, especially for beef. Lenihan, concealing as usual his deeper thoughts, said that "the Arabs are buying Waterford Crystal!" As to the deeper thoughts, Lenihan was always immensely interested in the collapse of empires, in their successor states, and in national rights, be they those of the Irish, the Germans or the Palestinians. Like the southern members of the European Union, he believed that the Arab world would soon "come into its own"; and he also, prematurely, looked forward to the day when the growth of the middle classes in Egypt and Iraq in particular (very much as he welcomed, again prematurely, what he saw as the *embourgeoisement* of the Soviet Union) would create West European-style democracy and respect for human rights in those countries.

Ireland has of course a Zionist lobby, smaller than that in major countries but active and influential. By 1980, however, Irish opinion had begun for a number of reasons to swing in favour of the Palestinian Arabs. Initially, Irish people in general had regarded the struggle for the creation of a Jewish state as analogous to our own struggle for independence from Britain. They admired Israeli successes, epitomised in the famous claim of "making the desert bloom". Few knew anything about the Palestinian Arabs or took much notice of the claims for Palestinian rights urged by Erskine B. Childers, son of President

117

Childers. When Irish troops went to Lebanon under the United Nations flag to seek to keep an uneasy peace there, their officers at first went, for the most part, as strong Israeli sympathisers, partly for the reasons just outlined and partly because of their indoctrination, which, for all the lip-service to neutrality, differed little from that of Nato officers. But they soon came to detest their Israeli counterparts, first for their arrogance and bad manners, and secondly for inspiring attacks on the UN forces by their Christian puppet in south Lebanon, the renegade Lebanese officer Major Haddad. As for Lenihan, always the practical politician, he reposed much of his hopes in the Israeli Labour Party, especially in Shimon Peres. He despaired of the Likud Party, and detested Jewish religious fundamentalism no less than the Christian and Islamic versions.

Matters came to a crisis with evidence of Israeli collusion in abominable actions including the murder of two Irish soldiers, Derek Smallhorn and Thomas Barrett. This is described in the book *Pity The Nation* by the great English reporter Robert Fisk:

> What, for example, was Lieutenant-Colonel Yoram Hamizrahi of Israeli military intelligence doing all the time in the south Lebanese village of Bent Jbail? Why was Lieutenant-Colonel Gary Gal of the Israeli army so frequently liaising with Haddad's gunmen in the Lebanese Christian enclave? And what was the shadowy figure of Major Haim — one of the most feared Israeli Shin Bet [intelligence] operatives — doing so often in Marjayoun?

An Israeli officer called a Dutch UNIFIL (United Nations Force in Lebanon) officer to warn him of a forthcoming artillery barrage. "A couple of seconds later," the Dutchman said, "shells started landing behind the United Nations lines. How was he so accurate? He wanted me to know he was next to the artillery battery. He was doing the shooting."

Of the murders of the Irish soldiers, Fisk writes:

What infuriated officers of the Irish 46th Infantry Battalion was ... intelligence information which suggested that a Shin Bet officer had actually been present at the murders and had stood by to witness the shots being fired into the necks of Barrett and Smallhorn.

Of much more long-term significance was the reaction of the Israeli government. Shlomo Argov, the Israeli ambassador ... in an interview on Irish radio petulantly lectured the Irish: "If you will permit me to say so, you sit there all so smugly up in Dublin and just pass judgement on things that are happening on the other side of the moon, on the other side of the world ... I should have expected a Christian nation to have a little sensitivity for people who are trying, among other things, in addition to preserving life and limb, also to preserve themselves as Christians."

The Irish ambassador demanded from the Israeli Prime Minister, Menachem Begin, an explanation for the murders but got none.

What had really angered the Israeli government was a statement made in Bahrain in February of 1980 by the Irish Foreign Minister, Brian Lenihan, acknowledging "the role of the Palestine Liberation Organisation in representing the Palestinian people". From that moment, the Irish had been singled out for vilification by the Israelis.

Lenihan was shocked by the murders and by the discourtesy shown to his ambassador, and angered by the assumption in some quarters that favouring Palestinian self-determination suggested antisemitism or opposition to Israeli interests: he never wavered from his defence of Israeli existence and security. But he was proud of the Bahrain Declaration, preceding as it did by a few months the Venice Declaration on similar lines by the European Council of Ministers. In an article in the *Irish Times* in 1993, he wrote:

The declaration incorporated two fundamental principles — "the right to existence and security of all the states in the region, including Israel, and justice for all the peoples, which implies the recognition of the legitimate rights of the Palestinian people."

The declaration further stated that the Palestinian people, "within the framework of a comprehensive peace settlement, must be placed in a position to exercise fully their right to self-determination."

Finally, the declaration stressed the need for Israel to put an end to the occupation of Arab territories, and most importantly spelled out that the PLO "would have to be associated with the negotiations."

I am glad to say that, thirteen years later, most of the elements in the Venice Declaration are included in the peace proposals now being fleshed out by Israeli and PLO negotiators.

He lived to see the Oslo Accords which created an embryonic Palestinian state, but not to see the ensuing calamities caused by Islamic terrorism and the obduracy of the Israeli government under Binyamin Netanyahu, who came to power in 1996.

With the more serious matters, a little diplomatic joke may be recorded. Lenihan had asserted the right of Palestinian self-determination, with all that that implied. Worldly diplomats suggested that it could be likened to a proposition, to wit, "will you have dinner with me, with all that that implies?"

*

In addition to his concerns in Northern Ireland and the Middle East, Lenihan on taking office as Foreign Minister found himself immediately embroiled in an international crisis. The Soviet invasion of Afghanistan, and gross infringements of human rights in Soviet satellite states, threatened detente and the "Helsinki process" of European security co-operation.

On 21 December 1979, as president of the European Foreign Ministers' Council, he issued a statement in which the ministers expressed "profound disappointment at the rejection of the appeals of the signatories of Charter 77 sentenced on 23 October [in the then Czechoslovakia] and at the recent sentencing of a further member of their group." Those imprisoned included the playwright Vaclav Havel, who would go on to become President of the free Czech Republic.

Two of Lenihan's most important speeches date from late 1980. It is worth noting that he did not confine himself to speeches: during a difficult meeting of the Conference on Security and Co-operation in Europe (CSCE) in Vienna earlier in that year he had helped Hans-Dietrich Genscher to negotiate with the Russians. But the speeches show his fear that, contacts like those of Vienna notwithstanding, the CSCE would become a dead letter and detente more widely would break down.

In Trinity College on 17 October he said that "joining the European Community was the most historic and decisive foreign policy [decision] made since the foundation of the state", and continued:

> The assertion is often made or at least the question asked if membership of the Community and participation in European political co-operation diminish our sovereignty and weaken our independence. It is a legitimate question which deserves to be answered. In my own view, in the view of this government and I believe previous governments, the answer is that membership of the Community and involvement in European political co-operation enhance our sovereignty and give more substance to our independence ...
>
> Freedom and independence to be meaningful must be exercised actively. An independent foreign policy is merely an empty slogan if it is not used to some purpose and to some effect ...
>
> Ireland and the other member states ... have a genuine opportunity and an effective instrument with which to work for peace and order, equity and fairness in the world. These are obviously worthy purposes. What do they mean in concrete terms for an

independent Irish foreign policy both within the Community and in the international organisations and negotiations in which we participate, and for the efforts of the Community itself?

The sixties and seventies were an era of negotiation when at global and regional and bilateral level governments established the machinery and began the task of coping with those urgent and dangerous problems which can only be solved by common action. The need to solve the problems is still there and increasingly urgent, and the means to do so are still available.

In Madrid on 12 November, at a review meeting of the CSCE, he said:

Detente seems to be faltering. If this is so, then the CSCE which is part of the process cannot but falter too. Armed interventions, international and internal instabilities have increased rather than diminished tensions. Mutual mistrust, the emergence of new weapons and the strategic doctrines that go with them threaten a new round in the arms race and to undermine the existing fragile arms control agreements. Indeed the preparatory meeting which has just ended has only too clearly reflected the current adverse state of East-West relations ...

Some things need to be said not only in the interests of honesty and plain speaking — but in the interests of the CSCE process itself. Some of us maintain that detente, like peace, is "indivisible". Others used to say that detente is "irreversible". If anyone thought that in making those assertions he was stating facts rather than expressing wishes, clearly he is wrong. In our view detente is neither an abstraction nor a mechanical process independent of our will and actions. It is unlikely to survive if it is expected to withstand another shock like the Soviet intervention in Afghanistan. Moreover the notion of an "irreversible" detente will soon be dissipated, if it is seen as threatening the political order or social system of any state. And the average person is likely to regard detente as an illusion and the CSCE as a fraud if he sees and hears of people imprisoned and harassed simply for invoking the rights which the [Helsinki] Final Act was supposed to accord to them.

While on this and other occasions Lenihan was severely critical of Soviet policy, and while he approved of US military moves in support of Germany, he by no means spared the Americans. The reference above to strategic doctrines means those of the so-called "neo-Clausewitzians" whose theories, borrowed from the utterly different conditions of the eighteenth century and early nineteenth century, led to Ronald Reagan's "Star Wars". Long afterwards, in an analysis of American postwar foreign policy, Lenihan would praise the work of President Harry Truman and General George Marshall but go on to castigate the policies of John Foster Dulles and of his disciples who aimed at establishing US influence, not to say domination, everywhere in the world.

*

The hunger strikes of 1980-81 by IRA and INLA (Irish National Liberation Army) prisoners in the H-Blocks of the Maze prison, formerly Long Kesh, resulted in ten deaths and gave the political wing of the republican movement, Sinn Fein, popular support which they did not previously enjoy. They may be seen as leading directly to the Sinn Fein electoral successes of the nineties.

The deaths must be laid at the doors, first of the IRA leadership and secondly of Margaret Thatcher. She held out adamantly, frequently ignoring the advice of her own ministers, against granting the prisoners anything that might be construed as "political status", such as the right to wear their own clothes. This and other rights were in fact eventually granted, which makes the waste of life and the advantage to the IRA all the more deplorable.

Lenihan looked back more than once in print at his own and Haughey's impotence in the face of the looming tragedy. His son Niall went to the New York launch of Lady Thatcher's turgid and self-serving book *Margaret Thatcher: The Downing Street Years*. He introduced himself and received from her a complimentary inscription to his father. Lenihan did not pay her back in kind, but reviewed the book in the *Irish Press* in October 1993 with uncustomary but well-deserved harshness. Referring to the famous phrase of December 1980, "totality of relationships", he wrote:

> The phraseology was carefully crafted by officials and ministers on both sides, and it is a nonsense for Lady Thatcher to suggest in her book that she "allowed through the statement because she did not involve herself closely enough in the drafting of the communique."

He contradicted her on the allegation that the Anglo-Irish Agreement of 1985 failed to improve security co-operation between the Republic and Northern Ireland. (Lady Thatcher gave security co-operation as her motive for signing the agreement. Her friend Alan Clark in his diaries attributed it entirely to American influence.)

On H-Blocks, Lenihan wrote:

> As early as 1 December 1980 she records Mr Haughey as urging her in the margins of a European Council meeting in Luxembourg "to find some face-saving device which would allow the hunger-strikers to end their fast."
>
> For five months until Bobby Sands's death in May, the Taoiseach and I tried every device and contact open to us, as did the late Cardinal O Fiaich, the Irish Commission for Justice and Peace, the European Commission on Human Rights, and Michael Foot MP, then leader of the British Labour Party, but to no avail.

Lady Thatcher was adamant but her intransigence
gave a new lease of life to the Provisional IRA.

*

It may also be said to have cost Haughey the 1981 general
election. Almost from the beginning, Haughey had gravely
disappointed those who thought that the new Taoiseach would
bring to the country the sadly-lacked and much-longed-for
"smack of firm government". He addressed the nation on the
subject of the public finances, telling us that we would all have
to tighten our belts, but once challenged he ran away and the
condition of the finances continued to deteriorate. His admirers
claimed that everything would change once he had his own
mandate, and whether or not he had the courage to back his
words with actions he certainly wanted to achieve that mandate
as quickly as possible. He decided to use the Fianna Fail ard-
fheis of February 1981 as the launching pad for the general
election, but a calamitous fire, with terrible loss of life, in the
Stardust ballroom in his own constituency of Dublin North East
caused the cancellation of the ard-fheis and the postponement of
the election. By the time the election was held, the deaths in the
H-Blocks had begun. "H-Blocks candidates" ran in several
constituencies. Two were elected at Fianna Fail's expense. The
loss of even two seats sufficed to deprive Fianna Fail of the
chance of forming a government.

FitzGerald formed a coalition with Labour which did not
command a Dail majority but needed for its survival the support
of two independents, Jim Kemmy and Sean Dublin Bay Loftus.
Kemmy had first encountered Lenihan while campaigning as a
Labour activist in the 1968 Limerick by-election. He defected
from the party and founded his own Democratic Socialist Party,
but later rejoined Labour and became the party chairman. Loftus
was an environmental campaigner and a member of a
"community" group on the Dublin city council.

In January 1982 FitzGerald's Finance Minister, John Bruton,
introduced a budget which proposed, *inter alia*, to impose value
added tax on children's shoes. Kemmy and Loftus voted against

the budget, bringing down the government. FitzGerald announced his intention of immediately seeking a dissolution of the Dail from President Hillery, but his meeting with the President was delayed because Hillery's secretary had to be fetched from the theatre where he was spending the evening.

The President has it in his or her power to refuse a dissolution to a Taoiseach who has lost his Dail majority. Haughey decided to ask Hillery to exercise this power. It was a strange decision. Since the government had fallen in ignominious circumstances, a Fianna Fail victory at a general election appeared a certainty, whereas it was very far from a certainty that Haughey could form a government in the existing Dail. In all probability he not only thought that he could cobble together the thinnest of majorities, but that he could go to the country a few months later looking for a majority on a platform of "stable government".

He held a meeting of the Fianna Fail front bench and issued a statement saying that he was available to the President for consultation. So far, so proper — but if Hillery had refused FitzGerald a dissolution, he could have been seen as interfering in political party matters. More dubious was the propriety of causing telephone calls to be made to Aras an Uachtarain, which Hillery viewed as improper pressure. These telephone calls, ultimately calamitous for Lenihan, will be discussed below in the context of the 1990 presidential election.

The dissolution was granted and the general election held. FitzGerald fought a brave campaign and made a great impact on voters who had started to think that fiscal rectitude might after all be a good idea. He lost narrowly to Haughey, who came back to office with the support of the Workers' Party. Thus began the Year of the GUBU, the acronym for "grotesque, unbelievable, bizarre and unprecedented".

Freed from the Colley veto, Haughey made a number of cabinet appointments which an astonished Lenihan described as "terrible misjudgements". Sean Doherty, deputy for Lenihan's former Roscommon constituency, became Minister for Justice. Haughey gave Lenihan Agriculture instead of Foreign Affairs.

This move provoked considerable mirth, not least within the Lenihan family, in which Brian was known as "the white-handed farmer" because he fancied himself as something of an expert on crops and stock while never doing any actual agricultural work. It could be rationalised on the grounds that a modern agriculture minister's work has little or nothing to do with farming as such and everything to do with European negotiations and developing markets, including Middle Eastern markets, and on both of these Lenihan was indubitably an expert. But the real reason was Haughey's attempted manipulation of the balance of power within his cabinet.

In a sense, Lenihan was lucky not to hold one of the most sensitive portfolios in a period in which everything went grotesquely, unbelievably, bizarrely and unprecedentedly wrong. He was certainly lucky to be out of Foreign Affairs when Haughey not only offended the British, but departed from EU policy, during the Falklands war. Ireland was at the time a member of the UN Security Council (an honour for which Lenihan as Foreign Minister had campaigned with skill) and therefore enjoyed greater than usual influence. The Irish ambassador, Noel Dorr, was instructed to seek "a ceasefire in place", leaving the Argentine forces in possession of most of their territorial gains on the Falkland Islands. Adroit diplomatic work by Dorr and the British ambassador, Sir Anthony Parsons, averted a full-scale Anglo-Irish crisis, but British anger persisted for many years. Lenihan profoundly disagreed with Haughey's departure from the EU line, and told members of his family that if he had been Foreign Minister at the time, he would have resigned. Had he had the misfortune to be involved, it would have been difficult for him to gain the trust of the British and score the successes that he subsequently achieved in Anglo-Irish relations.

*

Haughey used the GUBU phrase in relation to the arrest of Malcolm Macarthur, later convicted of murder, in the attorney-general's apartment. Many other GUBU events occurred in 1982, of which the one with the longest-lasting repercussions was the tapping of two journalists' telephones. These were Geraldine Kennedy and our old acquaintance Bruce Arnold.

Telephone tapping is so old and general a practice as to merit in normal times little attention. When Harry Truman succeeded Franklin D. Roosevelt as President of the United States, he was outraged to discover that Roosevelt had spied in this manner on members of his own government. Truman ordered the practice discontinued, but his successor Dwight Eisenhower reinstated it. In Britain, disclosures of telephone taps on members of the Blair government by the intelligence services caused a furore in 1997. In Ireland, pre-1982 targets had included Brian Lenihan as well as numerous politicians and journalists. The practice, as we have seen in Chapter 8, had reached a peak at the time of the Arms Crisis, with the Department of Justice holding enormous numbers of tapes, illegally obtained.

And that is just the point: tapping was usually carried out without authorisation, other than authorisation by nod and wink. The taps on the Kennedy and Arnold telephones were placed on foot of warrants issued by Doherty as Minister for Justice, ostensibly in the interest of national security — and Doherty embroiled Garda Siochana officers of the highest rank, with disastrous consequences for their careers. As the police reported, the taps yielded nothing at all in relation to national security. But they recorded a great deal of political conversation.

Although the incident did not come to light until the following year, many in Fianna Fail — and almost everybody outside Fianna Fail — regarded activities like these as typical of any administration led by Haughey. For this and other reasons, large numbers in the party also regarded him as an electoral liability. In two general elections within a matter of months, the second held in circumstances highly disadvantageous to the opposing parties, he had failed to win an overall Dail majority. And since Fianna Fail still held single-party government as a so-called "core value", he could not plausibly plead the 1959 and 1968 failures to change the voting system as an excuse. Not only his opponents believed that any other Fianna Fail leader would have easily won a majority in February 1982.

The first "heave" against him occurred before he came back to office in March. It was defeated by a substantial margin, though not substantial enough for comfort. The second came in the autumn, the third in early 1983.

Throughout, Lenihan supported him with a loyalty which must be called both excessive and self-sacrificing but which he justified on the usual grounds of party unity. He felt that Haughey, so far from acting dictatorially — the customary charge against him — handled the dissidents much too gently. By the summer of 1982, O'Malley had replaced Colley as the unofficial but acknowledged leader of the anti-Haughey faction. Lenihan and Ray Burke went to him and told him that if he kept quiet and kissed the rod he would assuredly succeed Haughey in time. O'Malley does not appear to have seen that Lenihan by making this demarche was in effect destroying his own leadership chances in favour of a man with whom he had little sympathy. More curiously, he does not appear to have understood the significance of the approach. He says that many others urged him to take the course urged on him by Lenihan and Burke. He evidently did not realise that they regarded themselves as a delegation representing middle-ground opinion, and assuredly did not speak only for themselves.

The incident, no less than Lenihan's loyalty to Haughey, was wholly in character. Lenihan would make almost any political sacrifice in the interest of party unity. His motives were honourable, and well understood by such as Brendan Halligan, who had ridden out so much turmoil in the Labour Party. The question, however, must be asked, whether Colley or O'Malley or any other leader could have united Fianna Fail. Among the scores of people interviewed for the purposes of the present work only one, Bruce Arnold, thinks that Colley or O'Malley could have achieved that. All the others believe that Haughey would never have bowed to the rule of either Colley or O'Malley.

A second attempt to unseat Haughey failed in the autumn. The third came at the beginning of 1983, after he had gone back into opposition. He had lost a vote of confidence in the Dail, simply because one Fianna Fail deputy had died and a second, none other than James Gibbons, was ill and unable to attend. After the second general election of 1982, FitzGerald returned to office in another coalition with Labour, this time commanding a Dail majority. His Justice Minister, Michael Noonan, disclosed the story of the telephone taps, giving Haughey's internal opponents a magnificent issue on which to fight. Doherty asserted that he had acted without Haughey's knowledge or authority, but he was not widely believed.

A matter of days before the decision on the leadership (confined to Fianna Fail deputies in a rollcall vote) Haughey had undoubtedly lost the support of a majority in the parliamentary party. He regained it after he appealed, on Lenihan's advice, to the party activists in the country over the heads of the deputies. Then a group of his close supporters engaged in a massive exercise in intimidation. Strange cars and vans were spotted outside deputies' houses, often late at night. Calls went through to unlisted telephone numbers, again often late at night. The callers told the deputies who answered that their seats, and more, were in danger. There was talk of a political "death list" drawn up in a Dublin hotel. One deputy described himself as "frightened beyond being frightened any more."

Haughey's opponents were handicapped by their lack of a candidate generally acceptable to the party. The middle-ground deputies feared that if they chose O'Malley they would provoke an outright split. Several names, including those of Gerry Collins and Michael O'Kennedy, were thrown into the pot at the instigation of Haughey himself or his associates. Lenihan, seen as too close to Haughey, was seldom mentioned. He intended, in the event of Haughey's defeat, to offer himself as a candidate, and went so far as to draft a statement declaring his candidature. But at the very same time he worked by day and night to woo the waverers by gentler means than those employed by the late-night callers. And his arithmetic was as superb as his knowledge of the parliamentary party was intimate. Before the crucial meeting, he showed a journalist a piece of paper on which were inscribed the figures 40-33. That was exactly the vote in favour of Haughey.

Haughey had survived largely thanks to Lenihan. He would give him poor payment for his loyalty. Meanwhile, the party settled down into a sort of battered and sullen unity, and into exploiting the numerous mistakes and misfortunes of the second FitzGerald government. The latter was easy work. The coalition somehow survived from December 1982 until the beginning of 1987, but had lost all cohesion and sense of purpose by the summer of 1986 at the latest. It had, however, one major achievement to its credit, the Anglo-Irish Agreement.

*

This was a bad period for Lenihan's reputation. Haughey treated him and the press secretary, P. J. Mara, as a pair of court jesters; the public saw him as the man who "warmed up" ard-fheis audiences for the Boss with flowery rhetoric, sometimes descending into nonsense. One sentence sticks in Olivia O'Leary's mind: "We must be negative in order to be positive." Liam Lawlor says that "the troops loved to hear Brian telling them things like 'we're a national crusading movement, a family — embracing the big man and the small' — that sort of junk." Deirdre Purcell wrote that nobody else could talk for so long and say so little. Lenihan felt a mixture of pride at his ability to rouse the delegates and embarrassment when he entered more sophisticated company. The public forgot that he had loyally performed a similar service for Lynch, and had made speeches indistinguishable from the Haughey warm-ups at pre-election rallies. Lawlor remembers that on one such occasion he was seated beside Lynch when the leader turned to him and murmured, "he's a terrible rabble-rouser, isn't he?" Gratitude is not the most salient quality of political leaders.

Lenihan also continued to be trotted out to parade the Fianna Fail line on television, often substituting windy rhetoric for detailed discussion of current issues. On one occasion he shared a studio with the present author and Gemma Hussey, FitzGerald's Education Minister, and spoke for the best part of fifteen minutes (this is not an exaggeration but an actual timing) without appearing to need to draw breath. The theme, if it may be so called, was Fianna Fail as "the repository of Irish nationalism". Attempts by Mrs Hussey and myself to get a word in availed us little, and he actually rebuked me for trying to interrupt him. I did not take the reproach to heart.

In May 1983 FitzGerald set up the New Ireland Forum, which sat in Dublin Castle on and off for a year and heard a number of interesting submissions. The Forum's unsatisfactory outcome, and the absence from it of unionist representatives, attracted much misguided criticism. The exercise was useful, though badly spoiled by Haughey.

The unionists' boycott was of little significance, because this was a constitutional nationalist forum comprised of the Republic's political parties and the SDLP: one of its main purposes was to prop up the SDLP against the growing electoral threat from Sinn Fein. Many valuable contacts were made or renewed, and in particular a close friendship, already of long standing, flourished between Lenihan and the SDLP deputy leader, Seamus Mallon. Secondly, a unique event occurred: representatives of the Catholic hierarchy, led by Cardinal Cahal Daly, were subjected to rigorous public questioning. Thirdly, the officials who serve these stage-managed shows, especially young high-flyers from the Taoiseach's Department and the Department of Foreign Affairs, gain profitable experience in drafting documents and in dealing with politicians. Fourthly and most important, the exercise concentrated the minds of nationalists, or at least such minds as were open, on the subtleties and complexities of the Northern question.

One man's mind, however, was not open. Charles J. Haughey, for all his attempts to create a new kind of Anglo-Irish relationship with Margaret Thatcher, had no intention of diminishing his credit with nationalists of the old-fashioned variety. He also believed that the business of an opposition was to oppose, and never to miss an opportunity to score a hit against the government. When it came time to draft the Forum's report, he insisted that among the various "options" for a settlement, a unitary Irish state must take pride of place over any alternatives, such as a federal arrangement or joint Anglo-Irish authority over Northern Ireland. Immediately after the report's publication his chief spokesmen went so far as to present a unitary state as the only option to be seriously considered. For this they were angrily, and properly, attacked, since it was clear to any objective student of the question that an ultimate settlement could not possibly feature a unitary Irish state. The other parties accepted the thrust of the report only with reluctance, and only after the Labour leader, Dick Spring, had obtained the insertion of a paragraph to the effect that other options would be considered. John Kelly refused to sign the report.

Kelly was not the only unhappy man. Dick Walsh in his biography of O'Malley gives an account of the next twist in the story:

> The Fianna Fail leader's refusal to hold internal discussions on the Forum report led to the first in his final series of disagreements with O'Malley. Haughey insisted that he alone had the right to speak publicly on the subject. O'Malley argued that since Ray MacSharry, one of Haughey's supporters, had been allowed to give an interview following the leader's line, he too should be permitted to present his views.
>
> In another party, at another time, on any other issue, there would have been no argument. But populist Fianna Fail fifteen months after its last leadership challenge was not like any other party; the national question was no ordinary issue; and Haughey and O'Malley were never likely to agree to differ. Haughey had always mistrusted FitzGerald and felt uneasy about the Forum; he had long been convinced that O'Malley's views were closer to those of the Fine Gael leader than to his, not only on the North but on the economy and on political standards . . .

Now, the answer to the question "Who will rid me of this turbulent priest?" was at hand. O'Malley made public his views, first on party discipline and democracy — he did stand closer to FitzGerald and John Hume than to Haughey — and the business of having him expelled from the parliamentary party was set in train immediately.

Charlie McCreevy says that supporters of Fianna Fail are different from supporters of all other parties. As the saying goes, he never said a truer word. In this instance, and in the greater divisions that followed, for the most part Fianna Fail at all levels thought that O'Malley behaved very badly, while almost everybody else who thought about the matter felt that he behaved very well. Lenihan, doubtless remembering the unsuccessful demarche of 1982, thought O'Malley had behaved badly. That opinion, right or wrong, would soon bring more trouble on his own head.

Eleven

We must opt for a formula of constructive ambiguity.
GIULIO ANDREOTTI

In his seminal work *Church and State in Modern Ireland*, Professor John Whyte noted the feebleness of clerical opposition to Lenihan's film and book censorship reforms in the sixties. As seen in Chapter 3, the main episcopal voices raised at the time were those of Archbishop John Charles McQuaid of Dublin and Bishop Cornelius Lucey of Cork. McQuaid demanded protection "from the public activities of those [film makers] who neither accept nor practise the natural and the Christian moral law"; Lucey wanted publication of pornographic books made a criminal offence. "Neither of these episcopal statements, however," Whyte wrote, "had any effect on government policy."

Later governments, regrettably, did not see off the conservatives with similar ease; nor could they see them off at all without a major and bruising conflict. The adoption in the nineties of most of the "liberal agenda" owed a good deal to chance, and perhaps more to imprudent strategy on the part of the lay fundamentalist leaders who largely took over the cause from a hierarchy that (with notable exceptions like Archbishop Kevin McNamara of Dublin and Bishop Jeremiah Newman of Limerick) would have preferred a more cautious approach.

The conservative movement, like all mass movements, had various wings. Behind it were the manipulators, of whom Emily O'Reilly has given an account in *Masterminds of The Right*. It had its intellectuals, like the brilliant lawyer Professor William Binchy, and parliamentary apologists of the highest respectability, like Des Hanafin. It also had a lunatic fringe, in touch with the American campaigners who used physical violence against abortion clinics and doctors who performed abortions, and suspected of receiving money from American fundamentalists. It was egged on by the long-serving Papal Nuncio, Monsignor Gaetano Alibrandi, a Sicilian and a man of many parts whose accomplishments extended to playing the theme from *The Godfather* on the organ.

With the censorship battle over, the next target was contraception. The importation and sale of contraceptives were forbidden, but the courts struck down the ban on importation on constitutional grounds in the McGee case. An attempt to regularise matters by law was defeated in the Dail in 1976 when Cosgrave, with several other Fine Gael deputies, voted against a measure brought in by his own Justice Minister, Patrick Cooney. On Fianna Fail's return to office in 1977, Lynch appointed Haughey Health Minister and handed him the poisoned contraception cup. Haughey introduced a laughable measure which provided that doctors could supply married couples with prescriptions for condoms. This he described, in a phrase that would haunt him, as "an Irish solution to an Irish problem".

The third issue was abortion. The fundamentalists saw their opportunity in the political turmoil of 1981-82, when three general elections were held in less than eighteen months and the politicians were at their most vulnerable. They persuaded — forced might be a better word — both Haughey and FitzGerald to support a constitutional amendment asserting the right to life of the unborn child, with due regard to the pregnant woman's equal right to life. Some thought the equation of the life of a foetus with that of an adult human being offensive, but "pro-life" campaigners have since stated that the wording did not meet their requirements and that they wanted a wording simply banning abortion in all circumstances (denying that it could be necessary to save the pregnant woman's life). At the time, perhaps a more significant question was why anyone should have thought a constitutional amendment necessary, since abortion had long been banned under a British Act of 1861, never repealed after Irish independence, and abortion on demand or otherwise was sought only by a tiny "pro-choice" lobby. To this the "pro-life" campaigners answered that it might be legalised on foot of the landmark English case Rex v. Bourne, or by European law. They cannot have foreseen that their employment of the latter argument would have shattering effects and lead indirectly to the fall of a government. Still less could they have foreseen that their campaign, so far from making abortion in the jurisdiction impossible, would result in legalising it.

This, however, was in point of fact forecast by FitzGerald's attorney-general, Peter Sutherland; and Senator Mary Robinson predicted, accurately, that the issue would in due course find its way into the courts. FitzGerald repented his commitment to the earlier wording and put forward an alternative form of words devised by Sutherland. It was defeated in the Dail in 1983, a referendum was held, and a constitutional ban on abortion on the original wording was agreed by a two-to-one majority.

Flushed with their success, the conservatives went on to oppose a modest liberalising measure on contraception introduced early in 1985 by FitzGerald's Health Minister, Barry Desmond. In his O'Malley biography, Walsh writes:

> Before and during the debate, lay fundamentalist organisations, some of them called into existence at the time of the abortion referendum, others long accustomed to equally forceful if less public lobbying, exerted considerable pressure on politicians to reject the measure.

When O'Malley came to speak on the Bill on 20 February 1985, he told the House:

> In the past ten days the most extraordinary and unprecedented extra-parliamentary pressure has been brought to bear on many members of this House. This is not merely ordinary lobbying. It is far more significant. I regret to have to say that it borders at times almost on the sinister.

Fianna Fail opposed the Bill, not for moral reasons but in the hope that defections from the governing parties would help them to inflict a defeat on the FitzGerald government. Although they had taken the parliamentary party whip away from O'Malley, they pressed him to join in this endeavour. He said in his speech:

> I am possibly unique in that I have been subjected to two enormous pressures, the more general type and a particular political one. They are both like flood tides — neither of them is easy to resist and it is probably more than twice as hard to resist the two of them ... I do not believe that the interests of this state, of our constitution and of this republic, would be served by putting politics before conscience ... I stand by the Republic.

He did not vote for the Bill (passed by eighty-three votes to eighty) but abstained. One might have thought that, since he was not subject to the party whip, he had a perfect right to do either. Fianna Fail thought otherwise. Haughey proposed at a meeting of the national executive that O'Malley should be expelled from the party for "conduct unbecoming", and the motion was carried by seventy-three votes to nine. Lenihan called the decision "democracy at its best". It was possibly the most shocking thing he ever said in his life, and his friends outside the party could not forbear to chide him for it.

Notwithstanding his personal friendships with many conservatives in his own and other parties, Lenihan deeply disliked the fundamentalist movement and thought it anti-democratic. But he viewed the O'Malley issue as political rather than a matter of conscience, and believed that one should always stand by one's party. There is profound irony here. Lenihan's loyalty would be rewarded by betrayal; O'Malley's standing by his conscience and the Republic would bring trouble on Fianna Fail's head; Hanafin on the other side of the debate would go on to suffer, albeit temporarily, for putting conscience before party. But here we are concerned with Lenihan's reputation, and in thinking of it one thinks of Hanafin's words: The Party, the Party, the Party!

*

Lenihan, predictably, supported the party line on the Forum, but not only for party reasons. He was always a proponent of the classic Irish negotiating style of starting with the maximum demand, in this case the unitary state. His closest political associate in the North was Seamus Mallon, who made no secret that had he been born on this side of the border he would have been an enthusiastic Fianna Failer, and who often stayed with the Lenihans in Castleknock; and Lenihan evidently entertained hopes that the SDLP would take the Fianna Fail view. But, knowing the illusory nature of the unitary state proposition, they gave equal weight to the other Forum "options" — not to say greater weight, since they had long been convinced of the necessity for compromise. The Lenihan family thought they detected, as a result, a cooling in relations with Mallon, but Mallon says the incident did not affect his warm relationship with Brian.

Fianna Fail, however, rejoiced in the humiliation of FitzGerald at a meeting with Thatcher at Chequers following the publication of the Forum report in 1984. At a press conference after the meeting, Thatcher took each of the three options and declared it "out". What was dubbed her "out, out, out" statement aroused bitter anger in Ireland, anger emphatically conveyed to the British establishment in general and the Conservative Party in particular. FitzGerald and his Foreign Minister, Peter Barry, kept their heads and (with more difficulty) their tempers and worked adroitly on British contrition to bring the Prime Minister into a more accommodating mood. A committee was established, consisting of four of the best officials on each side, to devise a new agreement. A cogent point made by the Belfast journalists Eamonn Mallie and David McKittrick is that the best minds in the Irish civil service work on Anglo-Irish matters, whereas that is seldom the case on the British side. In this instance, it was the case, and the British fielded a powerful team led by Robert Armstrong. The efforts of the official negotiators, and FitzGerald's conciliatory approach, bore fruit in the Anglo-Irish Agreement, signed at Hillsborough in

November 1985. The agreement gave the Irish government a guaranteed role in Northern Ireland and a physical foothold in the North, with Irish as well as British officials stationed at Maryfield near Belfast, a location known as "the bunker".

Haughey completely misread the situation and the public mood, which rightly identified the agreement as a triumph for the FitzGerald government and for Irish nationalism. He publicly opposed the accord on unconvincing constitutional grounds, but modified his opposition once the state of public opinion became clear to him. Lenihan, who saw much of his role as tempering Haughey's rashness and preventing him from making political blunders, unavailingly advised him against taking a stand against the AIA. But he agreed to go to the United States to "put the Fianna Fail view" to the Irish-American leaders. It was disgraceful for Haughey thus to try to undermine abroad a pillar of Irish policy, which should have been bipartisan policy. Was it disgraceful for Lenihan to consent, and to undergo a humiliation which, if not comparable to that inflicted on FitzGerald by Thatcher, was quite bad enough? Tip O'Neill, who had not forgotten the Donlon affair of 1980, received him with scant courtesy and dismissed him virtually unheard. Lenihan knew that the Haughey line was nonsensical, persuaded himself that he was just doing "another job for the party", and made no real effort to change the Irish-American leaders' minds. His true opinion, and that of other level-headed people close to the centre of the party, was summed up, not by himself but by Sean Duignan after Duignan briefly left broadcasting to work as press secretary to Albert Reynolds. Talking to Martin Mansergh about the AIA, he said, "we were very bold." To Duignan's alarm, Mansergh, a very tall man, drew himself up to his full height, seemed to look offended, drew a deep breath and finally replied, "yes, we were."

O'Malley for his part favoured the Hillsborough Agreement and saw Haughey's opposition as opportunistic and misguided. So did another deputy, Mary Harney, who had long had her differences with the party leader. Along with a number of defectors from Fianna Fail and Fine Gael — most notably Michael McDowell, a member of an eminent Fine Gael family who had chaired FitzGerald's organisation in the Dublin South East constituency — they founded a new party, the Progressive Democrats, on 21 December 1985.

The new party was seen by Fianna Fail loyalists as a mere breakaway group based on no better grounds than hostility to Haughey, and O'Malley as someone who, from jealous motives, refused to accept the democratic decisions of the party from which he had broken. That view was firmly rejected by the media and most of the public, who unlike Lenihan felt that O'Malley had been treated abominably and, further, that were he leader of Fianna Fail, the party could stay in power for two Dail terms or longer. Another way of looking at the PD phenomenon was to take the twin planks of its policies, liberalism on "social issues" such as divorce and contraception and (in theory) fiscal conservatism, and identify the party as a classic European Liberal party. It allied itself with the Liberal group in the European Parliament, and in another country might have found for itself popular support at a level it never would enjoy in Ireland. O'Malley and his associates would discover to their cost that the niche for a party supposedly adhering to strict fiscal policies is very small here.

But for the practising politicians, far more significant than any of the above views and considerations were the probable electoral consequences. Although the Progressive Democrats at the next general election in 1987 harmed Fine Gael more than Fianna Fail in terms of votes and seats, the overriding fact was that the split was expected to, and did, deprive Fianna Fail of the overall majority to which they had confidently looked forward in view of the misfortunes and unpopularity of the FitzGerald government.

Among those who immediately foresaw this consequence were Lenihan and Bertie Ahern, then Fianna Fail chief whip. The foundation of the PDs coincided with the participation of both of them in the last *Saturdayview* radio programme of the year. It was another odd chance that they were together, since normally the panel would not include two representatives of the same party. The news of the birth of the PDs made these two normally cheerful men so unhappy that they indulged in a gloomy drinking session beginning when the programme concluded in the early afternoon and continuing until after midnight.

Here again one sees the difference between Fianna Fail and other parties. Lenihan and Ahern had assumed that O'Malley would not defy Haughey over the Forum report; secondly, they had assumed that, notwithstanding the removal of the whip, he would continue to support the party in the Dail; and thirdly, they had assumed that even after all that had gone before he would draw the line at setting up a rival party. They were wrong each time.

The new party had its strongest support in O'Malley's Limerick East constituency, where he had a loyal following of impressive organisers and public representatives. These defected almost *en bloc* to the Progressive Democrats, but the Fianna Fail leadership got it into their heads that "moles" or "sleepers" or some such creatures of John le Carré-speak had remained in their own organisation. O'Malley dismisses the theory as a fantasy. Nevertheless, Lenihan was despatched to Limerick to conduct a weird inquisition into the loyalties of those who had stayed in Fianna Fail. As in the instances previously mentioned, his friends outside the party considered this demeaning, but whereas he had undertaken his American mission with reluctance and very obviously disbelieved in it, he seems rather to have relished his Limerick task.

His dislike of the PDs was intense. In newspaper interviews he described them as having "fascist tendencies", much to the astonishment of the interviewers, who thought his attitude out of character and the allegation outrageous. Interviewed by Declan Lynch for *Hot Press* (6 November 1986) he said:

> There's no doubt about it that we had problematic people within our party ... most of whom are now with the PDs, and we're very happy with that. I've

very little time for them, because I have no time for ultra-right-wing parties. All they can do is destabilise society. Just an extra splinter group in the body politic. And there are certain shades of the 1930s about them that I don't like, to be quite candid. Fascist tendencies. There's nothing personal in this at all. I've sat around a table with Dessie O'Malley. I've been in government with him, and I know his views. His views are very right-wing. I don't see any future in civilised society for that kind of politics.

Much earlier, he had given his views on party discipline in the *Irish Independent* in February 1983, when he referred euphemistically to "leadership meetings":

The first purpose of the Fianna Fail Party now is to unite under the leadership of Mr Charles Haughey, a leadership which has been agreed upon by 40 votes to 33 by the parliamentary party. We have had three such leadership meetings within twelve months and the almost unanimous view is that we do not want any more ... It is my belief that there will not be a residue of lasting bitterness after this third challenge to Mr Haughey's leadership. It was my belief from the outset that Charles Haughey was going to win ... I knew it was going to be narrow enough but I was confident that there was never going to be any real danger that he would be defeated. That was certainly not the view conveyed by the media, which largely sought to generate the idea that he was gone and finished. I do not blame the media for that. I think this line was fed to the media and they, by and large, accepted it. Of the hard core of dissidents, of whom there are probably no more than two or three, if they express themselves in any way that is antagonistic to the leadership or the party in the future, disciplinary measures will have to be applied. I see no reason why one cannot have a healing process within the party and a disciplinary process as well ... The two concepts are not in conflict.

Lenihan was absolutely sincere in his detestation of right-wing politics and in his view that right-wing parties — and splinter groups in general — were destabilising. His condemnations of the PDs were not just for public consumption; he expressed similar views in his family circle. Conor Lenihan says that "when we teased Dad about Haughey and his alleged jackboot tactics Dad would grow angry and say that the PDs, not Haughey, were the real fascists." Further, he considered the Progressive Democrats a bad influence on certain younger figures in his own party, who showed signs of sharing what he saw as their Thatcherite ideology. He was greatly amused when the present writer called them "Young Turks" — much more amused than this unoriginal quip warranted. But in the claim of "nothing personal" and the carefree attitude to the defections, one detects a certain economy of truth. Lenihan had a right to resent O'Malley's rejection of his overtures in 1982; and as we have seen, he knew that the defections threatened Fianna Fail. And sure enough, at the 1987 general election the Progressive Democrats took fourteen Dail seats, an achievement never to be repeated, and Haughey failed again to win an overall majority.

He was, however, able to form a minority government which enjoyed greater stability than most because of a unique departure by Alan Dukes, who had succeeded FitzGerald as leader of Fine Gael. Dukes proclaimed the "Tallaght Strategy" of not opposing the Haughey government's efforts to get the public finances under control. He had two reasons for taking this line, simple patriotism, and buying time; he did not want Haughey to call a snap election before he could copperfasten his authority over Fine Gael, badly bruised from its severe electoral losses. Haughey now had a wonderful opportunity, of which he seemed initially to be taking full advantage. But two years later he blew it.

*

When Haughey appointed Lenihan Tanaiste and Foreign Minister. Lenihan had all an Irish politician's heart could wish, short of the premiership or the presidency. He also had remarkable freedom of action.

Viewed superficially, this was exceedingly surprising. Haughey appeared to keep a tight grip on his government. It was acknowledged even by his opponents as one of our most competent administrations, and for that he got most of the credit. Ministers who served in his 1987-89 cabinet praise him for his admirable chairmanship and thought him a master of crisis management. His *modus operandi* on the latter was to call key ministers and officials to semi-social events at his Kinsealy mansion on Sundays, at which crises were briskly resolved. How could he forbear to interfere in high-profile policy areas like Northern Ireland and Europe? There are several answers, none of them very favourable to him.

We know from the 1997 Dunnes Payments Tribunal that he was deeply troubled about his personal finances, which, for all his surface insouciance, preyed on his mind. His decisiveness was to a large extent illusory. He was infinitely more timid and cautious than he liked the public to think. In private, he gave way to melancholy and fits of panic and doubt, so that at really bad times Lenihan and others were obliged, in the colourful words of one of them, "to go out to Kinsealy and pick him up off the floor". It is not too much to suggest that his excellent conduct of cabinet meetings, and his Dail performances, owed much more to style than content. That was certainly the case with his performance when Ireland held the European presidency in 1990; he treated it as an exercise in public relations. Strangely for a man of his intellect and political ability, he had relatively little grasp of the European enterprise and could not remotely match Lenihan in his understanding of European issues. As to Northern Ireland, he could not have relished the prospect of any more confrontations with Thatcher. But a more significant consideration was the American view in favour of the Anglo-Irish Agreement, forcefully impressed on him on a visit to Washington immediately after he returned to office. He now accepted the Anglo-Irish Agreement as a *fait accompli* and an international treaty, and gave his Foreign Minister a fairly free hand.

In 1984 John Kelly had said that "it might seem a desperate choice, but I think I would rather see Fianna Fail's Northern policy entrusted to the breezy recklessness of Brian Lenihan than to Mr Haughey's unerringly malignant touch." Kelly was usually a most perceptive as well as a friendly critic, but on that occasion he was wrong. There was nothing of "breezy recklessness" in Lenihan's approach. On the contrary, he was both cautious and imaginative, and he had every intention of building on FitzGerald's Anglo-Irish Agreement. Characteristically, he made it a priority to establish a good relationship with the Northern Ireland Secretary, Tom King. That was easy enough. King, despite a brusque manner, was a social animal, and like almost everybody else he liked Lenihan. In addition, he must have been glad to meet someone who treated him with sympathy and courtesy. The unionists, as part of their campaign against the Anglo-Irish Agreement, refused to meet British ministers: some did not speak to him for four years. Missiles were thrown at him when he visited the Belfast City Hall. Another hate-figure (unionists have a flair for instant demonology) was Peter Barry, and some unionists took to Lenihan if for no better reason than that he was not Peter Barry. That showed their invincible ignorance, since in the matter of implementing the accord there was hardly a hair's breadth of difference between Lenihan and Barry, but they persuaded themselves that some sort of distinction existed and called Lenihan "a practical man".

Three main points of what virtually amounted to a joint Anglo-Irish agenda were to ensure the smooth working of the Hillsborough Agreement through intergovernmental (ministerial) conferences and the secretariat at Maryfield; to see what could be done to get the Northern parties into round-table talks; and to improve security co-operation while at the same time conducting security operations in such a way as to give the least offence to nationalists and to prevent republican and loyalist organisations from establishing control over the ghettoes. Contrary to Thatcher's assertions, security co-operation improved markedly in this period, and King was grateful. But Lenihan had more radical ideas. He told this writer that he wanted to see the RUC broken up into three separate forces. However, King says that Lenihan never raised the proposal with him.

Their personal relationship flourished well enough to give birth to another classic Lenihan anecdote. An extremely unpopular figure at Stormont was dismissed by Thatcher. The story goes that twenty-four hours before the event, King telephoned Lenihan and said: "The bastard's gone!" Sadly, King says that he did nothing of the kind. The high probability is that the call was indeed made, but by somebody else.

King recalls the "notable change in temperature" that followed Lenihan's arrival in Foreign Affairs:

> Brian had a more easygoing nature and was pretty convivial. It may sound a bit bizarre, but in some unionist quarters he was seen as less of a threat. The idea that "my enemy's enemy is my friend" may have contributed. There was great hostility to the Anglo-Irish Agreement from the unionists. I said: "If you have confidence in the majority of people in Northern Ireland wishing to remain in the union with Britain it should be seen as a reassurance. Here we have an international treaty with the Taoiseach confirming that if a majority want to stay in the United Kingdom the Irish government will respect it." Haughey had accused FitzGerald of copperfastening partition and of writing the people of Ireland as a whole out of the decision. I got into trouble over a speech I made in Belgium. I was challenged, not for saying that partition could go on into perpetuity but for not adding a qualification. A senior official in the Department of Foreign Affairs said to me: "There would have been nothing wrong with what you said if you had added a reference to the will of the people in Northern Ireland".

Fianna Fail came into office pretty ambivalent as to what they were going to do about it — really, almost as to whether they were going to go on with it. But they had to take into account its popularity with the Northern nationalists and in the Republic and with Irish movers and shakers in the United States. After the AIA doors opened to me in the US. The Four Horsemen were extremely friendly. There was a feeling that the British had taken an important initiative, which they fully supported.

Brian and I had our first meeting shortly after the new Irish government came into office. I'm not sure we knew then what the attitude of the new government was going to be. In fact, we operated the agreement exactly as before. I was under no illusions about Brian. He was likeable and very good company, but underneath he was a very sharp chap. I liked him as a person, and I liked working with him.

I was surrounded by a lot of security, in the North and on my trips to Dublin. I was a target for the IRA and the Loyalists. Once we had a meeting in Iveagh House. There was a bit of a gap after lunch. I said, "why don't we go for a walk?" We walked around St Stephen's Green with television cameramen walking backwards in front of us. I wanted a bit of fresh air but I also wanted the pictures. Brian was not quite sure how to behave in regard of this public demonstration of the relationship. But I think he was pleased with the result.

I don't think he found it so easy when I first met Haughey in his company. There were always sensitivities about the timing of particular meetings. Some incident in Northern Ireland might have set Irish teeth on edge. I found Haughey perfectly charming but I got a feeling that there was a bit of unease about things like publicity.

We had intergovernmental conferences about once a month, except during holidays and parliamentary recesses. If the meeting was at Stormont, Brian would

Making friends with Tom King, Secretary of State for Northern Ireland, in 1987.

Government, opposition and parliamentary bigwigs celebrate an American presidential visit. From left: Peter Barry, Senator PJ Reynolds, Dick Spring, Dr Garret FitzGerald, President Ronald Reagan, Tom Fitzpatrick, Barry Desmond, John Ryan, Senator Tras Horan, Charles J Haughey, Brian Lenihan.

With Kevin McNamara, British Labour MP with whom Lenihan worked on fair employment in Northern Ireland.

Yasser Arafat presents Lenihan with a Christmas crib inscribed 'Jesus Christ – Jew, Palestinian and Christ'.

Sergeant Michael Dillon demonstrates a Steyr rifle to the Minister for Defence. With them is Major–General Jim Parker.

Lenihan with Haughey and Mikhail Gorbachev, who failed to effect the reforms in the Soviet Union for which Lenihan had hoped.

With Ann in Rochester, Minnesota, shortly after
the liver transplant.

Making a serious point to the broadcaster Rodney Rice, 1990.

St Patrick's Day, 1987, in Washington: Lenihan
with President Ronald Reagan and the U.S.
ambassador to Ireland, Mrs Margaret Heckler.

Evidently, they both enjoyed Pavarotti's
performance.

Down but far from out: Receiving the applause of the Fianna Fail ard-fheis in 1991.

Warming up an ard-fheis faithful to the delight of Maire Geoghegan-Quinn, under a giant picture of Haughey.

Have I done well on CAP reform or are you just pleased to see me?
Lenihan embraces Ray McSharry, European Agriculture
Commissioner, while John Wilson looks on.

With Albert Reynolds at the forum for Peace and Reconciliation in
Dublin Castle, 1995.

Ann and Brian in their garden.

All the family: from left, Niall, Paul, Anita, Brian, Ann, Brian Junior, his wife Patricia and Conor.

arrive with the Garda Commissioner and officials from the Department of Justice as well as his own department. People would then peel off. We would sit in my office before we went into the meeting proper and discuss what we would talk about. During our time there was a whole succession of incidents which caused a lot of disquiet. They led to periods of considerable strain but in the end they had to be ironed out. Some of the meetings became quite serious, difficult, protracted. With Peter Barry in part, but particularly with Brian, our relationship was helpful. He was keen to find ways through, not exacerbate problems. In between meetings, if there was a problem others could not solve I would ring him or he would ring me.

I asked his opinion as to whether I should accept an invitation to appear on the *Late Late Show*. I think it caused a slight uncertainty in other parts of the administration, but Brian was supportive. He didn't have the sort of hangups that one or two other people did. Shortly afterwards I opened a light industrial unit in Warrenpoint. The chairman of the committee was a Catholic solicitor. He said that before he had seen me on the *Late Late Show* he didn't know what to think of me, but now he was very pleased to welcome me. People had lived on a diet of news clips of me looking grave and stern and commenting on some serious incident. On that show you can relax a bit and people can see if you're a human being or not. I owe that to Brian's advice to appear on the show. That was the kind of relationship we had.

Lenihan for his part equally enjoyed working with King. In April 1990 he told the *Sunday Business Post*:

King and I had a way of working. We had very helpful and constructive private meetings which I found very valuable because you could talk straight to him. He was very upfront, from a military and farming background. There was nothing devious whatever about him. Whatever he said he delivered on. We trusted each other.

Their friendship survived Lenihan's departure from Foreign Affairs in 1989. King kept closely in touch with him during his critical illness. However, Lenihan was never a man to operate on one front only. While working with King, he also worked with the British Labour MP Kevin McNamara on the issue of fair employment in Northern Ireland. They discussed amendments put down by McNamara to legislation going through the Westminster parliament, with the object of strengthening the measure to ensure an end to discrimination against Catholics. One of their difficulties was that Haughey had supported the "MacBride Principles", an anti-discrimination schedule adopted by several American state and city governments, which if fully implemented would not have led to fair employment but to American disinvestment, a move deplored by McNamara, Lenihan and John Hume, now leader of the SDLP. It was necessary to "finesse" the MacBride Principles while pressing the British government to make their own measures as tough as possible, and worthy of Dublin support. It was the kind of operation in which Lenihan characteristically revelled. But even more characteristic of him was his practice of sitting down with Tom King before a meeting in order to massage the agenda. That was the true Lenihan style: "Stitch it up."

By no means all his relations with British politicians were as happy as those with King and McNamara, or as that with Carrington in an earlier period. Tony Benn in his diaries recorded a meeting Lenihan held with him and another Labour MP, Chris Mullin, in June 1987. The passage is delightfully but inadvertently self-revelatory:

> I formed an instant distrust of him. After C. Mullin asks him to delay ratification of extradition treaty until Birmingham Six are released: Lenihan looked cautious, and I realised that he did not want to endanger his reputation with the British government.

Benn: Look, you can do it very skilfully. You could let it be known that you are concerned and have raised it. Secondly, express your confidence publicly that when the case comes to the Court of Appeal in the autumn the government in Britain will not dare to have the appeal turned down. Keep the pressure up. Go to the United Nations, talk to the Americans — see that Britain is kept under pressure. You can do it perfectly well.

BL: I see you are a pragmatic man.

Benn: I'm just putting my ministerial experience at your disposal for this particular purpose.

Benn could not see that Lenihan was making fun of him and his unhelpful and unwanted advice.

*

In Europe, Lenihan was at his best in this period. He knew everybody, and everybody knew him. His officials loved him and for the most part knew what to expect of him — though he gave them a good many bad half-hours. He would go into meetings of, for example, the Council of Foreign Ministers without telling the officials his intentions, but would explain after the meeting why he had taken such and such a course of action — as if they had not already figured it out for themselves.

He did have his lapses. He called on occasion for one-page summaries. He could be forgetful. One lunchtime he started drinking with Liam Lawlor, and it took Iveagh House over an hour to track him down. They finally managed to inform him that a foreign ambassador had been waiting all that time to see him. Lenihan said he would go there post haste. They should tell the ambassador that he had been detained by divisions in the Dail — the most implausible of excuses, since the Dail was not sitting that day. Meanwhile he hoped they had given the poor man a newspaper to read. Lawlor was amused at his concern that the diplomat should have reading material.

But these lapses were exceptional, and the demand for one-page briefs misleading. By current standards, Lenihan was unusually diligent in his reading. Nowadays ministers spend far too much time attending meetings and travelling to and from them. They have little time to read anything except on aircraft, and then they commonly do not even read their briefs, but only their speaking notes. Lenihan was more assiduous than the norm in his reading, and if he had not read a brief he could usually "wing" it at a meeting by consulting officials and by his own uniquely deep and wide background knowledge. He sometimes drafted his own speeches — though for such a colourful man the speeches were mostly unmemorable, for the excellent reason that he seldom strayed from the mainstream, at any rate in public. Among the papers he kept at home for future use is a single sheet of paper on which he had scribbled, in the course of a ministerial meeting, the heads of issues ranging across every region in the world, along with queries for possible consideration and discussion. When awed diplomats saw him plunging into a huddle and emerging from it with some deal favourable to Ireland, he had not acted on impulse or instinct but out of detailed and deep knowledge of the issue.

Winging it, however, did not always work. One Lenihan legend has him speaking eloquently and at length at a foreign ministers' meeting, then asking a senior official, "how did I do?" and eliciting the reply, "excellently, minister, except that you have just given away our negotiating position on five points", which the official went on to enumerate. Lenihan then, according to the story, went back to each of his colleagues in turn to repair the position. In fact, this never happened, but the yarn is an exaggeration, not an invention. Undoubtedly he did on occasion get caught up in the excitement of the moment, go outside his brief, and on having the lapse pointed out to him use his bonhomie and powers of persuasion to undo any damage. The net result was a series of negotiating successes, if sometimes achieved at some cost to official nerves.

Here, it might seem, was a man at the height of his powers, engaged in useful and enjoyable work for Ireland, for Anglo-Irish relations, for the elusive Northern settlement and for Europe. Unfortunately, his appointment as Foreign Minister in

1987 had coincided with a rapid and alarming deterioration in his health, which two years later brought him to the point of death.

Twelve

Are there ghosts in the house?
        CHARLES de GAULLE, visiting Ireland

Lenihan's liver, which had first sent out warning signals in his youth, began to fail him in 1987 and by 1989 had all but ceased to function. Like Winston Churchill, he admitted that he had abused his God-given constitution, but as fate would have it neither of their deaths was caused by their habits. Churchill, preserved by alcohol and cigar smoke, survived past ninety. Lenihan did not smoke, and his liver condition was unrelated to alcohol.

Between 1987 and 1989 he was constantly in and out of the Mater private hospital in Dublin. All treatments failed, and in the end the only option was a transplant in the Mayo Clinic in the United States. It is hardly unfair to medical science to say that the operation was then at an experimental stage, and at fifty-eight he was the oldest person to undergo it to date. When he left for the United States, most of the Dublin political world gave him up for dead. They had not reckoned with the high courage which, as much as the surgeons' skill, kept him alive.

Before his departure he performed, or tried to perform, a characteristic service for his party. Characteristic, as so often, in that he gave good advice. Characteristic, too, in that it was not followed.

Haughey still saw before his eyes the mirage of an overall Dail majority, and he was impatient at the constraints placed upon him by the lack of it. He had been defeated on a number of minor issues in the Dail. They were mere irritants, and he could have won a vote of confidence had the necessity arisen, but it was not in his nature to accept his setbacks with good grace. The last straw was a defeat on a proposal to allocate £400,000 to

154

haemophiliacs infected with HIV through blood transfusions. The cause was just, the amount trifling, the responsibility of the state undeniable. That Haughey chose to go to the country on such an issue showed that for all his seeming competence he was losing touch, and in the ensuing general election campaign he showed himself even further out of touch by admitting that he had not grasped the general discontent over cuts in the health services.

He first threatened to call the election on returning, jetlagged, from a visit to Japan. There was time to resile, and when he went to see Lenihan in hospital the Tanaiste urged him not to go to the country. He listened to less astute, hot-headed advisers, who had never come to terms with the necessity for coalition and thought, wrongly, that at an early general election Fianna Fail could win a majority. The election took place while Lenihan was in the Mayo Clinic. His sons bore the brunt of the campaign in his Dublin West constituency.

The story of the transplant is told in his book *For The Record*, and in greater detail in *No Problem — to Mayo and Back*, with the attribution "by Ann Lenihan, written by Angela Phelan". Angela Phelan is a journalist with the *Irish Independent* and a personal friend of the family. The proceeds of the book's sales were donated to the cause of organ transplants.

For the previous year and more, Lenihan's manifest bad health and rapidly deteriorating appearance had alarmed colleagues and persons with whom he had dealings at home and abroad. Tom King recalls one "absolutely ghastly meeting" in London, when he was "very shocked by his appearance. He looked absolutely terrible." After their meeting they held a joint press conference, at which Lenihan was clearly in distress. None the less, on his return to the Irish embassy, he gave a television interview. "I didn't think he would survive the day."

Maire Geoghegan-Quinn, junior minister with responsibility for European affairs, accompanied him to an important meeting in Luxembourg. Lenihan, she says, had taught her "the art of European politics — quite different from Ireland. In Europe it's all about networking". In Luxembourg he was so ill that she and his old friend Hans-Dietrich Genscher insisted that he should leave. They went back to their hotel, where Lenihan, on a whim, decided that he would like a swim. She sat at the poolside while he went into the dressing room. When he emerged in bathing togs she was horrified by his skeletal appearance. Seeing her concern, he stretched out his arms and said: "Maire! What a body!"

King describes him as "tremendously brave". He was indeed brave, and he put on a brave face throughout. He continued to maintain it when he went to the Mayo Clinic, but he wrote in *For The Record*: "I was dying and I knew it." There was of course no certainty that a suitable organ would be found in time to save his life. The liver he received came from a young man killed in water sports on a lake not far from the clinic, a spot Lenihan had visited not long before the operation. Lenihan saw his own survival as providential. He recovered with amazing speed and success. Twenty-four hours after the transplant, he was up and shaving. The news of his recovery delighted Ireland, and in particular the electorate of Dublin West, who in his absence returned him to the Dail with a record vote. Against the doctors' wishes, he came back to attend the opening session of the Dail and to witness one stage in a colossal political crisis.

He would have to return shortly to the Mayo Clinic and subsequently to go many times for treatments to the Mater. Although his recovery was amazing, the doctors continued to fear the possibility that his system would reject the alien organ, and to combat that he had to take steroids, which had a most debilitating effect. Moreover, he had hurt a foot in an accident in the Mayo Clinic, and ever afterwards walked with a slight limp. Nevertheless, he played a noble part in the political crisis at home.

So far from achieving a majority, Haughey had lost four Dail seats on the same proportion of the first-preference vote as in 1987. Clearly the Irish electorate had no intention of ever giving him a majority. His options boiled down to opposition, or an alliance with the hated Progressive Democrats. These had lost eight of their fourteen seats at the election, but the six they retained, together with Fianna Fail's seventy-seven, added up to precisely half the Dail seats, effectively a majority.

On the night of the count, Haughey was in a television studio in Dublin. His look of distaste when O'Malley's face appeared on a link with Limerick was a wonder to behold. Many of those who saw it thought an alliance between the two old enemies contrary to nature. They were wrong. The parliamentary arithmetic mattered more than personal feelings. And the PDs could feel their power. They rejected the proposition that they could support a Fianna Fail minority government from the outside and insisted on coalition. Haughey delegated Albert Reynolds and Bertie Ahern to negotiate with them, while he himself dealt personally with O'Malley. To the dismay of much of his parliamentary party — and the comfort of important adversaries within it — he not only agreed to abandon a Fianna Fail "core value", single-party government, but gave the Progressive Democrats two cabinet seats, a junior ministry, and a number of minor goodies. As to his motives, lust for office would suffice; the national interest can be cited, and he has often been praised for bringing about a radical change in the system; but subsequent disclosures about his finances suggest that for less lofty reasons he not only wanted but needed to remain Taoiseach.

Lenihan for his part put aside his dislike of the Progressive Democrats and set himself to reconcile Fianna Fail to a new era in which coalitions would be a permanent feature of the scene. He was distressed to find that several of his colleagues persisted in their opposition and that the departure would be used as a device to undermine Haughey. Afterwards he believed that at this time he had witnessed the birth of the Country and Western Alliance, the coterie that would soon bring Albert Reynolds to power.

Haughey once again accorded him the title of Tanaiste but took him out of Foreign Affairs and sent him to Defence. This is normally regarded as one of the most undemanding jobs in the government, but as it chanced, in 1989 it was far from undemanding. Another development that Haughey — who was

rapidly losing touch with reality on the ground — had failed to
see since 1987 was that discontent over pay and conditions had
brought the armed forces into a state bordering on mutiny. An
"army wives' campaign" was one of the factors responsible for
the Fianna Fail setbacks of 1989. Lenihan had to calm the
discontents. He did so by setting up a commission under
Dermot Gleeson SC (afterwards a Fine Gael attorney-general).
The commission travelled to every defence installation in the
state, visited units serving abroad, took thousands of pieces of
evidence, and made recommendations on which Lenihan acted
with despatch. These included the establishment of
representative bodies for officers and "other ranks". It was not
hard for Lenihan to persuade himself that soldiers should not be
denied a privilege taken for granted by most civilian workers,
but long afterwards one of the representative bodies spoiled the
deal by making political statements instead of confining itself to
more appropriate issues such as pay and conditions. That,
however, is a minor criticism. Restoring the morale of the
defence forces was a success, towards the end of his career,
comparable with his censorship reform near the beginning. He
has greater achievements to his credit, but if he had had only
those two successes to boast of, few other ministers could match
them.

*

After fourteen years in the Phoenix Park, President Hillery
retired in 1990. The most obvious candidates for the succession
were Lenihan and possibly John Wilson from Fianna Fail, and
FitzGerald and Barry from Fine Gael. Not many thought of the
outstanding civil liberties lawyer Mary Robinson, whom
Lenihan had encountered in the Seanad in 1973. But Dick
Spring, and his advisers Fergus Finlay and John Rogers, thought
of her.

They were thinking of her, and negotiating with her, long
before anybody else had got out of bed. The negotiations began
on St Valentine's Day, 14 February 1990, but for the left wing of
the Labour Party the process was no love-in. Robinson had

resigned from the party in 1985, citing as the reason for her departure the lack of consultation of unionists over the Anglo-Irish Agreement, and she insisted on describing herself as an independent, not a Labour candidate. Spring bowed to her will, and in April "bounced" the nomination through Labour, wrongfooting the left wing of the party, who wanted to nominate Noel Browne.

In *Candidate: The Truth Behind The Presidential Campaign*, Emily O'Reilly calls Spring's choice "a piece of intuitive brilliance". So it was; but Robinson, whether on account of intuition, good advice or hard thinking, had also made the right decision. As a Labour candidate she could not have won; as a candidate nominated by Labour and supported by Democratic Left but appealing to a "constituency" up to three times the size of that held by both parties combined, she could win. From the beginning she set out to win, not to come a respectable second or third.

In the early days, however, the Robinson phenomenon was visible to very few outsiders. One newspaper report equated her candidature with an interest in running expressed by Carmencita Hederman, a former Lord Mayor of Dublin and a member of the same "community" group as Sean Dublin Bay Loftus — although Hederman had no chance whatever of obtaining the support of twenty Oireachtas members, or of four county or county borough councils, required for a presidential nomination. The general view was that if Fianna Fail nominated Lenihan, he would win easily, and even if they did not nominate him some other Fianna Fail nominee would be the favourite. The party had long held an iron grip on Aras an Uachtarain and now feared only two potential opposition candidates, FitzGerald and Barry. Neither had the remotest interest in running, and Dukes's efforts to persuade them to change their minds were adamantly resisted. After a series of manoeuvrings, a blend of the comical and the humiliating, Dukes finally found a candidate in our old acquaintance Austin Currie, who had forsaken Northern politics for a Fine Gael seat in Dublin West, Lenihan's constituency. It was virtually an admission of defeat.

Neither Dukes nor Currie, nor anybody else, thought Currie could win. The field seemed open for Lenihan.

But would he be the Fianna Fail candidate at all? His family, profoundly suspicious of Haughey, watched with dismay as they thought they saw him wavering on the nomination and toying with the idea of putting forward Wilson or some other candidate. They also suspected the Country and Western Alliance of backing the Wilson candidature. Their suspicions of Haughey turned to anger when a grotesque event occurred on 30 March. The immensely popular *Late Late Show* mounted what it called a "tribute" to Lenihan. The word tribute was singularly ill chosen.

The programme may be said to have marked the unofficial opening of the Lenihan campaign, but it hung on the publication of the Ann Lenihan-Angela Phelan book. The family were warned in advance, but not sufficiently far in advance, that Haughey and/or Haughey cronies would "hijack" the show. They therefore approached it with redoubled suspicions, which were more than justified. It featured Haughey at his most patronising. Worse, it featured everything that people most disliked about the party. It presented Fianna Fail in general, and Lenihan in particular, as rustic clowns and fixers. It carried film clips of Lenihan and his father which made both of them look foolish. The "pint or a transfer" story was told — badly. The cognoscenti observed Ann Lenihan eyeing Haughey and the programme's host, Gay Byrne, in a manner that recalled the proverbial "if looks could kill ..." The less observant saw the proceedings as the ultimate justification for never voting for a Fianna Fail candidate.

In the hand-picked audience was the veteran political writer and Haughey admirer John Healy. At the very end of the programme he rose to make a heartfelt, emotional and barely coherent protest. Lenihan, he said, should not be viewed as the clown prince but as the crown prince. He did not get the chance to elaborate on Lenihan's virtues and achievements. If the horrible incident brought any good result, it was to force Lenihan to consider the real nature of the man to whom he had given so much loyalty. He had already become aware that Haughey was supporting his candidature, if at all, without enthusiasm, and was taking soundings within the party on the possibility of finding an alternative candidate. The rationale was the difficulty that would arise, in the event of a Lenihan victory, of winning the by-election for the seat which he would vacate in Dublin West. Concern about Lenihan's health was also cited by Haughey associates. But one has to ask, in the light of subsequent events, whether there always existed here a disposition to treachery.

He had other reasons for disillusionment. He could make intelligent guesses about Haughey's unorthodox financial dealings. He knew that the lordly manner was a facade concealing indecision and worse. And while he might support opportunism up to the point where his reputation suffered from it, he was much too astute not to note that this man, who back in the sixties had been, with himself, one of the great modernisers, had subsequently gone backwards and appealed, whether directly or by nod and wink, to the most atavistic and unreconstructed elements in the party and the country: first on the "national question", secondly in taking the side of the fundamentalists on contraception, divorce and abortion. Lenihan had tried endlessly, to his own detriment, to argue, and to persuade himself, that competence made up for a multitude of faults. But where was the competence?

In April Lenihan told the *Sunday Business Post* that Haughey was "a tremendously loyal person to his friends, generous in spirit and a very kind and considerate person in all his personal relationships and dealings." He could not possibly have believed it. As to kindness and consideration, Haughey in power had brought rudeness to a fine art. As to loyalty, the party ard-fheis had come and gone without the expected announcement of Lenihan's presidential candidature. So far from blocking other candidates, Haughey permitted the issue to go to a vote between Lenihan and Wilson, which Lenihan predictably won. His official campaign began under these discouraging auspices.

The family were not wholly united on whether he should seek the presidency or bide his time for a stab at the premiership. His health had recovered sufficiently to make the latter proposition, though extremely unlikely, not entirely implausible in the event of Haughey's early retirement. When the family engaged in a lively discussion on the issue, only the youngest son, Paul, opposed a run for the presidency. Paul's opposition was not founded on the proposition that his father should seek better things, but on the belief that the country wanted a change and any Fianna Fail candidate would be beaten. Ann greatly favoured the candidature but, remarkably, something prompted her to order renovation work on her house, to the amazement of friends and neighbours who asked what was the point, since she would soon be living in Aras an Uachtarain.

What did Lenihan himself really want? A man so dedicated to day-to-day politics, and to the politics of power, could not but regard the powerless presidency as second best. After his transplant, he had become more religious, bordering on the mystical. Hanafin believes that he had "a spiritual experience" in the Mayo Clinic. O'Kennedy says that "he attributed his survival to Higher Power intervention, though he would have been the last to parade it." Even the more sceptical could accept that, although he never paraded his religious feelings, he believed that his life had been saved for some purpose. That, however, could as readily have meant the premiership as the presidency. Hanafin avers that Lenihan had always been interested in the office of the presidency, had discussed the question with him many years earlier, and felt that he could "make something" of the office. Whatever the fact, the Book of Job tells us that the old warhorse, sniffing the battle, shouts "Ha! Ha!" A politician as committed as Lenihan throws his heart and soul into the fight. Lenihan did not walk, he galloped, to disaster.

*

The Fianna Fail campaign, even at its limited best, was a dismal affair. This was not immediately apparent, because Robinson did not come to be taken as a real threat until the autumn and because the Fine Gael campaign was a joke. Dukes's many enemies within the party looked forward gleefully to using a wretched result for Currie to topple him from the leadership. Leading Fine Gael women refused to endorse Currie; they preferred Robinson. This should have been taken as a warning signal by Fianna Fail as well as Fine Gael, and the Fianna Fail strategists should have seen the need to appeal to a wider electorate than their own traditional voters. They should also have insisted on full endorsement of Lenihan by the Progressive Democrats, but Haughey's attitude to the PDs in government was to bend so far backwards as to fall over. More omens.

O'Reilly quotes a Fianna Fail deputy:

> There was a great lethargy within the party. On loads of occasions people simply didn't turn out to meet him. The feeling within the campaign team was that Brian's a great guy, just let him at it. The underlying aim was to promote Brian as good old Brian, the sort of man you'd meet in the street and he'd talk to you and he'd probably say, sure don't I know your mother? We should have been more attuned to what was happening on the ground. I remember early on in the campaign meeting an old Fianna Fail voter down the country, and he looked at me and he smiled and he said, Oh, I think I'll give the woman the stroke this time. But we didn't pick it up. Our feedback was faulty. People kept telling us that there was great turnout here, there and everywhere, but none of us had been wherever it was and so we didn't know and of course Brian was always saying that things were grand. And of course people were trying to cover their own asses in the campaign, saying that the advertising was wonderful and this was wonderful and that was wonderful when it wasn't.

Robinson was going to set much of the country on fire with an "inspirational" campaign leading to an "inspirational" presidency. Lenihan had his own ideas as to how the office could be gently and cautiously developed, with the President playing a political (though obviously not a party-political) role in conjunction with the government of the day, within the very tight constraints imposed on the President by the constitution. But to try to use those ideas in a campaign would have bored the voters even more than the actual campaign did. And he could not present himself as a more "exciting" President than Hillery, because that would have been unfair to Hillery.

Ann, still worried about his health, wanted him to go home every night. That made devising itineraries more difficult, and so did Lenihan's desire to visit every town of consequence in every part of the country. A campaign member told O'Reilly:

> All the local tour organisers wanted him photographed with them for when he became President so that they could stick it up on their mantelpieces and we ended up travelling to houses half-way up the sides of mountains just so they could get their picture taken. And of course the Boss was opening his papers every day and seeing pictures of Currie and Robinson and he was throwing tantrums which didn't help anyone's morale.

The party television broadcasts were, in O'Reilly's word, "uninspired"; the poster campaign a mess. When the candidates appeared together on election programmes, the more acute in Fianna Fail scored them as victories for Currie — not that it did Currie much good, but it should have dented their complacency. All this was frustrating for Lenihan, himself no mean campaign organiser (as witness his success with Childers in 1973) and a man who knew how things should be done. Paul remembers "a sense of powerlessness. Dad had no control. He had no say on who went on television. Fianna Fail just didn't play on his achievements as a minister." And he was irritated that he, who had struck one of the first blows for the liberal agenda with his censorship reforms, should be pictured as a conservative candidate as opposed to the liberal Robinson — and that some in Fianna Fail made the picture worse. At a meeting in Wexford, a Fianna Fail deputy asked whether Robinson, if elected, would set up an abortion referral clinic in the Phoenix Park. Lenihan looked down from the platform at the press table, and saw Miriam Lord of the *Irish Independent* taking a note. At the same moment she looked up and their eyes met. He knew, and he knew that she knew, that he had just lost another few thousand votes. A party running such a ramshackle, not to say such a stupid, campaign in relatively easy times was bound to panic in a crisis, and panic it did when the crisis arrived.

Thirteen

A man cannot be too careful in the choice of his enemies.
OSCAR WILDE

On 17 May 1990 Lenihan granted an interview to an unknown UCD research student (and occasional Fine Gael activist) called Jim Duffy, who was working on an MA thesis on the presidency. When Duffy entered the Tanaiste's office, he was shocked by his deathly appearance. Lenihan assured him that he was all right, he just happened to be on medication that made him "look drawn".

That was a good deal less than the truth. Lenihan had undergone a "rejection crisis" which had very nearly killed him, and the medication prescribed to prevent the rejection accounted for much more than his dreadful appearance, it gravely affected his memory and judgement and caused him to make statements which were both inaccurate and imprudent. He should not have been at work, much less acceding to requests like Duffy's. It was one more example of his inability to say no. This time his good nature would have ruinous effects.

It had long been believed, and had often appeared in print, that on the night of 27 January 1982 members of the Fianna Fail front bench had telephoned President Hillery in the hope of persuading him to refuse Garret FitzGerald a dissolution of the Dail. It was also believed that none of the callers had succeeded in speaking to Hillery personally. Now, however, Lenihan told Duffy that he had spoken to the President, who was understandably angry at the approach. "I got through to him and he wanted us to lay off." He had his wits sufficiently about him to emphasise that the conversation was confidential, and he naturally assumed that it would be used only for academic purposes — and that Duffy would send him a transcript of the tape for correction.

In September Duffy published a series of articles in the *Irish Times*. In one of them he wrote that telephone calls were made by Haughey "and, at his insistence, Brian Lenihan and Sylvester Barrett, two close friends of Dr Hillery. The President angrily rejected all such pressure and, having judged the issue, granted Dr FitzGerald the dissolution."

Life is full of strange coincidences, but few so strange as that Fine Gael seized on Duffy's article as a campaign issue. At the official launch of the Currie campaign on 1 October, reporters were handed a four-page statement. Two pages addressed the question of presidential independence, with specific reference to the events of 1982. Stapled to each handout was a photocopy of Duffy's *Irish Times* article. Currie himself asserted that as President he would be independent of the government of the day. He said he had "serious doubts about the capacity of Mr Lenihan to carry out the functions of the office of President independent of Fianna Fail, and particularly of a Fianna Fail government led by Mr Haughey ... It is difficult to see how the habits of loyalty to Mr Haughey for half a lifetime will be abandoned by Mr Lenihan if elected President."

On 22 October Lenihan appeared on the *Questions and Answers* television programme. Another panellist was FitzGerald, who had cut short a trip to Venice at the request of the Fine Gael Party. In the audience was Brian Murphy, former chairman of Young Fine Gael, a member of the Currie campaign team, and a friend of Duffy's. A veritable crescendo of coincidences.

But there was more. O'Reilly wrote: "On Duffy's own admission, by the night of the *Questions and Answers* programme, a significant number of people knew that he had interviewed Lenihan, other people had been told that Lenihan had been telling lies, that his research proved it, and at least one person had been given details of the taped interview by Duffy himself." Interviewed by the same author, he admitted having telephoned Murphy on the day of the programme, again the following day, and twice the day after.

Another *Questions and Answers* panellist was the *Irish Times* journalist Nuala O'Faolain, who observed with concern Lenihan's fatigued condition when he arrived in the RTE hospitality room before the recording of the programme, without the customary minder, and fell asleep in his chair. Shortly afterwards, she recalls, Niamh O'Connor from the Fianna Fail press office came in but decided not to wake him up until it was time for the recording to begin. In *For The Record* Lenihan gives a slightly different account of his arrival, but beyond question he was in a state of physical and mental exhaustion then and later, in a far more disastrous television performance.

When a member of the audience asked about "the role of the President in relation to Dail dissolutions", FitzGerald raised the issue of the 1982 telephone calls and alleged that seven calls were made to Hillery "to try and force him to exercise" his right to refuse a dissolution. Lenihan said, "that's fictional, Garret", and FitzGerald rejoined: "It is not fictional, excuse me, I was in Aras an Uachtarain when those phone calls came through and I know how many there were." In the course of the ensuing confused argument, Lenihan said that a President would refuse a dissolution only "in case of a very serious state of anarchy". Then Lenihan was asked: "Did he make a phone call or phone calls to Aras an Uachtarain in that period, when the Taoiseach, Garret FitzGerald, was seeking a dissolution of the Dail?" He replied: "No, I didn't at all. That never happened. I want to assure you that it never happened."

*

The following day, Tuesday 23 October, Duffy telephoned Dick Walsh, by then political editor of the *Irish Times*, and told him that a person who had made calls to the Aras had confirmed the fact to him. He meant Walsh to understand that that person was Lenihan. Walsh, according to Duffy's account to Emily O'Reilly, told him that the conversation with Lenihan should be made public. Duffy refused. Walsh then suggested that the newspaper might interview him instead, and that he could say that he knew from his research that Lenihan had lied. He said he would consider it. He then telephoned a number of academics to seek their advice. They came down, in the main, strongly against publication.

Nevertheless, that afternoon he played the tape of his Lenihan interview to an unnamed *Irish Times* journalist. Later the same evening, he played it to Walsh and the *Irish Times* political correspondent, Denis Coghlan. The editor, Conor Brady, listened to part of the tape. According to O'Reilly, Duffy then agreed that the newspaper could run a low-key story stating that they had corroborative evidence that Lenihan, Sylvester Barrett and Charles Haughey had made phone calls to Aras an Uachtarain, but not giving any hint as to what this evidence was. The editor, she wrote, "wanted the claim to be relatively modest and qualified." The story "might appear obscure to the general readership but ... would be understood by those directly involved." This version of events does not make it clear whether Duffy or the *Irish Times* journalists realised that the appearance of the report would create an irresistible demand for the publication of the tape.

When the story duly appeared on Wednesday morning, Bertie Ahern, Fianna Fail director for the presidential election, spoke to Lenihan, who told him that the report was without foundation. He had forgotten that he had ever spoken to Duffy, but a couple of hours later he met Ahern again and told him that his private secretary had reminded him that he had given a student an interview some months earlier. By lunchtime, word reached him that Sylvester Barrett, in Clare, was recording an interview for transmission on the *Today Tonight* television programme the following evening, saying that he had tried to get through to Hillery. Lenihan telephoned Barrett and asked him if he remembered that he too had made calls. Barrett said he had not.

At almost exactly the same time, O'Reilly describes Duffy as running around the UCD campus at Belfield, chased by reporters and also by Fianna Fail acquaintances who wanted to discover what the tape contained and, if damaging, to persuade him not to publish. Duffy, in a distressed and emotional state, telephoned Brady, who suggested that he should see a lawyer. A company car took him to the offices of the *Irish Times'* lawyers on St Stephen's Green. Within hours this fact was known to Fianna Fail.

Next morning Duffy went back to the lawyers' office and telephoned Brady. When Brady arrived, Duffy said that he wanted to publish part of the tape. In the afternoon two *Irish Times* executives accompanied Duffy at a press conference in the Westbury Hotel. The assembled journalists heard the portion of the tape on which Lenihan said that he had telephoned Hillery and spoken to him. Then, just before Lenihan would have been heard emphasising confidentiality, one of the executives switched off the tape recorder. This appears to have been done at Duffy's request, the rationale being that Lenihan wanted the next portion to remain permanently off the record.

Lenihan and Niamh O'Connor were on the campaign bus in the North Dublin suburbs. Sean Duignan, then presenter of the *Six One* television news, reached Niamh O'Connor on a mobile telephone, told her the contents of the tape, and urged her to get Lenihan to appear on his programme. When she told Lenihan, he at first refused to believe what had happened. On the way to the next stop, he spoke to Haughey on the mobile telephone, then said, "I'm going to ring Hillery." The person who answered the telephone at Aras an Uachtarain said the President was not there. Lenihan left a message asking Hillery to ring him back. He then headed, by car, for the RTE studios in Donnybrook. On his arrival, he had a brief conversation with Ahern.

In the news studio, he ascertained, to Duignan's puzzlement, which camera he should face in order to address the nation directly. Lenihan, familiar with television for decades, should have known that this is something one never does. Television is vastly different from a platform in a public hall: an interviewee should always talk conversationally with his interlocutor and take absolutely no notice of the cameras and the other equipment littering the studio — or of the numerous functionaries moving about.

In the interview, he said that his "mature recollection" was that he did not make the calls, and that he intended to seek a meeting with the President to bear out his assertion. The phrase "mature recollection" immediately entered the Irish political vocabulary as a synonym, to quote O'Reilly again, for questionable veracity. The tactic of looking straight into the camera made matters infinitely worse. Ann Lenihan said that whoever advised him to do it should be shot. Others might think such a punishment too mild. Lenihan's enemies laughed, his best friends cringed; in *For The Record*, as an example of the general reaction, he quoted the horror of the rugby international Tony Ward on seeing and hearing him. Virtually the whole country thought he was lying.

*

Was he? What really happened on the night of 27 January 1982? O'Reilly asserts that in Lenihan's conversation with Ahern before his interview with Duignan he gave the following version:

> He and Barrett (clearly under instructions from Haughey) left the room where the [front bench] meeting was taking place and went into Haughey's secretary's office just beside it. There, with Lenihan sitting beside him, Barrett made all the calls but was never put through to the President. Lenihan then apparently informed the meeting that their little scheme had failed and went off to the bar for the rest of the evening leaving the rest of them to it. He had no idea what happened after that.
>
> That version does seem plausible. Lenihan is known to hate making phone calls and, despite instructions from Haughey, urged Barrett to do the dialling instead. It is also possible that when Barrett got on to the Aras, he told whoever took the call that he and Brian Lenihan wanted to speak to the

President. This could then have been conveyed to the President in such a way as to have Hillery inadvertently believe that separate calls had come through from the two men. He may then have told FitzGerald that Lenihan had rung him. When Lenihan went back to the meeting he could have let on that he too had tried and failed. But either way the inescapable fact ... is that he did collude in the phone calls. The only thing Lenihan did not do, on his own admission to Ahern, is physically lift the receiver and dial the number.

This account, however, does not square with the story which Barrett told in his *Today Tonight* interview and which he repeated when interviewed for the purposes of the present work. He is adamant that he left the room, alone, on Haughey's instructions and tried to ring the President. "In my conversation with the aide de camp I said, 'I am speaking on behalf of Charles Haughey, Brian Lenihan and all the front bench.'" When he failed to reach the President, he returned and reported to the meeting to that effect. He was asked to try again. He did so, with identical results. He and Lenihan then left the meeting (which broke up in a casual fashion) and went down to the Leinster House visitors' bar. Ray Burke joined them shortly afterwards, and they "made a night of it" in the course of which they spoke to, and drank with, numerous other people. In *For The Record*, Lenihan gives a somewhat, but not materially, different account. He also asserts, and it has never been disputed, that he advised Haughey against making any approaches to Hillery. Another example of good advice disregarded.

Barrett is a man of unimpeachable reputation, and his story must be taken as important evidence of Lenihan's innocence. Two other pieces of evidence in his favour are his telephone call to Barrett and his desire to seek confirmation of his version of events from Hillery. What he told Duffy may be discounted, since it assuredly could not be true. It is, however, possible that a third party telephoned the Aras and used his name.

Another piece of evidence in his favour is a conversation in which Ulick O'Connor asked him about the tape incident:

> He said: "I didn't ring Hillery. I could easily have said I did. That was the awful thing. If I had said I rang him, it would have been all right." I thought, what a horrible thing to have used it against him in that way.

At the time of the Duffygate affair, members of his family questioned him closely on the subject; and he was again questioned by a legal team before *For The Record* went to press. In both cases the interrogators included his son Brian, who had already achieved greater distinction as a lawyer than his father. The references to the 1982 incident in *For The Record* were written with exceptional care.

Two other facts, however, must be recorded. Lenihan, while in his sober senses and not suffering from a medical crisis, told at least two journalists that he had telephoned Aras an Uachtarain; and in the immediate wake of Duffygate, Ahern, using channels that can only be guessed at, convinced himself that if Lenihan pursued his attempt to get Hillery to verify his story the answer, if forthcoming at all, would not be favourable. He prevented Lenihan from going ahead with this endeavour — which in any case was most imprudent. Had Hillery supported him, he would have been seen as interfering in party politics, much as he would have been seen as interfering in party politics had he entertained Haughey's overtures in 1982.

"Mature recollection" was an unfortunate phrase in more senses than one. At the time, Lenihan's memory was extremely confused, and he was unable to remember accurately precisely what had happened. It is not too much to say that he had forgotten all about it — highly probable, since he felt it necessary to ask Barrett whether or not he had made a call. Moreover, he considered the incident unimportant. He never thought there was the remotest chance that Hillery would accede to Haughey's request, and he was not involved in any conspiracy to subvert the system. In another country the affair would have been quickly forgotten, but in Ireland nothing is ever forgotten and controversies go on for generations.

*

The media, along with those amateur opinion-formers, callers to radio chatshows, agreed on one thing: the President had behaved well. They should have paused to reflect on what they were saying. Any private citizen is supposed to behave well, and the idea that the first citizen should behave badly was ludicrous. P. J. Hillery had an outstanding record of service and a reputation as a man dedicated to the niceties of his office. Had the point been worth making, which it was not, it could have been valid only in order to make a comparison with the bad behaviour of others. As it happened, most of those involved in the affair in their various ways behaved abominably.

Haughey, as we shall see in the next chapter, behaved worst of all. Fine Gael behaved not only badly, but idiotically. They boasted that they had laid a trap for Lenihan, then recanted when they saw that this was no way to occupy the "high moral ground". Of course they had laid a trap and Lenihan had walked into it. But how widely, and how far back in time, did the conspiracy extend? Lenihan to the end of his days believed that it was broader, and older, than ever publicly appeared, and more than once (for example, in an interview with a *Hot Press* journalist and in a conversation with the present writer) put forward an elaborate theory whose publication would cause writers to fall foul of the libel laws; *Hot Press* decided on legal grounds against publishing that part of the interview. Since it is still unpublishable, we must content ourselves with Barrett's comment: "Of course the whole thing was a setup by Fine Gael."

The behaviour of the *Irish Times* astounded the rest of the media. They were not bound by any rules of confidentiality. When they had Duffy and his tape in their hands, they were in possession of a thundering scoop. Why did they not publish it in the normal way as an exclusive story instead of sharing it with all their rivals at a press conference? Barrett surmises that they did so in order to draw the teeth of his television interview, broadcast a few hours after the press conference, but that seems improbable. Still less plausible is Lenihan's own theory, that they held the press conference in order to obtain the widest possible publicity. Had they published the story as a scoop the following morning, the rest of the media would have had no option but to follow it up, and it would have had equal publicity.

But it was the behaviour of those guardians of the high moral ground, the Progressive Democrats, that most concerned Fianna Fail in the wake of Duffygate. What would the PDs do to demonstrate their snow-white purity (or, in the Fianna Fail view, insufferable self-righteousness)?

They saw themselves as having a mission to clean up Irish politics, but had not been notably successful in the enterprise. By coincidence, soon after they joined Fianna Fail in government an unprecedented spate of business/political scandals broke out. To do them justice, they made valiant albeit mostly unavailing efforts to have the scandals thoroughly investigated (as Labour in coalition with Fianna Fail would do in their turn) and they forced their partners to set up a tribunal of inquiry into the beef industry.

Lenihan they regarded with great suspicion. They remembered with rancour the Limerick inquisition, and felt no gratitude to him for having helped to "sell" their participation in office to his party. They disliked his nonchalant utterances on practices in the beef industry disclosed by the judicial tribunal: he took the line that everything alleged in Ireland, and worse, went on in the same industry in other countries. They may not have realised that his private view of business and political scandals was entirely different. In public he maintained absolute discretion, but he let his family circle know his opinion of certain of his fellow politicians: "They're so greedy and so crooked!"

Two distasteful characteristics of moral guardians are the intense pleasure they take in inflicting punishment on others and their inability to detect any beams in their own eyes. They now set out to inflict on Lenihan the ultimate punishment, a political death sentence. Many accounts of the period are based on two assumptions: that they were in the right, and that they were united. Both assumptions are false.

There were those among them who knew that all members of the human race have beams, or at least motes, in their eyes. They knew that a strict insistence on the truth, the whole truth and nothing but the truth would empty every parliament in the world. They had sufficient sophistication to appreciate Lenihan's subtle joke, that "the only place to lie is in the House" — where economy of truth, as in all other parliaments, is the norm. They thought that he could have "finessed" Duffygate, in other words made some sort of admission. Arguably it might have been wise to consider that ignoble course before appearing on the fatal television programme. He did not, but it is clear from his conversation with Ulick O'Connor that he was aware of that possible recourse.

But when PD ministers and functionaries met to discuss the crisis, the more sophisticated view seems never to have been put. Indeed, no distinction was made between motes and beams. The meeting was followed by an appearance on *Saturdayview* by Pat Cox MEP, who asserted that credibility and integrity in small things were indivisible from credibility and integrity in large things. The party had already decided that either Lenihan must resign, or their deputies would vote with the opposition on a motion of no confidence tabled by Fine Gael, and bring down the government. Or had they? There is evidence of intriguing telephone calls between Dublin and European cities, and of PD figures saying that they could consider "a range of options".

Some accounts of the crisis are mistaken in another respect. They show Haughey as intending, at least initially, to stand by Lenihan. If so, why did he not seek a compromise? What is politics all about, if not about compromise? Why did he not seek to identify the "range of options", if indeed they existed? The official Fianna Fail answer was that no compromise was possible and that Haughey would have lost in a confrontation with the Progressive Democrats. Was he ever truly willing to risk that? It would have meant a general election fought on the issue, as Cox would have put it, of credibility and integrity, an issue virtually certain to put him out of office. And men like Haughey will cling on to office at any cost, for any length of time. Ten years is nice, but a year will do. A month? A week? They could echo Desdemona's despairing cry to Othello: "Kill me tomorrow, let me live tonight!"

If that assessment is hard on Haughey, let us be equally hard on the PDs. If Lenihan was innocent, they were demanding the head of an innocent man. If guilty, he was guilty of something Haughey had told him to do. Yet the PDs' preference was to remain in office under Haughey, with Lenihan's severed head on the cabinet table. Another characteristic of moral guardians is that they like to have the best of both worlds.

Fourteen

All government is founded on compromise and barter.
QUEEN BEATRIX of the Netherlands, quoting Edmund Burke

That weekend, Lenihan campaigned in the south-east. In Dublin, Haughey called a meeting of the Fianna Fail ministers, except for Lenihan and his sister, and presented Lenihan's resignation as Tanaiste and Defence Minister as the only way out for the government. On Monday evening, as Lenihan rested in the New Park Hotel in Kilkenny before addressing a rally, he received a telephone call from his son Brian, who had heard that journalists were being briefed to expect the resignation the following morning. Lenihan wrote in *For The Record*: "It now appeared that a public execution was being planned for the morning and the plot was already written in Kinsealy."

He also wrote that "I was certain of one thing. I would not be resigning." His firmness, however, must be questioned. He had spent too much of his life complying with the wishes of party leaders, and Haughey had every intention of exploiting his malleability. Luckily, his wife and sons were absolutely determined that, whatever pressure might be applied, he must not resign.

On Tuesday morning he met Haughey *tête-à-tête* at Kinsealy. Ahern was in the house, as were the campaign manager, Michael Dawson, and Conor and Niall Lenihan, but not in the room. Haughey told the Tanaiste that he had met O'Malley the previous day "and that O'Malley's bottom line was my resignation, or else the support of the PDs would be withdrawn the next day, which would, of course, mean a general election." Lenihan continues:

The Taoiseach advocated that the best option open to me was my resignation. He said my resignation would help rather than damage my campaign for the presidency. He said most people would respect me for standing down in the national interest, in order to avoid a general election. Pressing his point further Mr Haughey said that if I resigned, Dessie O'Malley would issue a statement congratulating me on my decision. The Taoiseach also promised that if I resigned, he would keep the Defence portfolio and the position of Tanaiste vacant, so that if I lost the election I would be immediately reinstated. Mr Haughey also intimated that Dessie O'Malley's statement on my resignation would include an endorsement of my candidature for the presidency, thereby improving my chances of victory.

I listened to all of this patiently. I then countered that my resignation would be tantamount to an admission that I had done something wrong as Tanaiste and Minister for Defence which rendered me unfit to serve as a member of the cabinet. It was public knowledge that I had performed well as Minister for Defence and at no stage had anyone suggested otherwise. If I regarded myself as unfit to be Tanaiste and Minister for Defence, then I was unfit to be President. If I resigned, I argued, my campaign would become unsustainable and I would be laughed out of court. The only thing against me was that I was telling the truth in regard to the telephone calls made over eight years ago. I put it to the Taoiseach that he and Mr O'Malley knew that I was telling the truth because both of them were on the Fianna Fail front bench on the night the phone calls were made.

I said to the Taoiseach that the people should be allowed to decide the issue in the presidential election and I guaranteed that if I was defeated in that contest I would resign from the government. I felt this proposal of mine was eminently fair as it would allow the election to proceed on its own merits and it would also avoid the need for a general election. I thought that from Mr O'Malley's point of view this alternative should be perfectly acceptable. The Taoiseach told me that O'Malley would not agree to it, that all options had been discussed and the only acceptable solution was my resignation. I asked for time to consider the matter and it was agreed that I would go into Leinster House to discuss things with any of my ministerial colleagues who happened to be about.

Haughey at that point dashed off to Dublin Airport to greet Queen Beatrix of the Netherlands, arriving on a state visit. Lenihan held a brief meeting with Ahern, Dawson, Conor and Niall. He then went to the Department of Defence, and from there to Leinster House, where he met Ray Burke, Padraig Flynn, Vincent Brady (the chief whip) and Albert Reynolds. Reynolds, who said he saw no reason for resignation, left for Granard, agreeing to meet Lenihan there in the afternoon on a tour of the Longford-Westmeath constituency which would conclude in Athlone.

At the airport Haughey told journalists: "I will not be asking for the Tanaiste's resignation from cabinet. I will not be putting him under pressure to resign, nor will his cabinet colleagues. It is entirely a matter for my old friend of thirty years." By now, economy of truth had given way to total absence of truth. When he again met Lenihan, this time accompanied by Ahern, after lunch, he handed him a prepared resignation statement. The document contained the preposterous assertion that "the decision is mine and mine alone. I have not been subject to pressure from any quarter."

It was lucky for Lenihan, and unlucky for Haughey, that the Tanaiste was on his way to his own "Shannon wave", to quote Bruce Arnold, where he was certain of the most fervent support, not to say adulation. But long before the battle bus went anywhere near Athlone a flood of messages was relayed to it, all backing Lenihan and urging him not to resign. In addition, Conor, knowing that pressure from Dublin was going to continue, took the only operative mobile telephone and hid it from the Fianna Fail functionaries on the bus. When Reynolds joined the bus at Granard, he again advised Lenihan not to resign.

> But I had a dilemma — the Taoiseach wanted my resignation and time was running out. In deciding not to resign I knew I would be drawing down a barrier between myself and most of my ministerial colleagues and all those urging me along a different path. I stood up from my perch at the front and walked down to the end of the bus where there was a small partitioned-off room. My wife Ann was sitting there on her own. I told her I was not going to resign. Her eyes filled with tears. I held Mr Haughey's resignation in my hand and suddenly, becoming aware of it, I held it up to her and joked, "I don't suppose I'll be needing this." She looked at it for the first time and threw it aside.

At Longford town he told Dawson to telephone Haughey and inform him of his decision. At Mullingar, he confirmed it for television and radio interviewers. On finally arriving, hours behind schedule, in Athlone, he and Ann went to the house of their old friends the O'Callaghans (retired Garda Chief Superintendent Brendan O'Callaghan and his wife Maureen) and from there to the Prince of Wales Hotel. Up to four thousand people had come out to express their sympathy with a man being hounded. About half of them were crammed into the hotel and the overspill was disrupting the traffic in one of the most notorious bottlenecks in Ireland.

Ahern had arrived, as had Padraig Flynn, despatched to Athlone by Haughey. Mary O'Rourke had already confronted Flynn at Moate, a few miles from Athlone on the Dublin road:

> It was at Moate that I first saw my cabinet colleague Padraig Flynn. He said, "how are you, my dear?" I said, from the bus, "you are not here on good business. You come not in friendship but in guile." He said, "I am your friend, Mary."

In the hotel, she was still out of temper with him. They had, she says, "a blazing row" in the course of which she told him to "get back across the Shannon where you belong." (She meant to his native Mayo.) On Lenihan's arrival, he was mobbed and had difficulty in making his way into the conference hall. He could hear chants of "no resignation". He later wrote: "The sound carried upstairs to where both Bertie Ahern and Padraig Flynn waited, unable to join me on the platform because they were afraid of what they thought was a hostile mob. Albert Reynolds and my sister made defiant speeches and I told a delighted audience that I would not be resigning." Messages of support kept arriving in the hotel, as also at his Castleknock house and Fianna Fail headquarters, where an anti-resignation picket was mounted. But the other side were active too. Charlie McCreevy telephoned Mary Harney and asked her to see to it that the Progressive Democrats postponed their meeting (to decide their tactics on the opposition no-confidence motion) until the Fianna Fail parliamentary party had met. "He assured her," wrote Lenihan, "that Mr Haughey would get a mandate to do whatever he liked."

At the O'Callaghans' next morning, the clatter of helicopter blades woke Lenihan. The noise came from an aircraft hovering ten feet above the roof. More telephone calls came through from Dublin, one insisting that Lenihan was needed immediately in the Dail, another contradicting it:

> An atmosphere of panic and paranoia was being created up in Dublin. An official from the Department of Defence rang through to my driver in his car suggesting that I was being held hostage by my family and that if I didn't come up soon, they would ask the Gardai in Athlone to get a search warrant. The driver told the caller they must be off their head ... With these antics over I came down for breakfast and sat listening to the radio as it broadcast the opening exchanges in the confidence debate. I listened to Mr Haughey denying opposition charges that he had

telephoned Aras an Uachtarain back in 1982 and threatened an Army officer.

*

It was borne in on Queen Beatrix that her hosts had other things on their minds than Dutch-Irish relations. At a lunch in her honour in Iveagh House, she made a passing reference to their preoccupations and quoted Edmund Burke: "All government is founded on compromise and barter."

Not much sign of compromise was visible in the Dail chamber, where the tone of the confidence debate was exceedingly bitter. Dick Spring set it:

> This debate is not about Brian Lenihan when it is all boiled down. This debate, essentially, is about the evil spirit that controls one political party in this Republic, and it is about the way in which that spirit has begun to corrupt the entire political system in our country. This is a debate about greed for office, about disregard for truth and about contempt for political standards. It is a debate about the way in which a once great party has been brought to its knees by the grasping acquisitiveness of its leader. It is ultimately a debate about the cancer that is eating away at our body politic — and the virus which caused that cancer, An Taoiseach, Charles J. Haughey.

Fianna Fail took great exception to that speech, comparing it with FitzGerald's "flawed pedigree" remarks in 1979 and condemning both as unfair. They would change their tune in 1997, when it was disclosed that Haughey had humbled himself before Ben Dunne. But notwithstanding the findings of the McCracken Tribunal, and notwithstanding all the allegations, true or false, launched against him throughout his long career, he never did anything worse in his life than to betray Lenihan.

By the time the Dutch queen spoke, that betrayal was well in train. Before attending the Iveagh House lunch, Haughey had told the parliamentary party meeting that it was "a matter of grave concern" that he could not contact his Tanaiste and Defence Minister. He was seizing on this as an excuse. Senator Eddie Bohan angered him by contradicting him, saying that "I was talking to him myself this morning on the phone." Just after the meeting adjourned until the afternoon, Haughey encountered Bohan and Liam Lawlor in the corridor. He told Bohan: "If I cannot contact my Tanaiste and Minister for Defence I'll have to sack him."

In the afternoon Lenihan arrived in Dublin and went to the house of his former private secretary Peg Fogarty. He sent to the meeting, via Lawlor, a dignified statement which hardened the resolve of deputies who were willing to face a general election in preference to sacrificing Lenihan. One of them, Sean Power from Kildare, asked Haughey this question: if he now handed the PDs Brian Lenihan's head, what would happen when they came looking for his own head? Power was a very young and a very new deputy, and Lawlor says that he "did not have the political IQ" to press his advantage. Could more experienced politicians have cornered Haughey and forced him to stand by Lenihan? In the atmosphere of crisis and bewilderment, most deputies thought Haughey would stand firm and face an election. But they were unaware of his manoeuvrings and the concocted letter of resignation. It has always remained the overwhelming opinion — and Power's own opinion — that a majority in the parliamentary party, once they saw a way out, would not risk an election. The meeting broke up inconclusively, but it was taken for granted that Haughey had its sanction, spoken or unspoken, to go ahead.

Albert Reynolds and Mary O'Rourke tried to arrange a meeting between Lenihan and O'Malley, and a room was booked in the Berkeley Court Hotel for the purpose. But Lenihan refused to attend. He wrote that "I did not trust O'Malley ... I was in no mood for what struck me as a macabre political encounter with my putative executioner." He might well have added that he did not trust Haughey. By then, it was impossible for him to have any trust in Haughey.

He came into Leinster House to vote with the government parties on the confidence motion. When he entered the visitors' bar, there were emotional scenes, inspired by guilt and love in more or less equal parts. A few minutes before the vote was taken, Haughey announced that he had dismissed him. The government won the division by eighty-three votes to eighty.

*

A lesser man would have looked for a hole to crawl into. Lenihan fought the last week of the campaign with renewed vigour, amazingly looking — as Spring's adviser Fergus Finlay noted in his book on Robinson — younger and fitter than Robinson. He was boosted by the enthusiasm of the Fianna Fail grassroots, who cast aside their earlier apathy and poured out on to the streets to canvass for him, and by opinion polls which showed him recovering from the low point he had reached after Duffygate. Robinson meanwhile began to show signs of fatigue, and no wonder: she had been on the stump ever since April. Suddenly Fianna Fail thought all was not yet lost.

Robinson had shrugged off her left-wing associations and achieved her aim of being identified as an independent and not a Labour candidate. Both Fianna Fail and Fine Gael determined, however, to brand her a socialist, and Fianna Fail dug out a 1982 statement in which she had said she favoured nationalising the banks. She denied it. Then they placed newspaper advertisements asking: "Is the Left Right for the Park?" This was done without consulting Lenihan, who thought the tactic absurdly belated and in any case pointless. Party headquarters seemingly thought that the scare tactics might frighten conservative Fine Gael voters into refusing to transfer second preferences to Robinson. In the event, and quite predictably, Fine Gael dropped their own attacks on her as a left-winger and stitched up a massively successful (but only for her) transfer pact the weekend before the election.

But in the end it was Padraig Flynn who unwittingly aborted the Lenihan recovery. Lenihan, eternally reluctant to criticise his colleagues harshly, lets him down lightly in *For The Record*, so we may as well let Emily O'Reilly take up the story:

> Ronan O'Donoghue, the producer of *Saturdayview* on the weekend before polling, had one aim in mind. On the programme he had Fianna Fail minister Padraig Flynn and PD chairperson Michael McDowell. This was the first time the two parties had come together on such a programme since the sacking. And O'Donoghue was hoping for fireworks.
>
> What happened went beyond his expectations.
>
> Flynn, instructed by party bosses to go for Robinson on the socialism, "reds under the bed" angle went gloriously off his brief accusing Robinson of having been reconstructed by her handlers in Labour and the Workers' Party, of having discovered "the new interest in family, being a mother and all that kind of thing. But none of us, you know, none of us who knew Mary Robinson very well in previous incarnations ever heard her claiming to be a great wife and mother."

To do Flynn justice, his intention was not to cast aspersions on Robinson's wifeliness and motherliness. What O'Reilly calls his "stream of consciousness vein" was inspired by Fianna Fail frustration at her handlers' clever "remake". They knew that they could rely on the left-liberal vote but needed a much wider constituency, and accordingly set out to emphasise her family life and to play down her former radical views and associations. But Flynn should not have engaged in an argument he could not win, much less couch it in what sounded, both to those in the studio and the wider audience, like deliberately insulting terms. McDowell, white-knuckled and furious, berated him, told him to mind his manners, and described his intervention as "disgusting".

That afternoon Ahern, who had not heard the programme, was canvassing with Lenihan in the west. As he was leaving a rally in Ballina, O'Reilly writes,

A woman approached him muttering about Padraig Flynn and saying, "if that's the way you lot are going to behave ... " A short time later, two women Fianna Fail supporters, both pushing prams, accosted him.

"It's despicable," they said to an increasingly puzzled Ahern. What was despicable, he inquired. Flynn, they said. Ah sure, Padraig Flynn is a nice guy, answered Ahern, totally mystified. Then he went on to Tuam, then to Ballyhaunis, each time encountering irate women, each time pondering how strangely unpopular Flynn was in his own neck of the woods.

Finally ... a young woman literally grabbed Ahern by the lapels. "It's bastards like Padraig Flynn," she spat, "that are ruining the party my father loves. Why do you let him on the media?" But what did Flynn do, begged Bertie. So she told him.

Later that night Ahern checked back with HQ and heard in detail what had happened. The incident, he told people later, had cost Lenihan between two and three percentage points. The Robinson camp, he knew, had been devastated that weekend. They felt the campaign had run away from them, that Lenihan would romp home. The "Flynn thing" had changed all that.

At a grisly final campaign rally in Dublin, the Lenihan family cold-shouldered Haughey and mounted an operation to prevent physical contact between the Taoiseach and the Tanaiste he had sacked. Haughey, however, watched closely and waited for his chance. When it came, he seized Brian by the arm and held it up. This gesture was designed to persuade the naive that the dismissal had been no more than a ploy, that it would if anything enhance the candidate's chances, and that the two men remained friends. It took in some observers, but not those who knew the real story, and it enraged the family.

Lenihan's penultimate action of the campaign was to have his bus convey Gene Kerrigan of the *Sunday Independent* to his local polling station. There Kerrigan voted for Mary Robinson, an action he later came to regret. Lenihan's final action was to switch off the tape of Tina Turner singing *Simply The Best*. He had grown thoroughly sick of it.

*

The country went to the polls on Wednesday 7 November, and the counting of the votes began the next morning. The count went into a second day, but the result was clear from the start.

Lenihan received 44.1 per cent of the first preferences, Robinson 38.9 per cent, and Currie 17 per cent. More than 200,000 of Currie's votes, 76.7 per cent, transferred to Robinson. On the second count, Robinson won by 52.8 per cent to Lenihan's 47.2 per cent.

Without Duffygate, without the Flynn intervention, with a better Fianna Fail campaign, would it have been any different? We can never know. The opinion polls, usually so reliable, fluctuated crazily during the campaign, and inevitably so in view of its sensational nature. But one of the leading opinion pollsters points out that Lenihan obtained what was then the normal Fianna Fail percentage of the vote — five percentage points higher than that achieved at the next two general elections. His view coincides with that of Liam Lawlor and that of Paul Lenihan, earlier recorded here, that no Fianna Fail candidate could have won with 44 per cent first preferences. But it holds good only in the event of substantial transfers between Fine Gael and Labour, as was the case in 1990. It also runs contrary to Lenihan's own belief, expressed in typically colourful terms the very day before the fatal *Questions and Answers* programme. When a foreign diplomat with whom he was friendly asked him how the campaign was going, he replied: "I'm home, if only I can keep my fat mouth shut."

The consequences of this election were seismic. Lenihan was the first victim, but he was quickly followed by Dukes, whose internal opponents in Fine Gael used the calamitous Currie result to dump him and replace him with John Bruton. The third victim would be Haughey. Sean Power's question about surrendering heads to the Progressive Democrats had been prophetic. He had got the timing only slightly wrong.

Fifteen

The good things of prosperity are to be desired, the good things of adversity to be admired.
    SENECA

Lenihan may have looked to Finlay younger and fitter than Robinson, but the shattering experiences he had undergone had taken a terrible toll of his health. He had to return to the Mater for tests and treatments. Yet with a resilience bordering on the superhuman, he emerged full of confidence and fight.

He set at once about restoring his reputation. He wrote *For The Record* in about two months. It was published in May 1991, and became, like his wife's book, a bestseller. The launch, in the Berkeley Court Hotel where he had refused to meet O'Malley, was a jolly and bibulous occasion. But he had more serious business on hand.

In a pre-publication interview with me for the *Irish Independent*, he declared his continuing interest in the premiership, if only as a "caretaker" or "interim" Taoiseach. Many dismissed the idea as implausible, but Lenihan was in deadly earnest.

Haughey's powers were visibly waning. His betrayal of Lenihan, and his supine attitude to the Progressive Democrats, had alienated large sections of his party. Scandals continued unabated, as did what Fianna Fail like to call "innuendo", a word they often apply to specific and concrete accusations. To all his real or imagined offences from the Arms Crisis down were added his mishandling of the scandals, in which he made more enemies for himself, and the allegation that he had uttered threats to an Army officer, an aide at Aras an Uachtarain, on the night of 27 January 1982. He made a lachrymose denial of this charge in the Dail. Like all the other stories, however, it simply would not go away. And when the question arose publicly of how long he would stay in office, he made himself seem foolish by mentioning the great age of Chinese rulers.

At the end of November 1990 a five-hour parliamentary party meeting had held an inquest of sorts on the presidential election debacle. The chairman, Jim Tunney, described the meeting as "delightful", and the chief whip, Vincent Brady, said that most speakers had been complimentary about the Taoiseach's "first-class and totally satisfactory" performance. In what respects Haughey's performance merited these epithets was not at all clear to the many disgruntled deputies and senators. The meeting was more noteworthy for a suggestion from Liam Lawlor that the leader might seek "a fresh mandate" from the parliamentary party.

The event coincided with a curious move, evidently uncoordinated, by a number of cumainn in various parts of the country to put forward Lenihan's name for the presidency of the party at the next ard-fheis. The Fianna Fail leader is always president of the party, and Haughey's coterie read the move as a direct challenge. They put it about that if he lost the leadership it would mean a general election — an obvious attempt to frighten backbenchers. Haughey sent for Lawlor, who had never been on friendly terms with him and who describes their meeting with some relish:

> Haughey said: "Brian Lenihan should never have been our candidate. I knew something would go wrong. What's he up to now, saying [sic] that he will stand for the presidency of the party? That would create a two-headed monster. I want you to talk him out of it." I replied: "I know nothing about it and I owe you nothing. I'll be here when you're gone."

On 11 December Lenihan knocked the proposal on the head in a statement in which, however, he hinted at Haughey's early departure and his own candidature:

I have been overwhelmed by the volume of support I have received from members and units of the Fianna Fail organisation throughout Ireland for the office of president of Fianna Fail.

However, it must be noted that in the history of our party, the office of president of the Fianna Fail organisation has been combined with the leadership of the parliamentary party. The experience of political parties at home and abroad who have taken a different course has not been a happy one.

The traditional practice of Fianna Fail has been for the parliamentary party to determine the leadership. As a committed believer in our system of parliamentary democracy I accept that practice.

I also believe that a contested election for the post of president of Fianna Fail at the next ard-fheis would not serve the unity and wellbeing of our party or our nation. For these reasons I do not wish my name to be submitted for the position of president at the ard-fheis.

At their meeting of 4 December the Fianna Fail organisation in Dublin West called for a review of the party leadership in the context of the present commission of inquiry into the party. The commission of inquiry is the chosen instrument of the parliamentary party to investigate the affairs of the party. The parliamentary party has accepted that the scope of the commission should not extend to the leadership of Fianna Fail. As a democrat I accept that decision and Charles Haughey will continue to receive my support as the elected leader of the Fianna Fail party. My support of successive leaders of Fianna Fail has never been in question.

I want to contribute to the wellbeing of our country in Dail Eireann to the full extent of my abilities. I believe that the economic achievement of the government must be translated into equal rights and opportunities for all sections of our community. I believe our high reputation as a state in world affairs

must be preserved. As honorary secretary of the
Fianna Fail organisation I want to assist in the renewal
of the Fianna Fail party.

Of course, in the event of a vacancy arising on some
future occasion in the leadership of the Fianna Fail
party I intend to contest that vacancy.

As the pressure on the Taoiseach continued, deputies, even
certain ministers, convinced themselves that he had given them
some kind of promise that he would step down soon, choosing a
time at which he could go with "honour and dignity" and
arranging for a smooth succession. There is some question as to
whether Lenihan at this time constituted himself a "committee"
with one other deputy, a person close to Haughey, with a view
to overseeing the exercise. Whether two persons can make up a
committee is perhaps a semantic point. The certainty is that
three or four different factions in the party believed that Sean
Power had got it right and that Haughey would go, at the
bidding of the PDs or otherwise, probably by the end of the
year. Once again they were wrong about the timescale, but only
slightly.

A stark example of his fading powers came very soon with a
mid-term (and in the view of hard-headed politicians, pointless)
"renegotiation" of the government programme, on which the
Progressive Democrats insisted. The negotiators of 1989,
Reynolds and Ahern, were charged with the task. Their PD
counterparts assumed that the normal pattern would prevail
and that they would get anything they sought. Reynolds had
other ideas. To the PDs' distress, he fought them every inch of
the way. Although they put a good face on it, they had to settle
for much less than they wanted. To make it all the more galling,
they had to settle with Reynolds, who had described the
coalition as "a temporary little arrangement" and held out to the
Fianna Fail grassroots the prospect of an overall majority.

Reynolds had looked about him and decided that there were
only two plausible successors to Haughey: himself and Ray
MacSharry, European Agriculture Commissioner. MacSharry
insisted again and again that he had no intention of returning to

domestic politics, and displayed considerable fortitude when endlessly chivvied by journalists who did not believe him. Reynolds did believe him, and once persuaded of MacSharry's lack of interest in the premiership he saw himself as the heir apparent.

He had the firm support of the Country and Western Alliance, but decidedly not of the party establishment — if a party in such a battered condition can be said to have had an establishment at all. In so far as one existed, it included Ahern, Burke, Lenihan, and O'Rourke (the "centrist" principle again). They underestimated the growing strength of Reynolds, and could not foresee the further sensational events that occurred in late 1991 and early 1992. Had they foreseen them, and countered the Country and Western Alliance, they would probably have prevailed. But by now their candidate would have been Ahern, not Lenihan.

In the autumn of 1991 the "Gang of Four" — four of the younger deputies, Sean Power among them — openly challenged Haughey with a motion for debate by the parliamentary party. Reynolds and Flynn refused to support Haughey and were dismissed from the cabinet. The country was electrified by the spectacle of one of the leading Fianna Fail ministers, Gerry Collins, on television, tearfully pleading with Reynolds not to "burst up" the party. The Gang of Four motion was defeated, but the party was already well and truly "burst up".

Having dismissed Reynolds and Flynn, Haughey proceeded to make a major blunder by proposing the appointment of Dr Jim McDaid as Minister for Defence and Noel Davern as Minister for Education. Lenihan disliked these nominations simply on the grounds of the two deputies' inexperience. But it was not their lack of experience that led to the next blow to Haughey. McDaid was falsely accused of IRA sympathies, and the Progressive Democrats objected to his appointment. He withdrew with dignity (and eventually reached the cabinet under Ahern in 1997). The sight of another head on a PD plate infuriated many in Fianna Fail and contributed to the undermining of Haughey.

One of the most remarkable features of these months was the confidence exuded by Reynolds. Lenihan would limp into the chamber when Haughey spoke and sit listening to the proceedings, a little smile on his lips: "watching the game .. . loving the game." But he did not see closely enough into the game being played in the corridors, where Reynolds impressed all who saw and heard him with his calm assurance. His supporters meanwhile persuaded themselves that when the crunch came Ahern would switch sides and that they could put forward a Reynolds-Ahern "dream ticket". What made them think that remains unknown, and the crisis came in a manner wholly unexpected by Ahern or Lenihan.

Sean Doherty had always maintained that he had ordered the telephone taps of 1982 without Haughey's knowledge. Now, early in 1992, he suddenly changed his story. He called a press conference and told the assembled media that Haughey had known all along about the taps. Haughey called his own press conference and issued a strong denial. Doherty, he said, was a self-confessed liar: either he had lied in 1982 or he was lying now. This did not satisfy the Progressive Democrats. As Power had foretold, they demanded Haughey's head and got it.

He made a flowery resignation speech, in which he said that he wanted as an epitaph the words "he served the people, all the people, to the best of his ability." He quoted Shakespeare's *Othello*: "I have done the state some service." And he quoted Yeats: "My glory was I had such friends." More than one journalist sat in the press gallery and thought of Brian Lenihan.

Lenihan was not thinking of the irony, but of the succession. Before Doherty's intervention, he was annoyed by what he saw as naivety on the part of the Gang of Four, and infinitely more annoyed by what he saw as an attempted *Putsch* by the Country and Western Alliance. He strongly supported Ahern. But Ahern, only recently promoted to Finance, was struggling with the details of a budget, and his internal party soundings led him to believe that Reynolds would win a contest. He declined to go forward, much to the dismay of Lenihan, who issued a statement which made his feelings about "dream tickets" very clear:

> I am disappointed by the decision of Bertie Ahern TD not to contest the leadership of Fianna Fail. In my view he was in a position to unite the different strands of the party and meet the challenges of today's Ireland.
>
> Every Fianna Fail councillor, TD and government minister is on the Fianna Fail ticket. No two individuals in Fianna Fail constitute a dream ticket. The qualities required of the next Fianna Fail leader are a record of public service and loyalty to the party and its institutions.
>
> In the circumstances I have decided to support Mary O'Rourke TD for the leadership of Fianna Fail.

However, the Fianna Fail deputies elected Reynolds by an overwhelming vote over the opposition of Dr Michael Woods and Mary O'Rourke. Lenihan, knowing the certainty of a Reynolds victory and as always intensely concerned for party unity, supported his sister's nomination only with great hesitation.

*

Reynolds's first actions in office did little enough for unity. In the "St Valentine's Week Massacre", he astounded the party and the country by sacking most of the Fianna Fail cabinet ministers and junior ministers. They included Ray Burke, Gerry Collins — and Mary O'Rourke. This last dismissal caused such an outcry that he partly relented and offered her a pick of the junior ministerial jobs. She chose one in Industry and Commerce, where the senior minister, O'Malley, treated her decently and gave her considerable independence.

Reynolds would have done better to pause and reflect that this was no time to make enemies. He was facing a series of crises of an unparalleled nature, crises which would interact upon one another and result in utter disaster. The disaster was largely of his own making, but the first crisis owed its origin to our old friends the fundamentalists.

He learned of it with horror immediately on taking office. He was informed that on foot of the amendment to the constitution consequent on the 1983 abortion referendum, an injunction had been issued against a fourteen-year-old rape victim to prevent her having an abortion in England. The "X" case was something the conservatives in 1983 had said would never happen. Now it had, and the country was in turmoil.

Luckily for the politicians, the Supreme Court ruled in favour of the girl. The court held that, since she had threatened suicide, this constituted a threat to her life and she therefore had a constitutional right to an abortion. But politicians, being politicians, displayed little gratitude to the court for solving their dilemma. Certain Fianna Fail politicians in particular were incensed by the criticism levelled against them by Mr Justice Niall McCarthy for their failure to legislate on foot of the amendment and thereby clarify the position. As to the "pro-life" lobby, they refused to accept that their own campaign of 1983, designed to prevent abortion, was to blame for legalising it. They launched a new campaign, demanding a stricter wording.

Reynolds had more pressing concerns than that demand. The Haughey government, almost entirely unnoticed, had caused a protocol to be inserted in the Maastricht Treaty on European Union, protecting the abortion amendment from European law. Did this mean that the thousands of Irish women who annually travel abroad for abortions could be deprived of freedom of movement? And if so, did it mean that a bewildered electorate might vote against Maastricht in the imminent referendum in which they had to decide whether or not to endorse the treaty? So alarmed was the Reynolds government that it made a feeble effort to have the treaty itself amended. When that predictably failed, it obtained from its EU partners a declaration asserting the rights of freedom of movement and information. That would have to suffice. Reynolds campaigned for the treaty on the basis that it would assure European subsidies of £6 billion a year for Ireland, and a huge majority voted yes in the referendum.

However, the issue had already caused a split between Fianna Fail and the PDs in the government. Reynolds wanted the Maastricht vote held before a referendum on freedom of travel and information, O'Malley argued for the opposite order. Privately, some significant Fianna Fail figures agreed with him, but Reynolds insisted on having his own way. In his account of his period as press secretary to Reynolds, *One Spin on The Merry-Go-Round*, Sean Duignan wrote that he thought it ominous that Mary Harney said the abortion row would not bring down the government. "She seemed to be insinuating that the breakup was on its way, but on a different issue." Indeed it was. The Progressive Democrats had reason to believe that associates of Reynolds were manoeuvring to fight a general election in which they would paint all their opponents, the PDs included, as abortionists. They failed, and would go the country at the wrong time on the wrong issue.

Meanwhile, Hanafin had the party whip removed from him for voting against the Maastricht referendum Bill in the Seanad. He would go on to lose his seat at the next election, but recovered it in 1997.

The bishops did not match his courage. The hierarchy issued a statement saying that they had noted with alarm that the right to life of the unborn "does not appear to be on the government's agenda at the present time", but when Reynolds telephoned individual bishops and berated them, they backed down.

*

If Reynolds could overcome the most feared and respected power group in the country, the Catholic hierarchy, surely he could put down the PDs, with their pathetic four per cent public support? Some of his closest friends had been sick of the pampering their junior partners had received from Haughey, and were now avid for confrontation. At the Fianna Fail ard-fheis in March, Brian Cowen delighted the delegates by saying of his party's partners, "when in doubt, leave out." Duignan records Cowen as telling him: "The PDs have already seen off a Fianna Fail Taoiseach, Tanaiste and Minister for Defence. They are now trying to bring down Albert. Well, they can shag off."

Older Fianna Fail ministers and deputies did not share this taste for confrontation. They could see that a showdown was looming, not on abortion, an issue favourable to them, but on the most unfavourable issue imaginable. Actions by Reynolds during his period as Minister for Industry and Commerce were under challenge at the Beef Tribunal in Dublin Castle. Both he and O'Malley gave evidence. Reynolds called O'Malley's evidence "reckless, irresponsible and dishonest". Under cross-examination for two days, he refused to withdraw the allegation. Even then, over the next few days Fianna Fail continued to hope against hope that O'Malley might swallow it. Duignan wrote: "We were disabused of this illusion when Bobby Molloy demanded an 'abject' withdrawal of Reynolds's dishonesty allegation, and the PDs told pol corrs [political correspondents] that the only reason O'Malley was remaining on as a minister was to ensure that files were not tampered with, or a civil servant intimidated in relation to the Beef Tribunal." On 4 November the Progressive Democrats called a press conference at which O'Malley announced the death of the coalition, citing "non-consultation and exploitation of loyalty" as the reason. After the word loyalty, Duignan interpolated [sic] and well he might.

These shenanigans were very distasteful to Lenihan. Regardless of his reservations about the Country and Western Alliance on the one hand and the Progressive Democrats on the other, he held that the first duty of a government was to stick together and that all differences could be resolved. His own greatest fault was his dislike of confrontation, because there are times when confrontation is unavoidable, but he was perfectly right in deploring avoidable confrontations.

Nor could a politician of his experience approve of the batty government decision to present each voter with no fewer than four ballot papers on 25 November: the constituency voting paper, and three abortion-related, the rights of travel and information, and the "substantive issue". Moreover, the government got the last of these hopelessly wrong. It came up with a wording which invited the voters to opt for abortion in the event of a risk to the life, but not the health, of a pregnant woman, and excluded a threat of suicide as a risk to life. The travel and information proposals were approved by big majorities, but conservatives and liberals combined to defeat the proposal on the "substantive issue", so that more trouble was stored up for the future.

In addition, he knew from the start that in the general election Fianna Fail were on a hiding to nothing. But even while the campaign went on he determined to try to turn their certain losses to advantage. His services to the party and the country were by no means over.

*

How to describe the Fianna Fail campaign? Frightful, desperate, hopeless: all these and more; a search for adjectives sufficient to describe its awfulness would exhaust the resources of Webster and Roget. Reynolds instructed Duignan to tell the political correspondents that "Fianna Fail traditionally start high and finish low, but this time we're starting low and we'll finish high." An academic observer commented mockingly that he achieved the first of these aims. There was never the smallest chance that he would achieve the second, and everything from the ominous opinion polls to the half-empty streets in which Reynolds campaigned to the silent telephones to the confused strategy, or lack of strategy, showed it. But the worst element of all was the disorganisation and low morale of the party. Duignan wrote:

> I was struck by signs of indiscipline and even insubordination in the organisation at large. A steady stream of HQ instructions to FF notables, recommending particular responses to opposition criticisms, were being widely ignored. Certain ministers and other personages who had been requested to represent Fianna Fail on various TV and

radio election programmes were begging off with all manner of specious excuses.

It seemed the prevailing party wisdom in the teeth of the storm was to remain well below decks. Heads dutifully poked through constituency portholes as we passed by, but were as quickly retracted. There was rarely any outright dissent, but it struck me that the much vaunted iron discipline of Fianna Fail was a myth. Many of the party warlords fought the election within their own territorial fastnesses — in their own way — with little or no reference to Mount Street.

Lenihan was one of these magnates. He had to ensure his own re-election and (notwithstanding any local feuds their respective supporters might engage in) bring Lawlor back in with him. It was not easy work; in the event, Lawlor survived by a margin of a mere fifty votes. But Lenihan did not confine himself to Dublin West. As Fianna Fail went from bad to worse to catastrophic, he knew that their only hope of remaining in office was a coalition with Labour, and he made contact with major figures in Labour: tentative contacts, but opening lines was well worth while. He was not helped by another batty Fianna Fail decision, to employ the legendary British consultants Saatchi and Saatchi. This decision foreshadowed the use of that last resort the "red scare", by now watered down to the proposition that voting for left-wing parties meant higher public spending and higher taxes. It had worked in the last British general election, but it had not worked for Fianna Fail in 1990 and it had not worked in the 1992 American presidential election, weeks before the Irish general election. And Irish voters are not easily put off by talk of high public spending; on the whole, they think it A Good Thing. As for Lenihan, he thought stable government infinitely more important than policies of right or left, and in any case he longed for a centre-left government, meaning a Fianna Fail–Labour coalition.

In his diary entry for 19 November, Duignan noted Reynolds's reaction to the latest adverse opinion poll:

Albert very quiet. Then he says, almost to himself: "Labour will strike a hard bargain." Labour will strike a hard bargain! Is that the way he thinks we'll escape? — *L'appertura a sinistra?* — Politicians are something else.

On the following day, Duignan accompanied Reynolds when Padraig Flynn greeted the Taoiseach on the outskirts of Westport:

> Driving into the town, after a brief council of war, "Pee" suddenly came to the point. There were, he said, "elements" within Fianna Fail trying to push the party into a post-election alliance with Labour. That, he declared, would have to be firmly resisted.
>
> Well, now ... I glanced at the Taoiseach to see how he was taking the advice of his close confidant. Reynolds kept listening and nodding as if Flynn were pointing out some interesting sights along the route. The hortatory monologue continued but Reynolds never ventured yea or nay. ... waiting until it was all over before going big game hunting. Like Charles Haughey before him, he was prepared to break historic moulds if that was what was required to continue as Taoiseach.

In other words, Lenihan was about to get his wish.

Sixteen

Being in politics is like being a football coach. You have to be smart enough to understand the game and dumb enough to think it's important.

SENATOR EUGENE McCARTHY

During the election campaign Bruton proposed that a "rainbow coalition" should succeed Fianna Fail in the next Dail. Spring ignored him, but the idea caught fire.

Something very like a rainbow coalition already existed in the Labour-led "civic alliance" on the Dublin city council. In addition to Labour, its components were Fine Gael, Democratic Left (successors to the Workers' Party), the Greens and the "community" group. (This last group later switched sides and allied themselves with Fianna Fail.) The Progressive Democrats were excluded from the civic alliance. The significance of the exclusion apparently eluded those who thought that any anti-Fianna Fail coalition, regardless of the colours in its spectrum, constituted a rainbow.

When the election returns came in, it was immediately clear that the parliamentary arithmetic would permit a Fianna Fail–Labour coalition with an enormous majority, or a coalition of Fine Gael, Labour and Progressive Democrats, but not a coalition of Fine Gael, Labour and Democratic Left. Nevertheless, Spring affected to believe the Fine Gael-Labour-Democratic Left option possible, and entered into negotiations with DL which ensued in the drawing up of a joint policy document.

He kept his negotiations with Democratic Left going for weeks. He plainly had two purposes, to buy time and to prevent a flanking movement on his left. When he finally entered into talks with Fine Gael, he demanded that the DL should participate in a minority coalition and that he should become a "rotating Taoiseach", sharing the premiership with Bruton. Bruton was willing to consider both propositions, but the Fine Gael front bench vetoed them.

Now the sagacity of Reynolds and Lenihan (who had not only made contacts with Labour during the election campaign but had discussed the question of an alliance between Fianna Fail and Labour with Brendan Halligan years earlier) made itself felt. But a Fianna Fail–Labour coalition could not come into being without difficult negotiations, without a special Labour conference, and without overcoming the deep suspicions felt about Fianna Fail in Spring's personal coterie. In the end it came down to a vote in which Spring's advisers split evenly, leaving the decision up to himself. Reynolds, Lenihan, Bertie Ahern and Dr Martin Mansergh, adviser to three Fianna Fail Taoisigh, were ready for him.

Ahern and Lenihan, the two greatest enthusiasts for a Fianna Fail–Labour coalition, worked closely together both before and after the election. After the election, they also worked very closely with Mansergh, who did most of their drafting for them. Ahern, having cleared the proposal with Reynolds, commissioned Mansergh to put together a paper on what the latter calls "shall we say, Fianna Fail–Labour community of interest":

> Brian Lenihan was probably the only person who expressed openly in advance of the election that it was desirable to go for a coalition with Labour. He had very particular reasons, apart from general tendency, not to want a renewal of the coalition with the PDs. It was they who had sought and got his head. I had observed before the election that Brian had gone out openly with this line. Fianna Fail were attacking Labour particularly hard in the last ten days. Bertie was anxious that we should not burn our bridges entirely. We took very good care that in various advertisements the attacks were political and not in any way personal.

Mansergh and others in the Fianna Fail inner circle have defended the electoral tactics on the ground that in their absence Labour might have done even better. That certainly was not Lenihan's opinion; and it has to be questionable in view of Labour's record result, 19 per cent of the first-preference vote as against 25 per cent for Fine Gael and a record low 39 per cent for Fianna Fail. The attacks were also unhelpful because they angered Labour and could have made the post-election negotiations even more difficult than they proved. Lenihan and Ahern were well aware of that, but the contacts continued after the election when, as Mansergh says, Fianna Fail had to play it cannily:

> The feeling within the party was that it was essential to lie low and not look as if we were trying to cling on to power. Albert Reynolds was alive to the possibility of doing a deal with Labour even though they might not be his natural partners. I remember reckoning at the time that we had about a one in ten chance of coming back into office. I had been involved in tentative offers to Labour in June 1981 and November 1982. Fianna Fail lost office both times. Haughey made a speech saying how much the parties had in common. We never understood at that time why Labour so underplayed their negotiating options. Based on that experience, I would not have had enormous confidence that the 1992 exercise was going to turn out any different.
>
> Bertie Ahern came into my office and commissioned a document which contained a lot of Labour policy. It was designed to show the compatibility of the two parties. The introduction was particularly important. It talked about partnership and said that it would be much more on a basis of equality than any previous coalition. It gave me great satisfaction to send it back half an hour after we received the Labour-DL document. We had got an unofficial version several hours before.

Bertie was the guiding spirit, but responsibility for the drafting was left very heavily to me. Albert Reynolds may have made one or two changes. I remember Padraig Flynn being distinctly quizzical about a sentence about us being a different sort of government.

Our document was delivered to Labour in the late afternoon. That night we went out in a large delegation to the Edinburgh summit [when Reynolds claimed that we would get £8 billion, not £6 billion, in European funding, his "dowry" for Labour]. I'm sure the result in Edinburgh helped. I was still there when Albert met Dick Spring two or three days later. Labour were interested in our paper, but worried about whether Albert could deliver Fianna Fáil. A certain number of people, mainly associated with the Haughey faction, wanted to go into opposition. It would then have been easier to get rid of the current leadership.

Not only did the prospect of a coalition with Labour delight Lenihan, nothing could have been less to his taste than another leadership coup. He was as loyal to Reynolds, their very different characters and backgrounds notwithstanding, as to all other leaders of the party, and he eagerly, if quietly, "sold" the new departure to the party. It was not an easy task. The "community of interest" argument pushed by Lenihan and Ahern did not appeal to substantial sections among the backbenchers and grassroots. These disliked another and presumably final abandonment of the "core value" of single-party government, or resented a much greater dilution of power than that involved in the previous alliance with the Progressive Democrats, or (as Mansergh saw) would not have regretted a change of leadership, or had less enthusiasm than Lenihan and Ahern for the formation of a centre-left government, or were influenced by some combination of the four. Large concessions had to be made to Labour in view of their Dail strength, including an exceptional number of cabinet and junior ministries and a poorly defined special role for Spring as Tanaiste. Lenihan was very much alive to dissent, and had to listen to at least one leadership hopeful hinting broadly at his intentions. While he listened, the Lenihan smile remained on his lips while his eyes narrowed: the leadership hopeful missed these warning signs.

Besides reconciling his party to the alliance behind the scenes, Lenihan stoutly defended the proposition in public. In what he called his favourite interview, with Mark O'Connell in the *Sunday Business Post* on 20 December 1992, he derided the idea of an overall majority: "Times have changed. It's just not on any more." He said that Fianna Fail had been pulled to the right by their experiences in government since 1977, and particularly by the coalition with the Progressive Democrats, and sought a return to the party's roots:

> Fianna Fail was originally founded in 1926 as a social-republican party. During the 1930s it had a strong social democratic base as well as a republican base. That was its great strength at that time. That's why it achieved so much success. It was the real Labour party in the country.

As to the internal opponents of coalition, he called their proposal to go into opposition outrageous:

> It's so simplistic it baffles me. I can't understand how the major political party in the country would voluntarily go into opposition. Politics is all about achieving power to do good. You can do nothing in opposition in the way of benefit to the community . . .
> It's sometimes a role for political parties to go into opposition, but it's a role which should only be thrust on a party by political events. A party shouldn't voluntarily seek that role. That is, in effect, reneging on all the public responsibilities of a major political party. It is to say to the people we don't want to be in government. I don't understand the politics of it.

In the same interview, he complained of the Fianna Fail attacks on Labour towards the end of the election campaign:

> I deplored the Saatchi and Saatchi anti-Labour themes adopted. They smacked of the reds-under-the-bed syndrome. I thought they were totally counter-productive and, in fact, I think they lost us seats.

Had he had an opportunity of observing the Labour special conference which endorsed the deal, he would have been better pleased. The conference overwhelmingly backed Spring's proposal for a coalition with Fianna Fail. Those in favour largely represented the small-town upper working class, the people whom Lenihan considered the backbone of the country and whose support he most valued. The left-wingers, mostly Dublin middle class by origin, conferred in corners and decided to "let the hare sit."

*

Before the new government took office, Reynolds briefed Spring (about to become Foreign Minister as well as Tanaiste) on the uniquely delicate and dangerous negotiations which would become known as the Northern Ireland peace process. Spring was shocked to learn that they involved talks with Sinn Fein, meaning talks with the IRA at one remove, or no remove at all if one regarded the two organisations as one.

At government level, the process had begun in Haughey's last months. Working in conjunction with John Hume, he initiated talks with Sinn Fein, using a Belfast priest as an intermediary (subsequent intermediaries would include a Presbyterian minister who has close contacts with loyalist paramilitary groups). In December 1991 he informed the British Prime Minister, John Major. Would Reynolds, on taking over, "run with it"? Indeed he would, intensifying the contacts, pushing harder than Haughey had felt able to do, and ultimately achieving historic successes. His detractors have often questioned his interest and grasp of the subject: they are entirely wrong. He had a deep interest and, in this as in other areas, a formidable grasp of detail. He thought violence not only abhorrent but stupid and wasteful — "killing," wrote Duignan, "he sees as the ultimate stupidity" — and felt that politicians in the past had approached the question back to front. It was pointless, in his view, to hold talks that dragged on for years while violence continued: the thing to do was to stop the death and destruction, and let the Northern parties wrangle indefinitely thereafter if they pleased. In addition, his business experience had convinced him that one could make a deal with anyone, and that he personally could make deals both with the British and with Sinn Fein, offering the former (and the Irish people) peace and the latter a British declaration accepting the right of Irish self-determination on an all-Ireland basis.

The peace process, however, may be said to have started much earlier, when Hume and other SDLP leaders held inconclusive talks with the IRA in 1988. The talks were followed by a conference at Duisburg in Germany, organised by a local lawyer who claimed to be in touch with Chancellor Helmut Kohl. The Germans had a special interest in stopping IRA attacks on British military installations on their territory. One of the participants in the conference, while not himself a member of Sinn Fein or the IRA, knew their mindset, and it may have been this person who pointed the organiser in the direction of Lenihan, who also knew the "Provo mind". Lenihan became the principal, though by no means the only, point of contact between the Dublin government and the various elements in the Provisional movement. Further, he made contact through another intermediary with the Loyalist paramilitaries and made some progress towards gaining their confidence. Right up to the time of his final illness, he was deeply involved in the peace process and working hard to break impasses.

And there were plenty of impasses, not least because so many people were working on "parallel tracks". Hume was engaged in separate talks with the Sinn Fein leader, Gerry Adams, with a view to producing a joint document. Mischievous accounts of these proceedings have asserted that the objective was to create a "pan-nationalist front", a phrase first used by Sinn Fein but seized on by unionists and unionist sympathisers as evidence of a nationalist conspiracy. In fact Hume was trying to devise a subtle form of words which would incorporate both self-determination and the principle of consent; in other words, very much the same thing Reynolds was trying to achieve in his talks with Major, which he now pressed with ferocious determination.

Reynolds triumphed with the Downing Street Declaration of December 1993, in which the British government acknowledged the Irish right of self-determination and the Irish government (as at Sunningdale and Hillsborough) the principle of consent, to be expressed by endorsement of a negotiated settlement by simultaneous referendums in the North and the Republic. But at the end of the summer a crisis had occurred when Hume announced that he had come to an agreement with Adams. Frantic efforts were made by Dublin officials to obtain a copy of the joint document, whose very existence some in the establishment doubted. (The truth appears to be that a joint paper had existed for some considerable time, but that no new document had lately been drawn up.) Hume left the country on a trip to the United States, leaving the government in a quandary. Reynolds and his confidants knew that the Hume-Adams agreement was almost identical to what Reynolds was trying to achieve with Major, but the last thing they wanted was a document with Sinn Fein "fingerprints" on it, arousing intense suspicion in Northern Ireland and in the British Conservative Party, and jeopardising Reynolds's complex and often stormy negotiations with Major. This, however, was poorly understood by the public and particularly by Fianna Fail activists, who saw the government as at best treating Hume coolly and at worst repudiating him.

It was in this atmosphere that the party ard-fheis was held. Contrary to reports at the time, Reynolds did not change a line of a carefully crafted speech in response to the delegates' anxieties. At the same time, he had to face down the "pro-life" lobby, who were demanding another abortion referendum. There were therefore two foci of dissent instead of one.

The ever-loyal Lenihan courageously entered the breach. He chaired a meeting packed with pro-lifers, at which a motion proposed by them was moved and voted on. Lenihan had vast experience of turbulent meetings. Years before, chairing one from which the national executive for some reason wanted a unanimous vote, he let the proceedings go on for hours until he finally settled the issue by the device of seeking a majority vote to decide that they would have a unanimous vote! This time he had to resort to blunter methods. There was clearly a majority for the motion, but he simply declared it lost on a show of hands and then proceeded, with difficulty, to try to leave the hall. He was confronted by a furious Hanafin, whose protests Lenihan shrugged off: he saw what he had done as just one more service to the party. Happily, they would be reconciled before his death.

*

Sinn Fein and the IRA were slow to respond to the Downing Street Declaration. The campaign of violence continued, albeit at a low level. Reynolds grew impatient. And he had another crisis on his hands, this time of his own making.

Relations between the Taoiseach and the Tanaiste had worsened to the point where, on 29 June, Reynolds told Duignan that he foresaw the beginning of the end for his government. He was not alone. What would the long-awaited report by Mr Justice Liam Hamilton on the Beef Tribunal say of his conduct as Minister for Industry and Commerce? On 1 July, before the Dail adjourned for the summer recess, Spring said that under no circumstances would Labour hide or walk away from the verdict. On 3 July the *Sunday Business Post* carried a report by Emily O'Reilly under the headline "Spring Ready to Leave Coalition if Tribunal Report Censures Reynolds". To the Taoiseach's anger, the story had obviously come from a source close to Spring. On 26 July Spring telephoned Duignan and told him to be careful how he briefed political correspondents on the findings of the tribunal report. Reynolds received a copy of the report on the evening of 29 July. Duignan was summoned to the

Taoiseach's office, where he found a team of top lawyers and civil servants examining the document:

> After about a half hour, a quick check around the table produced a consensus that the findings, apart from criticising certain of the Taoiseach's decisions, did not question his motives or impugn his integrity.
>
> Someone said: "You're in the clear." "Are you sure?" asked Reynolds. "Yes," came the reply. "OK," said Reynolds. "I've taken this shit long enough. I'm not going to take another minute of it. Tell the pol corrs I'm vindicated, Diggy." I hesitated: "Taoiseach, Labour are going to go spare. They've warned me against this." Teahon [Paddy Teahon, Secretary of the Taoiseach's Department] rowed in: "You don't need to do this, Taoiseach. You don't need to have a row with Labour. You've won." Reynolds said: "They've told the dogs in the street they would bring me down on this if they didn't like the judgement. Now I've been cleared, and I don't need their permission to tell it as it is."
>
> Then, as I made no move, he glanced at his watch and said: "You're already losing the country editions of the papers, Diggy. Now, if you don't do it, I'll bloody well do it myself." "OK. But I still believe we should tell Labour what we're doing. Let me at least ring John Foley [Duignan's Labour counterpart]." "I don't care who you ring. Just do it."

Duignan telephoned Foley and found that he already suspected that Reynolds would unilaterally release the sections of the report which he saw as vindicating his actions. He urged Duignan to prevent this if he could, and said that a deal had been made at cabinet that it would not be done. Reynolds has always denied that such a deal was made.

Duignan jotted down selective quotations, favourable to Reynolds, from the report, and began to telephone the newspapers from his own office. At this point Spring's adviser Fergus Finlay burst into the room. "I'm confronted by this Old

Testament whirlwind of wrath, biblical beard quivering, like Moses about to smite the idolators of the Golden Calf." Finlay told Duignan: "This could mean the end of the government."

It did not — at least not yet. The government would not survive the next crisis. It might not have survived this crisis, had not Reynolds come up with a triumph that trumped the Downing Street Declaration. By the time the Dail interrupted the summer recess for a special debate on the Hamilton report, the Taoiseach was a hero. He had cajoled Sinn Fein and the IRA, he had bullied them, he had not shrunk from the fiercest confrontation. He had given them a deadline for declaring a complete and, he hoped, permanent ceasefire, and threatened that if they did not meet it he would attempt to negotiate a settlement with Major which ignored and excluded them. They gave in. The ceasefire came into operation at midnight on 31 August-1 September 1994. Nobody would bring him down at a time like this.

Part of the credit for the ceasefire goes to Brian Lenihan, and his role should not be forgotten. One of the most acute observers in Northern Ireland, David McKittrick of the London *Independent*, wrote to him: "Like you, I hope and believe the peace is genuine and will be permanent. I watched your activities with interest during the peace process — noting on a number of occasions how well you gave valuable cover at some sensitive and delicate points." And Austin Currie, frequently so critical of Dublin politicians' attitudes, makes an exception for Lenihan: "When you talk to politicians here about Northern Ireland, it's not pragmatism that comes across, it's hypocrisy. That was not the case with Brian."

During the period immediately preceding the ceasefire Lenihan had maintained daily, sometimes hourly, contact with Reynolds and with the paramilitaries. When ill, he pressed his son Conor into service to pass on messages. The operation gave him immense satisfaction, both because of its own enormous value and because it showed that he could render an important public service without being a member of the government. Indeed, his lack of office was an advantage. He could hold secret meetings in which it could have been impossible for a minister to participate for fear of disclosure.

*

Lenihan was far too optimistic about the government's survival prospects. Spring might say, and did say, that trust had been damaged but could be restored. The reality was that trust between him and Reynolds no longer existed, and that another clash was in the making within two weeks of the Taoiseach's greatest success.

On 14 September Labour threatened to block the appointment as Chief Justice of Mr Justice Liam Hamilton unless they got a guarantee that the attorney-general, Harry Whelehan, would not succeed Hamilton as President of the High Court. They never spelt out their objections to Whelehan, saying only that he was "too conservative", but they evidently went back to his role in the "X" case.

Duignan professes himself puzzled as to why Reynolds was so determined to appoint Whelehan. Labour backbenchers were equally puzzled as to why Spring was so determined to prevent the appointment. The attitudes of both Reynolds and Spring baffled other close observers of politics, and still do. After a confrontation on the subject between Reynolds and Spring on 5 October, several Labour backbenchers revolted and demanded that their leader should back down, or at least find a face-saving compromise. The compromise was found at a midnight meeting at Baldonnel military airport, at which Reynolds agreed not to appoint Whelehan until the government approved a major reform of the courts. Whether Spring agreed to the appointment in return for the courts reform measure has been disputed, but undoubtedly Reynolds believed that he had and that the crisis was settled.

On 24 October it emerged that an application for the extradition to Northern Ireland of a priest, Brendan Smyth, had languished for seven months in the attorney-general's office before Smyth voluntarily went back to Northern Ireland and surrendered himself to the authorities there. Smyth, as would subsequently be disclosed at his trials in the North and the Republic, had spent most of a lifetime engaged in child sex abuse of an appalling kind. He served prison sentences in both jurisdictions, and died in prison in 1997.

Reynolds not only defended Whelehan, but went ahead with his appointment as President of the High Court. The argument that the attorney-general's office was faultless in the matter of the delay in the extradition rested chiefly on the assertion that the Smyth case, involving a lengthy "lapse of time", was unique and required deep consideration. But a comparable case, that of one John Duggan, was then discovered. Wild conspiracy theories flourished. Labour withdrew from the government, went in again for a matter of hours, then out again. Whelehan resigned as President of the High Court. Labour went after another head, that of Reynolds. He resigned as Taoiseach and Fianna Fail leader, and Ahern was unanimously elected leader in his place. He was within twenty-four hours of becoming Taoiseach when a story by Geraldine Kennedy in the *Irish Times* gave a different version of the timing of events in the crisis from that previously accepted. It was held by Labour somehow to inculpate Ahern, who afterwards said that he would never understand what had happened until the day of his death.

The plain fact of the matter was that everybody panicked. Labour were very far from blameless in this regard, but the most remarkable feature of the crisis was the headless-chicken reaction of the Fianna Fail ministers, graphically described by Eoghan Fitzsimons, the attorney-general who briefly replaced Whelehan, in evidence to a parliamentary committee which investigated the fall of the government — as usual, inconclusively. Lenihan for once was unforgiving. "Imagine," he said, "our people went to the committee and said they didn't know what they were doing in government." Reynolds was accused of misleading the Dail, but it is reasonable to say that this was a case of utter confusion, not of deliberately misleading the Dail. In a conversation with the present writer, he rejected the phrase "monumental cockup" in favour of simple "cockup"; and in another, similar conversation at Christmas 1994, Ahern said that "we made terrible blunders." Ahern came out of the fiasco with considerable if battered dignity, comparable to that of Currie after the 1990 presidential election.

In addition to the grotesque mishandling of events, Fianna Fail had taken too little notice of a point made by John Bruton a few months earlier. Labour's proposal of a Fine Gael-Labour-Democratic Left coalition after the 1992 general had suffered from the gross defect that the three parties together would not have commanded a Dail majority. But in the interim, Fine Gael and DL by-election victories had changed the parliamentary arithmetic. Bruton noted that not only did a credible alternative exist in 1994, but that it could come into being without any need for a general election.

A sardonic confidant of Spring had told his colleagues during the crisis: "Courage, comrades! You have nothing to lose but your mobiles." Now, chivvied about the difficulties of the alternative, the same man said there was never any doubt that a government would be formed before Christmas. "It would have been like stuffing Santa Claus back up the chimney."

Duignan, too, permitted himself a sardonic comment. In his diary entry for 7 December he wrote of Spring's acceptance of office in a Fine Gael-Labour-Democratic Left coalition under Bruton, with no nonsense about a rotating premiership: "He has only a small price to pay — knocking on that office door every morning, being told to come in, and then having to say to John: 'Good morning, Taoiseach.'"

Seventeen

The wheel of fortune has finally stopped turning.
SEAN DUIGNAN, One Spin on The Merry-Go-Round

Lenihan saw the storm coming, but tried to persuade himself and others that it would blow over. Days before the fall of the Reynolds government, he insisted that the crisis would be resolved and that the government was in for the long haul. One of his reasons was a refusal to believe that Labour would endanger the peace process by bringing down Reynolds.

On the morning of 14 November, an emergency meeting of Fianna Fail ministers heard Labour's conditions for the survival of the coalition. The same morning, Sinn Fein representatives met the Taoiseach, and elements in the republican movement sent stark messages to the government, via Lenihan, warning of what might follow if the coalition fell. These messages, described as "hair-raising" by one of the government advisers, were to the effect that the event would be regarded as a betrayal by hard-liners in Sinn Fein and the IRA; that the movement could split, and that leading individuals might be shot. Since Lenihan had his own "maverick" sources in the movement — a fact well known to the Sinn Fein leadership — it is a virtual certainty that some of the messages came from these. Both he and Reynolds took the warnings very seriously.

Clearly the fate of the peace process weighed with Spring when, two days later, he agreed to continue the government. This agreement, however, lasted less than an hour. He changed his mind after a mysterious telephone conversation — or conversations — in which he apparently received information concerning the existence of the second case in which the "lapse of time" consideration applied, which he felt undermmined the Taoiseach's defence of the attorney-general's office.

217

Ahern's subsequent failure to make a coalition deal with Spring was at least as traumatic for Lenihan as the fall of Reynolds. With himself out of the reckoning, he saw Ahern as the ideal person to lead a centre-left government, and Ahern's conciliatory approach as much more conducive to the smooth running of a coalition than the Reynolds I'm-the-boss-take-it-or-leave-it style. And he sorrowed more over Fianna Fail's loss of office than over the personal consequences which he suffered.

These included the loss of his chairmanship of the Oireachtas foreign affairs committee. That position was hardly comparable with the two great offices he had missed, the presidency and the premiership, but failing these it was almost the perfect job for him. He was a superb chairman, not only because of his unparalleled knowledge of foreign affairs but because of his style of chairmanship, learned from Lemass all those years earlier. For all his dislike of confrontation, he tolerated no nonsense and no waffle and did not flinch from shutting people up; in Michael Lanigan's words, "he cut through all the bullshit."

He continued, whenever his health permitted, to play an important role in the Forum for Peace and Reconciliation, set up by Reynolds as a device to get Sinn Fein into talks and to teach them constitutional politics. The enterprise was much more successful than has ever been acknowledged. Sinn Fein learned, as Fianna Fail had learned before them, that what Lenihan politely called "the classical republican position" had to be drastically modified. They learned that for mainstream nationalists, long gone was the simple demand for British withdrawal and a united Ireland, forgotten was the unitary state, a Northern settlement must be a very complicated business and it must be based on the principle of consent. Gently and subtly, Lenihan argued with them — and with Neil Blaney. He expressed sympathy with Blaney's position on Irish unity, but asked him how in practice did one bring it about; and he looked for a form of words which would assert the principle of consent while rejecting the phrase "unionist veto".

In his politics, Blaney remained intransigent to the end, but in his personal dealings he had mellowed. He knew that he was dying, and that reconciliation befits a dying man. One day during a break in the Forum proceedings he invited his old adversary, Sean Donlon, for a drink in a fashionable establishment close to Dublin Castle. When Donlon said he would like a glass of wine, Blaney ordered a bottle of Lynch Bages. He then confessed his involvement in the 1980 affair, about which of course Donlon had long known, and said that while he did not repent, he wanted it understood that it derived from no personal animus. For a man of honour, if often of poor judgement, it was a good way to go.

*

For Lenihan, this was a fruitful period in other ways too. Throughout most of 1995, as in the previous few years, he gave numerous interviews and wrote numerous newspaper articles, especially book reviews. These appeared in several publications, but he developed a special relationship with Bruce Arnold, literary editor of the *Irish Independent*, the same man whose telephone had been tapped and who had approached Lenihan thirty years earlier on the subject of censorship. He read the books at his usual lightning speed, and in discussing them he naturally drew on his own wide reading. One might suppose that he also dashed off the reviews at lightning speed, but Arnold says that was far from the case. They often went through two or three drafts before Lenihan was satisfied. Arnold compares him with Haughey, greatly to the latter's disfavour, and speaks of his admiration for Lenihan as a writer:

> Haughey's only knowledge of someone like Helmut Schmidt was how to make himself bigger. He glowed with self-importance. Brian Lenihan might be half drunk, but he stepped on to the world stage with penetrating analysis.
>
> I really valued him as a reviewer. He absorbed long books very quickly. We would often have lunch or

talk on the phone. I wrote some terrible things about
him and he never held it against me.

Unlike Blaney, he did not know that he was in the twilight of
his life, and he had determined to develop his writing style
(something virtually impossible during his ministerial career,
when he had to speak and write in officialese). Again unlike
Blaney, he did not need the prompting of approaching death to
move him towards reconciliation. The example of his
exceptional magnanimity most often cited is his statement that
Mary Robinson had made a better President than he could ever
have done. Much more remarkable is that he forgave Haughey
and even continued to regard him as a friend, an opinion
decidedly not shared by his family. In one sense Lenihan and
Haughey had never been close friends — they and their wives,
for example, did not socialise together, and Lenihan's visits to
Kinsealy were for political purposes — and as to their political
friendship, anyone might have thought that Haughey had
destroyed it once and for all in 1990. But Lenihan lunched with
him, and chewed over old times.

Other incidents towards the end of his life were similarly
characteristic. He and Ann went on holiday with Vinny Mahon
and his wife Bridie on a remote island. One fine day they sat on
the rocks and gazed at the Atlantic. But solitude is hard to find
in the remotest parts of Ireland. A shepherd came in view over
the hillside. He recognised Lenihan and began a conversation.
For the next two hours, Lenihan sat on his rock and listened to
the details of the shepherd's eighteen hospital operations. That
evening, he "left" a couple of pints for him in the local pub.

During his last summer, he and Ann, accompanied by Ray
Burke, visited the United Nations in New York. There he
spotted Giulio Andreotti, now in disgrace, sitting alone in a
corner. Lenihan went over and greeted him warmly.

In mid-September, he undertook a sentimental journey to
Roscommon. He and Ann had only got as far as Athlone when
he fell ill. It was not liver failure, or a drink-related condition,
but a blood clot. They took him, in terrible pain, to Portiuncula

Hospital in Ballinasloe and from there to the Mater. This time no medical skill could save him. He died on 1 November 1995, sixteen days short of his sixty-fifth birthday.

They brought his mortal remains from the hospital to the local church in Castleknock. The removal was delayed because crowds of mourners thronged the hospital grounds. At Castleknock, they were received with all due ceremony. Archbishop Desmond Connell of Dublin presided. So many people attended that hundreds were unable to enter the church. After the ceremony, the mourners crowded into Myo's pub. For hours on end, people kept leaving to join those in the church, still queueing to pay their respects to the family.

Then they took his coffin to Athlone and buried his remains near the Shannon. It was as he would have wished.

The mourning was deep, and wide, and genuine. Tributes flowed in from home and abroad. His every fine quality was wholeheartedly, and accurately, praised. The tributes were mixed with humour. In the Dail, Bertie Ahern said that "he was able to develop confusion to a very fine art." Too fine an art, sometimes, for his own good. The newspapers rose to the occasion. They might have concentrated on the bluff and bonhomie and bluster, on the Brianisms, on "no problem"; they did not. They recorded his personality, but they also recorded his achievements.

But this is Ireland, where we have our special forms of hypocrisy. There were those who falsely claimed friendship with him, and those who foolishly asserted that he had no enemies. Had he had no enemies, Emily O'Reilly acidly commented in the *Sunday Business Post*, we would have been taking his coffin out of Aras an Uachtarain.

At the by-election to fill his Dublin West seat, Brian Lenihan junior narrowly defeated the independent socialist candidate, Joe Higgins, with the help of Fine Gael transfers. His father would have appreciated the irony.

Professor Martin O'Donoghue had served with Lenihan senior in the Lynch cabinet of 1977-79. He shocked a dinner party in Dublin 4, where Lenihan's abilities were little understood, by saying that he was the best-read man in the cabinet (he might well have said, in the Dail). He observed the new generation with interest, remarking of Brian junior that "he has his father's intelligence but unlike his father he doesn't conceal it." He was far from the only person to spot the young Lenihan's ability. Many immediately identified him as a suitable future Taoiseach, and were dismayed when Bertie Ahern did not include him in the coalition government which he formed with the Progressive Democrats after the 1997 general election. They found it incomprehensible that neither he nor Eoin Ryan junior — whose father had worked closely with Lenihan senior under Lemass, and whose grandfather had been a founding member of the Fianna Fail Party — was appointed to the cabinet, or even to a junior ministry. Ahern, however, gave Lenihan some little compensation by appointing him chairman of the All-Party Oireachtas Committee on the Constitution.

If, unlike his father, Brian junior did not conceal his intelligence, he resembled him strikingly in many ways; and two aspects of the resemblance were demonstrated during and after the referendum on the Good Friday Agreement of 1998. This agreement brought to a culmination the noble work of many, including Brian senior, and achieved the long-held ambition of John Hume for simultaneous referendums North and South on a Northern settlement. In the Republic, the voters overwhelmingly endorsed the changes in Articles 2 and 3 of the constitution proposed in the agreement. The Fianna Fail grassroots took some persuading to abandon the words "written in stone" by de Valera, and Lenihan senior would have been proud of the part his son played in that persuasion.

But Lenihan junior showed himself even more uncannily like his father when he participated, along with the present writer, on a radio panel which discussed the referendum returns and their implications. There had been severe criticism of the Ahern government's decision to hold a referendum on the Amsterdam Treaty on the same day. The treaty was endorsed by a relatively small majority. Brian theorised that voters always like to say no if they have the chance; that they had exercised that option in

relation to the treaty; and that the vote in favour of the Good
Friday Agreement, close to 95 per cent, was probably higher
than it would have been had they not been able to indulge
themselves in the matter of the Amsterdam Treaty. The theory
may have some validity, but it would take a Lenihan to
adumbrate it. I turned to its begetter and said, "Brian, you're
your father's son all right."

At the 1997 general election, Brian's brother Conor had been
elected as one of the Fianna Fail deputies for Dublin South West,
a constituency shared with Mary Harney, Des O'Malley's
successor as leader of the Progressive Democrats. He did not
conceal his intention to make life uncomfortable for her and her
party. He went so far as to make a statement calling on Ahern
not to enter into a coalition with the PDs.

Later in the year, Professor Mary McAleese regained Aras an
Uachtarain for Fianna Fail after the resignation of Mary
Robinson and after the Fianna Fail parliamentary party chose
her as their presidential candidate in preference to Albert
Reynolds. She had been a member of the Catholic church
delegation to the New Ireland Forum. Brian Lenihan was her
presidential election agent.

Earlier, events in the autumn and early winter of 1996 had
brought a disgusting coda to the fatal Haughey–Lenihan
relationship, which infuriated the Lenihan family.

Sam Smyth disclosed in the *Irish Independent* that a highly
unorthodox business relationship had existed between a Fine
Gael minister, Michael Lowry, and Ben Dunne, who had been
ousted from control of Dunnes Stores. Cliff Taylor in the *Irish
Times* followed up the story by disclosing that Dunne had given
over a million pounds to a former senior figure in Fianna Fail,
unnamed but generally and correctly assumed to be Haughey.
Both stories evidently had their origin in aborted litigation
between Dunne and members of his family.

When the Taylor story broke, intimates of Haughey put it
about that the money had gone to pay for Lenihan's liver
transplant. That was utterly stupid, since it amounted to an
admission that Haughey had received the money. It was also

totally untrue. The operation, and associated treatments in Dublin and in the United States, cost a total of about £200,000, paid in part by the Voluntary Health Insurance Board and in part by a subscription raised from friends of Lenihan and his party. The prime mover of the subscription was Peter Hanley, a businessman in Lenihan's former Roscommon constituency and a personal friend.

The 1997 McCracken inquiry established that Dunne had given Haughey £1.3 million. Haughey initially denied having received the money and was slow to co-operate with the tribunal, even delaying a long time before appointing a legal team to represent him. He eventually went. to Dublin Castle and gave evidence which the inquiry report described as "unbelievable". He attracted derision when he denied that he had a lavish lifestyle; it was estimated that his outgoings amounted to almost a quarter of a million a year over and above what he received from the state in salary and pensions. Where did the rest of his money come from? In September 1997 the Dail agreed to set up a second tribunal to inquire into other donations that he and Lowry might have received.

In July 1998, Haughey appeared in the Dublin District Court, charged with obstructing the McCracken tribunal.

When Ahern formed his government, he appointed Ray Burke Foreign Minister. Burke held the job for only a few months before resigning in the midst of a controversy over business donations he had received in 1989. He also resigned his Dublin North Dail seat, which Fianna Fail lost to Labour at the ensuing by-election.

Eighteen

We are in the process of creating what deserves to be called the idiot culture. Not an idiot sub-culture, which every society has bubbling beneath the surface and which can provide harmless fun; but the culture itself. For the first time, the weird and the stupid and the coarse are becoming our cultural norm, even our cultural ideal.
CARL BERNSTEIN

Brian Lenihan was a delightful man, kind, generous, warm-hearted, amusing, intelligent, the best of company, idolised by his family, and brave beyond words in the face of adversity, in the face of death. This is first and last a political biography, and it is his political career, his achievements and failures, that must now be summed up. But they reflected his good qualities; and they reflected his faults, the other side of that coin. His sheer niceness went hand in hand with his softness, his pliancy, his hatred of confrontation, his difficulty in bringing himself to say no.

He would have made a terrific President. What kind of Taoiseach might he have made? Would his shrinking from confrontation, the fault so often emphasised, have prevented him from making tough decisions? Not necessarily. Many "grow into" the highest office, and Lenihan might well have been one, especially if he had had the opportunity to lead a Fianna Fail–Labour coalition. He could be decisive: as Sylvester Barrett says, "he could sum up a situation on the spot and make a decision." We have seen his admiration for Harry Truman, expressed precisely because Truman did not flinch from tough decisions. We have seen Michael Lanigan's praise for him as a brisk, Lemass-type chairman, and we have seen his willingness to dump John Silkin when Irish interests prevailed over "a temporary little arrangement" with the British on fisheries. One of those who knew him best says that "there was a cold, calculating political mind behind the mask all the time. You don't survive forty years without one." In short, Lenihan had his harder side. He could not have survived so long, or achieved so much, without it.

His relationship with Haughey is constantly condemned for the damage it did to his reputation, and he must be faulted for placing his trust in a man who, in a crisis, betrayed him. To be brutal, he should have repudiated Haughey in 1970, but that would have been entirely out of character: unlike Haughey, Lenihan would not betray a friend; instead, he urged Haughey to stay in Fianna Fail at whatever cost, and not consign himself to the political wilderness like Neil Blaney. And his subsequent misplaced loyalty to Haughey was more than personal, it was given in the interest of party unity.

There is little point in conjecture as to what might have happened if Lenihan had made greater efforts for a rapprochement with Labour in 1981 or 1982. Part of the price of a deal would assuredly have been Haughey's departure, and Haughey would not have gone quietly as he finally did in 1992. Nor is it likely that O'Malley would have abandoned his own leadership ambitions. Conceivably Fianna Fail might have split into two or even three separate factions, an eventuality that nobody would have deplored more than Lenihan, who gave so much of his life to trying to keep the party together.

There never was a really suitable time for Lenihan to take the leadership. Had he been more vigorous, and had he been in a position to forestall the rise of the Country and Western Alliance, he would have been a made-to-measure leader for a Fianna Fail–Labour coalition, the role he vainly hoped Ahern would fill in 1994. The temptation to look at "ifs and buts", something in which he himself loved to indulge, is irresistible. Had we joined the EEC in 1963, and had Lenihan become minister for Europe, not only his career but his reputation would have been vastly different. There is another possibility: that Lynch might have appointed him Foreign Minister, as Lenihan expected, in 1969. Can one detect the hand of de Valera in vetoing any such appointment, as the Lenihan family suspected? We know from Lemass's own mouth that de Valera did attempt to interfere in matters of state after his departure for the Phoenix Park; and we know from other sources that although Lemass speedily put paid to interference with himself personally, de Valera certainly had some involvement in political affairs at least as late as 1969. Lenihan's difficulty in either event would have been to do a job involving so much absence from the country while representing so demanding and unforgiving a constituency as Roscommon. No wonder he campaigned so assiduously for the abolition of the Irish system of proportional representation.

So much for speculation. Let us look at his concrete achievements.

Early in his career, he reformed the censorship laws and completed Haughey's work on the Succession Bill. Towards the end of it, he quelled the discontent in the defence forces. These were no petty successes. But his reputation must rest chiefly on his record as Foreign Minister, and here it rests on the firmest possible ground.

He was unquestionably one of the best foreign ministers ever to serve this state. He brought to the job his personal qualities, his depth and breadth of reading, his subtlety of mind, his pragmatism on the Northern question, and his exceptional grasp of European and world affairs. In his assessments and forecasts he frequently leaned too far to the optimistic side. He believed, for example, that Mikhail Gorbachev could reform the Soviet system from within; and, after the fall of communism, that liberal democracy could quickly replace it. These beliefs were founded to a great extent on the proposition that a large educated class had grown up in the Soviet Union and would insist on Western-style democracy and civil liberties: he failed to see that the rot had gone too deep. But both in the broad thrust of his thinking and his policies, and in his detailed analysis of subjects to which he set his mind, he rarely went wrong. He lived to see the triumph of the cause of German reunification, which he had unswervingly supported, and he could, had he wished, claimed to have chipped away some small part of the Berlin Wall.

Lenihan, who seldom engaged in harsh criticism of anyone, vehemently attacked Margaret Thatcher on this point. He was furious with her for opposing German reunification and for trying to enlist the French government on her side. Had the French been foolish enough to ally themselves with her, they would have broken the Franco-German axis on which so much of the peace of Europe has rested for half a century. His dislike of Thatcher was intense and extended to mockery; he loved to tell the story of how Helmut Schmidt when German Chancellor, tired of listening to her tirades at meetings, would ostentatiously open and read a newspaper. In his *Irish Press* review of the Thatcher autobiography, mentioned above, he brought his biggest verbal guns to bear on her, while giving a summary of East-West relations before and immediately after the end of the Cold War:

> From the Gorbachev-Reagan meeting at Reykjavik in 1985 to the Nato summit meeting in May 1989 it was growingly evident that Gorbachev wanted to reduce every category of weapons expenditure. Lady Thatcher refused to see the enormous shift of ground that was taking place, and in the months before the collapse of communism became isolated as the last of the Cold War warriors advocating increased expenditure on the modernisation of short-range nuclear weapons for use against the Warsaw Pact countries.
>
> However, Bush and [James] Baker with Kohl and Genscher refused to go down that road, and it marked the end of the special relationship between the US and Britain. From now on Germany became the major European player in the American scheme of things, and the Franco-German axis was cemented as the centrepiece of the European Community . . .
>
> Alone now in 1990, and hysterically opposed to a united Germany, she dreams up the craziest idea to

emanate from this book. She seeks to draw Mitterrand into joint diplomatic and military talks "to check the German juggernaut". She proposed in effect an Anglo-French alliance against Germany, which would effectively scupper the European Community. Mitterrand of course refused to abandon the Franco-German axis of friendship, which she describes in her book as a mistaken decision.

He was equally critical of US policy during the Cold War. In a review of a biography of Allen Dulles in the *Irish Independent* in March 1995, he praised the Marshall Plan and the American success in containing communism in Europe, but continued:

> Under the Eisenhower presidency, from 1953 to 1961, the Dulles brothers were hugely influential in the administration, with John Foster as Secretary of State and Allen as Director of Intelligence. This was the time when John Foster Dulles, mistakenly in my view, extended American foreign policy from the containment of the Soviet Union to one of interference in the affairs of countries throughout the world, in order to frustrate or prevent the governance of these countries by parties alleged to be communist or anti-American. His brother Allen simultaneously extended the intelligence-gathering functions of the CIA to the area of covert actions, in the form of clandestine operations to assist friendly parties in subversion, revolt, suppression, and assassination. Guatemala, Iran and Indonesia were just a few of the countries infiltrated by CIA agents in the 1950s. The result was support for very dubious dictators particularly in Central and South America. These policies finally led to the Bay of Pigs fiasco in Cuba, and to the tragedy of Vietnam. The legitimate postwar policy of containment had degenerated into international criminality.

On Northern Ireland, Lenihan unblushingly engaged in traditional Fianna Fail rhetoric but in office behaved in a manner both subtle and pragmatic, pursuing policies virtually indistinguishable from those of Garret FitzGerald and Peter Barry. His pragmatism had made itself visible back in the early sixties, when he advised Austin Currie to apply for a job with Fianna Fail and learn about real politics. He was always on the alert for new departures, and open to ideas like a new Anglo-Irish relationship, exemplified by his interest in the proposition that we might rejoin the Commonwealth. Whatever policies might be forced on Lynch, or incontinently adopted by Haughey, he knew that the Sunningdale and Hillsborough agreements were steps on the right road and that acceptance of the principle of consent was inevitable. His relationship with Sinn Fein, meanwhile, was curious. Currie noted at the Forum for Peace and Reconciliation that some of the Sinn Fein leaders appeared suspicious of him. That may well have derived from their knowledge that he was in touch with "maverick" elements in their movement. They may well have known also that during the two years 1992 to 1994 he was engaged in delicate and secret contacts with Loyalists as well as the IRA. Contact with the "hard men" on both sides is essential, and throughout the entire course of the Northern conflict there has never been a time when the Irish and British governments have not maintained contact with them at some level. Lenihan regarded bleats about not talking to terrorists as so much humbug.

In the Middle East, he considered that sooner or later the Arab nation would come back into its place in the sun. There and everywhere, he insisted that world peace, human rights and economic progress must have as their foundation the rule of law. He constantly referred to the UN and European human rights declarations, and to the need for the observance and development of international law.

He never had any sympathy with communism, but his rejoicing at the collapse of the Soviet Union and the fall of the communist regimes in Eastern Europe was not unalloyed. These events were not followed by serious debate on the future of socialism (or indeed of capitalism) and he saw the new triumphalism and complacency as contributing to "dumbing down", as it has since come to be known: to the "idiot culture" and what he frequently called "modern kitsch and non-thought". He deplored modish nonsense about the definitive triumph of capitalism and "the end of history". He knew that the game he loved ("the only game for grown-ups", according to the American writer Robert A. Heinlein) was not played out and would never be concluded while there were men and women to differ in their opinions. To back up his views, he cited sources as varied as Milan Kundera and John Kelly. In a *Sunday Tribune* review of Kelly's speeches, published posthumously under the title *Belling The Cats*, he wrote that he and Kelly differed on many things, but they were at one in their hatred of "modern kitsch and non-thought":

> [Kelly] rejected the kitsch of modern society comprising the stupidity of received ideas processed by computers and the mass media. He dealt in the common sense of facts based on the decency of human values, and would never conform to the non-thought of received ideas or conventional wisdom ... He always questioned the banality of modernity.

Had Lenihan lived, he would have made the perfect elder statesman, disposing of his vast knowledge and experience in the search for the compromise and the centre. He would of course have brought to the role, in addition, his emollient qualities and taught younger people the value of resilience, seen in him at its best after the catastrophe of 1990 but visible much earlier — as in his advice, recalled by Haughey, to the Lynch cabinet after their comprehensive defeat in the 1968 PR referendum:

> Brian said, "we must bend like the reed. Bend, and then spring right back up again." After the Gaullists had an electoral setback he told them that they must regroup and go on "to a new plateau of expectations". The French loved it.

Although he did not have the time to grow fully into the role of elder statesman, he spent much of the period between 1990 and his death — in addition to his work in the Forum for Peace and Reconciliation and as chairman of the foreign affairs committee — giving his blessing to good causes. He supported with characteristic enthusiasm the project, successfully completed by Philip Hannon, to put the Fianna Fail archives in order. He chaired the Irish Council of the European Movement. He helped Brendan Halligan's Institute of European Affairs in many ways, visiting the premises at least once a month and launching one of the many books published by the institute, speaking wittily and knowledgeably without a single note.

Whenever he was well enough, he turned up at any function attended by President Mary Robinson in his constituency. *Noblesse oblige.*

In his later, or not so late, years he put aside much of the discretion he maintained while in office and spoke with greater freedom, especially in surroundings in which he felt himself comfortable. In the autumn of 1986 he made a wonderfully cynical and knockabout speech at a convivial function organised by the Association of European Journalists. He had always been fascinated by journalism, but had not hesitated to chide his friends in the trade, privately, for their habit of getting things wrong. On the 1986 occasion he threw discretion to the winds and elaborated, hilariously and at length, on the faults of the media. So far from taking offence, his audience joined him and laughed at themselves. Regrettably, numerous inquiries among those who attended have failed to uncover a tape of the speech.

The journalists laughed all the more heartily because they knew Lenihan's ability, so unusual among politicians, to laugh at himself. The artist Wendy O'Shea was the author of a famous comic strip called "O'Brien". O'Brien may be described as the kind of Irishman who takes his laundry home to his mother every weekend. He bore a striking physical resemblance to Lenihan. When Wendy O'Shea collected her O'Brien strips in a book, Lenihan launched the book.

While in government or on the opposition front bench he had generally, as we have seen, and contrary to the public perception, been extremely discreet on important matters. Some of his indiscretions were calculated, some arose from over-enthusiasm, some were not indiscretions at all but party and nationalistic rhetoric. After 1990 he loosened the curbs on his tongue. As Paul Lenihan says, "he was no longer such a party man, but much more independent." Paul also notes that in his last years, when he had grown less impatient and more philosophical, he had one of the best spells of his political life. His mental faculties were as sharp as ever, possibly sharper than ever since he no longer had to engage in confusion or in the "blather" for which John Kelly had criticised him.

He was quite well aware that many of the hopes of the "glad confident morning" of the sixties had not been realised. Along with economic prosperity had grown up the idiot culture and the greed-is-good culture condemned by himself, by John Kelly and by Carl Bernstein among others — and which would have been equally condemned by his father, who had made a good deal of money as a businessman but did not believe in inherited wealth. The education reforms in which he had played a notable part had brought higher education, in theory, within the reach of everyone, but had not created an egalitarian society. In 1993 he took note of a statement by the Provost of Trinity College that only 1.3 per cent of his students came from a semi-skilled or unskilled background. Lenihan called for "positive discrimination measures" to remedy what the Provost had called a "caste system".

That was an admission that one of the fundamental aims pursued by him and by all three of his predecessors in Education — P. J. Hillery, George Colley and Donogh O'Malley — had not been properly realised. Neither had another fundamental aim, development of the aptitudes of the individual pupil. Sean O'Connor had written:

> The concern for examination results overrides all else
> in many of our schools. Now that the prizes have been
> increased fourfold and that competition is no longer

between pupils but "against the clock", the hunger for examination results will be fiercer than ever, I fear. What is to happen to the non-examination subjects and the other activities that are characteristic of the good school? ... I do not see how, without help, a school will be able to hold out against the pressures.

In the decades that followed, when the "prizes" increased much more than fourfold, his gloomy prophecies were borne out, but towards the end of the century the "demographic dividend" began to ease the pressures he deplored.

As to Irish society more widely, Lenihan disliked the growth of class distinction and class consciousness. According to Michael Herbert, "Brian like Lemass never foresaw that society would develop as it has done. Not only Lemass — Dev, the lot — thought all the children would be cherished equally. We saw independence as an egalitarian enterprise. Pearse and Connolly would turn in their graves if they could witness the way we have developed. It's sad that this should happen after seventy-five years of freedom."

Lenihan joked about the chaos in the Balkans following the decline of the Ottoman empire and later the collapse of communism. He told Mike Burns that "we should dig a Black Pig's Dyke around the Balkans and keep the Turks out!" But his true opinion was more serious. He strongly favoured Nato intervention in Bosnia, believing military force necessary to uphold international law and preserve the peace of the continent. Earlier he had supported American intervention in Grenada. He always wanted disputes solved by conciliation, but recognised that a time comes when only force will serve. And at home, he revealed his harder side when he implicitly, and sometimes explicitly, rejected the simplistic fondness for an unreal neutrality widespread in his party. In an important article in the *Irish Times* in 1993, he wrote:

In response to events since 1989 Nato is undergoing a dramatic reorientation into an organisation with a broader range of political as well as military tasks. The communiqué issued after the Nato ministerial meeting in Athens on 10 June 1993 emphasised the co-operative relationship between the Atlantic Alliance and Eastern European countries, and its support for CSCE and United Nations peacemaking and peacekeeping activities. It focuses on the military backup which the alliance is providing for the UN and the CSCE in supporting security, peacekeeping, and humanitarian measures in Bosnia and elsewhere in the Balkans. Ireland has now formally become an observer member of the Western European Union, and more significantly the passage of the Defence (Amendment) Act 1993 enables this country to participate in an international United Nations force, with the safeguard that any mission of twelve or more Irish troops must have Dail approval. The essence of this concept of collective security, elaborated in the UN Charter, is that if peaceful means fail to prevent a breach of the peace, or an act of aggression, coercive measures agreed by the international community may have to be used. In joining the United Nations, and in subscribing to the Charter in 1956, Ireland accepted that coercive measures, including military action, might need to be taken. In the last analysis all laws at every level require sanctions. Domestic law would be disregarded and anarchy would prevail in the absence of enforcement. Similarly if we are to preserve peace, and prevent aggression, the international community must be in a position to enforce its collective will for peace ... The next twenty years will decide whether mankind can provide a rule of law between nations to achieve and maintain peace, and a rule of law within nations to ensure human rights and the protection of minorities, together with a system of enforcing the rule of law nationally and internationally, that will cope with terrorism and war or threats to the security of peace. It is our manifest duty as a civilised nation to play an active part.

Lenihan showed his harder side again when he questioned what he saw as an excessive vogue for "open government" and for judicial inquiries, which he feared would lead to ministers and officials "minding their backsides" instead of getting on with their jobs. And an article in the *Sunday Press* in September 1985 revealed a genuine political thinker — typically much more conservative in his views on administration than in his approach to social policy — sketching how a liberal democratic state should be run, and citing authorities ranging from Thomas Aquinas to Edmund Burke:

> Cabinet government is ... the coping-stone which spans and blends the twin pillars of the rule of law and representative democracy. The mortar, which keeps the edifice safe, is the democratic but disciplined political party. The foundation of the whole structure is the sovereignty of the people.

He went on to discuss cabinet and ministerial responsibility and to oppose proposals to shunt responsibility onto civil servants:

> I believe that all necessary reforms of the Oireachtas and civil service can and should be carried out within the framework of this principle. To do otherwise would undermine the whole delicate balance that gives us democratic government. It is essential that the Dail, and the public, look closely at the specific transfers of executive functions from ministers to the proposed executive offices ... It is not enough to state glibly that policy and executive functions can be neatly divided into compartments between minister and executive office. In the absence of ministerial responsibility for the actions of his civil servants, the minister would be emasculated, without any responsibility to his government colleagues, to the Dail, or to the people. It is suggested that faceless bureaucrats are enabled to exercise power in the minister's name, while sheltering behind the doctrine

of ministerial responsibility. If this does happen it is not the fault of ministerial responsibility, but caused instead by ineffectual and incompetent ministers.

At the level of personal conversation, Vinny Mahon was one of those to whom he showed that harder side and with whom he cast off the mask of exuberance and colourful language:

> He despised cant and lickspittles. He said it was unfortunate that we had inherited so many of them. He believed firmly in strong leadership. Vacillation had no place at all in his vocabulary. Contrary to his public image, he said that "I never shied from a rough decision in my life and felt, having taken it, very relieved."

He planned to publish several books, including his collected journalism, a thesis on European integration, a history of Ireland's relations with the European Union, and a biography of Lemass. These projects, like so much else, were cut off by his untimely death.

*

At least as much as the praise from the Great and Good lavished upon his memory, he would have appreciated the tributes from humbler folk, especially the officials who had worked with him. Like the civil servant who wrote to Conor Lenihan that it had been an honour to serve his father. Like his onetime constituency secretary Peg Fogarty, who calls him "the perfect gentleman ... a loveable character ... unique ... a lovely, lovely man to work for."

He would have loved Olivia O'Leary's reminiscences. When women writing on politics were a new phenomenon in the early seventies, he protected her from "the boys in the bar", with their antediluvian attitudes:

> Could you match them drinking? They would buy doubles and trebles. They were trying to humiliate

women, not facilitate sexual advances. It was a sort of a battle.

Brian never had that. He was very much at home in the company of women and he did not mind if he got jeered at by the "boys". Brian liked talking to journalists, and he liked women. He was one of those men who genuinely enjoy the company of women. He never felt threatened by having a woman in his presence. He was the soul of honour, the utter gentleman. He would always look after you. He never made a chauvinistic or hurtful remark.

Once on television he called me "my dear young woman". He was trying to flatter me, to dodge answering a question. On the way out I said, "don't ever dare to call me that again." He looked innocent and said, "a term of endearment, my dear."

It was she who said, when asked why she chose to live in Ireland instead of making a career in British television: "I'd miss Brian Lenihan. What would I do without him?"

Seamus Mallon, a Northerner with a deep insight into Dublin, and especially Fianna Fail, politics, offers this summation:

A man who put party before himself. A man who in the interests of his party very often hid his own breadth of vision and his own understanding of the whole business of politics. A man who hid his immense abilities very often behind bluster, especially in public. A man of great humanity who had the capacity to build personal relationships right across the political spectrum and with people in every walk of life, here and abroad. His compassion and humanity are the two things I think we'll all remember Brian for.

But the last word must belong to Lenihan himself.

In 1992 a young man went to see him, to seek his help in getting a job with the European Commission. He found him reading *The Prince*. Curiously, in all Lenihan's vast reading he had not previously encountered the work of Machiavelli, the master of the devious. "Funny," he said, "I never read this book before. If I had read it years ago, things might have been very different.

"But then," he twinkled, "it would never have been my style."

Index

Index

Select bibliography

Adams, Michael, *Censorship: The Irish Experience* (Alabama, 1968)

Allen, Ciaran, *Fianna Fail and the Irish Labour Movement* (London, 1997)

Arnold, Bruce, *Haughey: His Life and Unlucky Deeds* (London, 1993)

Boland, Kevin, *Up Dev!* (Dublin, n.d.)

Bowman, John, *De Valera and The Ulster Question 1917-1972* (Oxford, 1982)

Brown, Terence, *Ireland: A Social and Cultural History 1922-1985* (London, 1985)

Browne, Noel, *Against The Tide* (Dublin, 1986)

Browne, Vincent, and Michael Farrell, eds. *The Magill Book of Irish Politics* (Dublin, 1981)

Collins, Stephen, *The Haughey File* (Dublin, 1992)

Cooney, John, *The Crozier and The Dail: Church and State 1922-1986* (Cork, 1986)

Duignan, Sean, *One Spin on The Merry-Go-Round* (Dublin, 1996)

Dwyer, T. Ryle, *Haughey's Thirty Years of Controversy* (Cork, 1992)

Fanagan, John, ed. *Belling The Cats: Selected Speeches and Articles of John Kelly* (Dublin, 1992)

Fanning, Ronan, *Independent Ireland* (Dublin, 1983)

Farrell, Brian, *Sean Lemass* (Dublin, 1983)

Garvin, Tom, *1922: The Birth of Irish Democracy* (Dublin, 1996)

Horgan, John, *Sean Lemass: The Enigmatic Patriot* (Dublin, 1997)

Joyce, Joe, and Peter Murtagh, *The Boss* (Dublin, 1983)

Keatinge, Patrick, *The Formulation of Irish Foreign Policy* (Dublin, 1973)

    A Singular Stance (Dublin, 1984)

Kenny, Shane, *Go Dance on Someone Else's Grave* (Dublin, 1992)

Lee, Joe, *Ireland 1912-1985: Politics and Society* (Cambridge, 1989)

Lenihan, Ann, and Angela Phelan, *No Problem — to Mayo and Back* (Dublin, 1990)

Lenihan, Brian, *For The Record* (Dublin, 1991)

Mallie, Eamonn, and David McKittrick, *The Fight for Peace* (London, 1996)

Nealon, Ted, *Nealon's Guides to the Dail and Seanad 1977-1997*

O'Byrnes, Stephen, *Hiding Behind a Face* (Dublin, 1986)

O'Connor, Sean, *Troubled Skies* (Dublin, 1986)

O hEithir, Breandan, *The Begrudger's Guide* (Dublin, 1986)

O'Reilly, Emily, *Candidate* (Dublin, 1991)

Masterminds of The Right (Dublin, 1992)

Routledge, Paul, *John Hume: A Biography* (London, 1997)

Siggins, Lorna, *Mary Robinson: The Woman Who Took Power in The Park* (Edinburgh, 1997)

Sinnott, Richard, *Irish Voters Decide: Voting Behaviour in Elections and Referendums since 1918* (Manchester, 1995)

Smith, Raymond, *Haughey and O'Malley: The Struggle for Power* (Dublin, 1992)

Smyth, Sam, *Thanks a Million Big Fella* (Dublin, 1997)

Walsh, Dick, *The Party: Inside Fianna Fail* (Dublin, 1986)

Des O'Malley: A Political Profile (Dingle, 1986)

White, Barry, *John Hume: Statesman of The Troubles* (Belfast, 1983)

Whyte, John, *Church and State in Modern Ireland* (Dublin, 1971)